Other People
Other Places

MARZIEH GAIL

GR

GEORGE RONALD
OXFORD

GEORGE RONALD, Publisher
46 High Street, Kidlington, Oxford OX5 2DN

ISBN 0-85398-122-1 (cased)
ISBN 0-85398-123-X (paper)

Printed in the United States of America

Contents

Acknowledgements

I wish to express my thanks to the National Spiritual Assembly of the Bahá'ís of the United States for permission to reprint the following essays: "The Days With Mark Tobey" (*World Order* magazine, Spring 1977); "Juliet Remembers Gibran" (*World Order* magazine, Summer 1978); "For John, With Love" (*Bahá'í News*, July 1974); "The Diamond Bough" (which appeared in *World Order* magazine, Spring/Summer 1981, under the title *Four Kinds of Love*).

My thanks go also to Kalimát Press for permission to use in "The Star Servant" material from my diary notes first published in my introduction to *Ṭáhirih the Pure* by Martha Root (Kalimát Press 1981).

I am also most grateful to May Hofman Ballerio, for her valuable editorial suggestions, and to Marion Hofman, who is responsible for the shape of this book (as she was for that of *Dawn Over Mount Hira*).

And to Russell Busey, for his most helpful correspondence on matters both business and literary.

And to my husband Harold, for preserving my notebooks through many moves, and for believing in their possibilities. It was Harold who made the initial selections and gave the manuscript its original form. Without his efforts, it is unlikely that my notes would have turned into a book – at least at the present time.

I

Victoriana

It was down in the basement in an open trunk, a big, warped, expensive cabinet photograph on a pile of faded lace. I took it over to the ground-level window where there was some light. I saw a formally-dressed man – just his head and shoulders; white collar, stickpin not vertical but aslant under the knot of his tie. He looked to be slender and blond, and he was leaning against the panel of a door. His dreamy blue eyes gazed up into mine. There were spots on the photograph, blurring the date. Before 1900, anyhow. Back upstairs again, I asked my mother.

"Why, that's Philip," she said. "That's Philip Savage. He was a New England poet. A New England Wordsworth was what they called him – what Louise Imogen Guiney called him in her book."

I wondered why the photograph, so elaborate. And why still with us, after all these years of travel: Washington – California – France – Istanbul – Ṭihrán – the Caucasus – New York – all through the long years.

"You see, Grandmother didn't want us to marry," my mother said. "Philip only had something like ten thousand a year, or whatever. It wouldn't keep me in dresses, Grandma said. After all," she added, "I used to change my clothes seven times a day. I used to drop each outfit on the floor for the maids to pick up."

No do-it-yourself in those days, I decided, with nostalgia.

"What happened?" I asked Mother.

"We used to sit on the beach in the moonlight at Deer Cove," she said. "Philip would look at me and tell me, 'Say *burnt ivory* again. I want to hear the syllables again: *burnt ivory*.' " (Dimly I recalled my mother's next-to-youngest

3

brother, Francis W. Breed, Jr, telling me he used to be sent down to announce dinner, breaking up those sessions on the beach.)

"What did Philip do for a living?"

"We didn't think of 'for a living' in those days. At least, our family didn't," she said. "It took me years to find out that most people have to work to live. Philip had a *position* with the Boston Public Library. He was assistant to the Librarian. But his work was being a poet."

"We lived in our beautiful house at Deer Cove," Mother said.

It was never given to me to see that house, which she always named on an upward note. Parents' tones and gestures and facial expressions are what children go by, not their words. I knew from the beginning that Deer Cove was an important name, from how she said it. Long after this time of Philip's photograph, when we buried my mother at Lynn, we found there was only a Deer Cove Avenue left, crowded with houses, from where my grandparents' home had been. Uncle Ralph, Mother's youngest brother, was with us that day, and he did recognize one of the few remaining trees, because long, long before, he had buried his dog at the base.

Of course I had seen many a picture of the place. For instance, that photograph of all the children on the lawn near the stables, each one mounted on his thoroughbred horse. The opening of the drive looked like the curving, casual driveway in the old film *Rebecca*. The house itself was stately, as you can tell from Grandmother's silver spoon. Grandmother was a great spoon collector, and once when she had guests to a large garden party, each guest received a sterling gift spoon, showing the Deer Cove house and tennis court. On the back of the spoon you can read her name: Mrs Alice Ives Breed. It is all we have left of the never seen by us children and now vanished forever home, but I still go back there now and then in memory.

For instance Mother used to tell us about the breakfasts, each one better than a week of breakfasts now. In those days, she said, older people could be as obese as they liked, under their layers of clothes. (This would remind me of the minister who told his parishioner to give up alcohol, because it would ruin his stomach. "Won't show with my coat on," the parishioner said.) A single breakfast might include egg dishes, meat dishes, cereal, high stacks of pancakes swimming in maple syrup and butter, and hothouse grapes.

That was a cosseted life, long before income tax. A time of charity. Grandmother would have her stale bread and cookies given away to "the poor" at the back door. "Mother," my mother, seven years old, asked Grandma one day, "do the poor have better teeth than we?"

In the spring – I think people had their main house cleaning in spring because the brighter light would show up spots invisible by winter in those dark Victorian interiors – Grandmother would marshal her maids and the opulent house would be gone over, attic to cellar. And afterward Grandmother would remark, tired out: "Blessed be nothing."

I learned from Mother that she herself soon wearied of the endless social rounds. "Oh," she once said, thinking out loud at one of the infinite, delicate, elaborate, débutante banquets, "I could eat nails!" She used to tell me, piercing through my self-absorbed teenage fog, that she had "led the German." (Who he? I would feel like asking, when in a bored, rebellious mood.) She would go on to tell about the young girls' pre-ball "beauty-baths." Necessary, I used to think. The dancers must have perspired a lot in those pre-antiperspirant days, wearing as they did not one but several "shields." (One of the things Father immediately loved about Mother was her special fragrance, he said.) A leftover of that time (Grandmother's? Mother's?) is the three-inch, flat, silver flask on my mantel. It was a "bosom bottle," worn in the dress, for dancing young ladies to keep their brandy in, should they grow faint.

That life of parties officially began for Mother when she made her début at Mrs Potter Palmer's in the Chicago castle, big until it shrank against the skyscrapers later on, and became a rather ludicrous and embarrassing landmark, which by one of fate's coincidences was pulled down in 1950, the year Mother died. That life of hers was all pulled down, everything was swept and blown, shoveled and forked away, like floral wreaths the day after the funeral.

In that world there was also Grandpa, tall, arrogant, magnificent, charming. When he lost everything from strikes or one of the panics or something, his father-in-law Ives had only this comment: "That's Frank. Up like a rocket, down like a stick."

I understand Great-grandfather was an affluent doctor and clergyman, both, but apparently of no tangible benefit to his descendants. "All your great-grandfather Ives ever left you," Father would say to the posterity, "was his long upper lip." The way I remember it, there was also a silver-headed cane. Great-grandfather's money went to convert the heathen, I forget from what to what.

Come to think of it, he did leave us a bit of history – which as the years went by and every single new guest to the house had to learn of it, I sincerely came to regret. It seems that when Father heard that Mother was part Ives he cried: "Christianity was first introduced into the Isle of Great Britain by a Persian monk named Ives. I have simply married back into my family." This Persian monk is supposedly reported on, *inter alia*, by Green.[1] I am still looking for him, but not very hard. In any case, Persian monk or no, there were those among the people of Boston (where the Breeds moved from Lynn) who did not approve the widely-reported wedding of a New England young lady to a dark stranger from the East. "Some didn't speak to me for forty-five years," Father would cheerfully observe. (However, the first to call on the young couple after their honeymoon was William James.)

Certain young ladies were not uniformly enthusiastic about the wedding either. The beauteous Laura Barney (Natalie's sister) remarked: "He has married that eccentric Miss Breed." "It was the first important Persian–American marriage," Mother always said. "Of course, there had been a few before – of no consequence." (The Master, 'Abdu'l-Bahá, said it was the first Bahá'í Persian–American marriage.) Mother adored Father, and adored his whole nation for being his.

We have never known who Grandfather Breed was. He was brought over to this country as a six-months old baby and adopted by the well-to-do Breeds. "English–Irish aristocracy," Mother always said, adding that there was one New England minister who knew where Grandfather came from. "How do you know Grandfather is an aristocrat?" I once asked my father. "Look at him," Father answered. Father was from a country, Persia, where royalty and nobility were recognized and valued. Born in the ancient city of Káshán, which tradition says was the home of the Three Wise Men, Father was proud of his family tree, going back to the Sásáníyán ruler, Núshírván the Just. According to Mother, you could see my nose on Sásáníyán coins. (Discouraging, if you are familiar with these coins.)

On a European journey, in some stately-home portrait or other, they found a probable ancestor for Grandfather: a blue-eyed, black-haired beauty, exactly like my Aunt Alice. It stood to reason, our family always agreed, that just any baby would not have been transported across the sea. Mother never said illegitimate: "born of a secret marriage" was the proper New England term.

Grandfather had an endearing, childlike quality, under his arrogance. His manners were perfect. The day that 'Abdu'l-Bahá came to Grandfather's to preside over the marriage of my Aunt Ruby, Grandfather, not a Bahá'í, humbly thanked Him for being kind to Mother on her Eastern journey. "Why do you thank me?" 'Abdu'l-Bahá said. "You are my own family."

"Your grandfather was very ethical," Mother would say. "He paid his bills before the ink on them was dry," which means little to this generation, that lives on credit, and lists your financial status as poor, if you don't owe money.

Sometimes he and Grandmother did have words. Once during an argument he told her: "Look at all I've done for you! I've given you seven children!" which became a family joke.

Two of the seven were in the graveyard, the first one born dead, so that Grandmother "wept her eyes out." The other was Helen – younger than Mother – who lived to be seven years old. Just as I have missed Deer Cove, I have always mourned the never-known Helen. "She was too sensitive to live in this world," Grandmother tried to explain; "she would cry when she saw the wind rippling over the grass." Besides

7

the first, stillborn one, and Helen, the ones that lived were Mother, Alice, Ruby – all Bahá'ís, along with Grandmother – and the two boys, Francis W. Breed, Jr, who said he wasn't good enough to be a Bahá'í, and Ralph, the youngest. Ralph met Shoghi Effendi in Paris and was in our photograph with the Guardian-to-be in the wheat fields at Barbizon, and in after-years, Ralph accepted the Faith. ("There is something very noble about Ralph," Shoghi Effendi said.) Frank was the family humorist, although they were all funny, from witty to droll, each in different ways.

One time there was a coolness between Grandmother and Grandfather, and she took her daughters and departed on the "Grand Tour." But he sent her a copy of a poem beginning

> Just awearyin' for you,
> All the time afeelin' blue,
> Wishin' for you, wonderin' when
> You'll be comin' home again . . .

And she came home. They survived together, well past their Golden Wedding Day. They had a splendid Golden Wedding, but our family could not attend; we were in Persia then and had to go by the reports. For the occasion, Uncle Ralph gave a speech to the multitudes. "Florence was their love child," he told the audience, "but I was their pièce de résistance." As part of the proceedings, the drama of Father's and Mother's unlikely Persian–American marriage was emphasized in the declaiming of a poem that begins something like this:

> Two shall be born the whole wide world apart,
> And speak in different tongues . . .

There must be somebody left who remembers it. It embodies that medieval awe at the magic of a man's and a woman's love, in this case a man and woman who came together from opposite ends of the earth. The planet was much bigger then.

But what about Philip and his photograph? Over the years I have slowly pieced him together – recomposed this

8

man who in some maddening way might have been part of me –
only then I would have been only part of me, myself.

He was born in 1868, entered Harvard in 1889, was a divinity
student, inwardly at least a freethinker, became a Harvard
English instructor, librarian, Thorovian, poet. What about
him?

I have his two traditional "slender volumes" here on the
shelf. One is *First Poems and Fragments*, by Philip Henry Savage,
Boston, Copeland and Day, 1895. The design on the title page
shows a sheaf of lilies with the Latin, *Sicut lilium inter spinas*: "As
the lily among thorns, so is my love among the daughters." The
other, *Poems*, same publisher, same lilies, was brought out in
1898. This second one is the volume he dedicated to my mother;
or as he wrote, to "Citriodora," the Lady of the Lemon
Verbena. (A third, comprehensive edition of Philip's poems
was published in 1901, by Small and Maynard, Boston.)

The dedication sonnet shows how Philip, like so many
others, would follow her about. Father told me in after years
that as a young boy in Persia – a country of heavily-veiled
women – he had much enjoyed the European fashion
magazines. He said Mother was like the pictures in those
magazines, those stately, frilly, nipped-in ladies of his
boyhood. Sometimes when they were walking together he
would drop behind, to watch.

"But then what happened about Philip?" I asked my mother.
And she told me, in her pensive, faraway voice. They didn't
know much about appendicitis in those days. They would
operate, that was all. Philip was off playing tennis somewhere.
Too soon after luncheon, he was on the courts. That seemed to
be the cause, anyway. It was the last day of May, 1899. Three or
four days went by. They sent for Mother, to come to the
Massachusetts General Hospital, because Philip was asking.
The engagement had never been formalized, but Philip was
asking, and she went. I am not sure when, but in that hospital
room their engagement was announced. Then it was June 4,
1899. She stood beside his bed and Philip looked at her, perhaps
just as his eyes had looked into mine, from the photograph
down in the basement.

"Florence!" he cried to her, "Florence!" from wherever he was going. He thought in some mixed-up way that dawn was breaking, and that she was the sun coming up. "Florence!" he called, "the sunrise!" And he died.

Mother told me that afterward she invited people to her wedding, meaning Philip's funeral. And once, she said, she saw him on the stairs.

In Boston on June 23, 1899, Louise Imogen Guiney, essayist and poet, wrote these lines in a letter, telling about that time: ". . . I lately lost a very dear old friend, who was also a colleague of mine at the Library: Philip Savage. Did you ever run across either of his two slender books? He had a greater intimacy with the open-air world than anyone I ever knew: a genuine poetic temperament, shy, gentle, brave, positive. His verse was just a bit quaintly scholastic, for all that. It reminded me sometimes of the seventeenth century lyrists, though he was Wordsworth's son. Well, he died suddenly, went out in three days, quick as a candle, from the full of his life and energy. He was one-and-thirty, the best-beloved of his father's children, and engaged to the loveliest of girls: an exquisite little creature, grey-eyed and gold-haired, who breaks my heart with her tearless courage. There are a good many circumstances which made this dying especially hard to bear."

And here is Philip's dedication poem:

To Citriodora
I turn and see you passing in the street
When you are not. I take another way,
Lest missing you the fragrance of the day
Exhale, and I know not that it is sweet.
And marking you I follow, and when we meet
Love laughs to see how sudden I am gay;
Sweetens the air with fragrance like a spray
Of sweet verbena, and bids my heart to beat.
Love laughs; and girls that take you by the hand,
Know that a sweet thing has befallen them;
And women give their hearts into your heart.
There is, I think, no man in all the land
But would be glad to touch your garment's hem.
And I, I love you with a love apart.[2]

II

Letters Home, 1932–1934

Author's note: Shortly before we received our degrees (Howard Carpenter's was the M.D. from Stanford University, and mine the M.A. from the University of California at Berkeley) a letter reached me from Shoghi Effendi, the Guardian of the Bahá'í Faith, requesting me to leave for Persia (Iran), to serve there as a link between the Bahá'ís of East and West. Waiting only for our diplomas, we sailed for Europe September 9, 1932, on a freighter from San Pedro, California, to Genoa, a trip which lasted the Biblical forty days and forty nights. We then stayed several months in Vienna, where Howard took further advanced courses in ophthalmology, and we both assisted the world famous Bahá'í teacher, Martha Root, helping to arrange lectures for her and spending four weeks in her company. With her we taught in Györ and Budapest, then went on to Belgrade where Martha left us February 23, 1933, on her continuing world journeys, and we proceeded to Sofia, Bulgaria. Here we spent five weeks teaching with the noted Canadian Bahá'í pioneer Marion Jack. Since in the meantime the Guardian had written us to visit Tirana (which we had never heard of before), we also put in a week in that city before leaving Albania to make our Haifa pilgrimage. We then traveled to Ṭihrán, where, because of Howard's serious illness, we could remain only two years. We returned, via Haifa, to California, hoping for a cure, but Howard died, November 24, 1935.

These notes are from letters we wrote home during our travels.

Vienna
Oct. 23, 1932

Dear Family –

Well, so far life in Vienna is satisfactory. We each have a hot bath every day, which is more than most tourists . . . Our room is kept very warm always, but the rest of the house isn't heated yet – they're waiting for cold weather. When I poke my head into the corridor I expect to see a sled and a line of dogs . . .

On Sundays the Viennese all go out of town and trudge for hours through the countryside. There are very few cars on the roads – you stop when one passes. Most people just walk, with thick clothes and large canes and fat dogs. It's a wonderful idea, too, because nothing makes you feel so virtuous as having had a long walk. I wondered how they could walk so much and still have no waistlines till I saw where the walk ended – at a sumptuous restaurant, with acres of chairs painted yellow, and trees and a view. Howard had thick soup and a dish of veal-and-mushrooms with rice, and a huge dessert made of chocolate, whipped cream and cake. I had lettuce salad but weakened when the dessert man came round with his tray for us to choose and had a sort of custard pie though it's almost sacrilege to call it that. The dessert man was separate and had to be tipped between two and three cents. When we'd eaten, the head waiter came around and asked what we'd had, and how many pieces of bread; that's the system here, and apparently no one thinks of keeping anything back. I suppose they have the good old Stanford University honor system, and if someone says he had only two rolls and you saw him have three, you stand up and say, "Someone is cheating in this restaurant."

The countryside is beautiful – hilly, with vineyards, and the leaves are changing; there are a few little shrines along the roads. I honestly think the people enjoy themselves more than we do in America, because a long quiet walk, a leisurely meal and then a concert in the evening is more recreation than our own Sunday traffic and the talkies.

Anyhow, we're homesick, because everybody speaks English but nobody can understand us, so we're getting sour and introspective, and Howard has to mutter each new pun to me alone because otherwise we'd have to make a long explanation which wouldn't be understood either.

Vienna
Oct. 23, 1932

Dear Family,

. . . One thing that bothers us here is the left-hand drive –
you have to take street cars on the wrong side of the street, and
look in the wrong direction when you want to cross. The
autos go at a great rate, and when they near a crossing they
crash right along except for tooting, but if two cars happen to
be approaching the same crossing, the one that toots most
emphatically seems to have the right of way. The policemen
are gorgeous in dark green and salute when you speak to them
and don't call you "dear" or "hey-you" either. The few
policemen who direct traffic look as if they were leading the
congregation in prayer. Most of the horns are musical and the
fire engine practically croons. The Viennese specialize in nice
noises and their voices are so sweet I often wonder how they
quarrel . . .

Vienna
October 25, 1932

Dear Family,

The first thing we did on arrival was to write Dr Maier, and
on Friday Mr Kluss – a friend who has been to America – came
and took us to the meeting. They made each of us get up and
talk, and translated what we said into German – after which,
to our embarrassment, they read our letter of introduction out
loud; you know it's as complimentary as if we'd passed on, so
now they think we're just wonderful. We met several of the
friends after the meeting, and many of them speak good
English – but for the rest I had to get along with French,
laryngitis and Esperanto. There are about fifty Bahá'ís here,
and they are a beautiful group. Sunday, Mr Kluss took us on
our trip out of town, and Monday we asked four of the group
here. The German way is to serve tea and cookies (etc., etc.) a
short time after the guests come, and apparently you're
supposed to spend the rest of the visit sitting around sipping
and nibbling – at least that's what our apartment owner told
us, and she's our authority on everything . . .

They are making plans to have a study class in English and a weekly English lecture. Martha Root is quite near here – Prague, I think – and Mrs Gregory is near too. Some of the problems the Bahá'ís have here are the strong prejudice against Jews, and the political disturbances. There are several Esperanto groups, but they aren't united because they're divided into Catholics, Jews etc. The Germans are great for clubs and organizations. They say if you find five Germans there are six clubs. Most people here think of America as their dream, and I believe anything America sponsored would be accepted here and probably through most of Europe. The more we travel the greater seems the responsibility of the American Bahá'ís.

Vienna
October 28, 1932

Dear Family – I've decided to drop "dearest" entirely – everyone shall be "dear" from now on, without distinction of creed or color . . . Mother Carpenter's letter came yesterday . . . The clipping made sense on both sides, and we weren't quite sure which to read; you'd checked the Habbakuk side, but the other side said, "Alcohol produces a delirium tremens of the imagination no less than of the body." I guess we were to choose whichever we needed most.

The Bahá'ís here are planning two English meetings a week, one public, the other for *The Dawn-Breakers*; there is one copy in Vienna, and you may be sure I've got it, and am keeping on with my notes.

October 29, 1932

We just had lunch in a restaurant situated in one corner of the Rathaus, which has nothing to do with rodents, being the town hall. We're more and more converted to Vienna desserts. There was a man near us with his wife and two children, and I noticed the waiter bringing him an enormous cake and thought one of the children was having a birthday, but no, that was his private dessert – and the next time I looked up the waiter was serving him two huge cream puffs as a chaser. The children weren't left out though, because they

16

were liberally supplied with "Indians" – short, squat chocolate pastries . . . and the wife was joyfully spooning up
whipped cream.

Vienna

Dear Family,
Mother Carpenter's letter came yesterday, and by the
way we get more fun out of them than out of any others, so
you mustn't be modest and say you "pity anyone who has
to depend on your letters," etc. Anyhow, yesterday's letter
was about the opera, and last night Howard dreamt he went
to an opera called "Coolidge" and there was a racing car on
the stage, which he interpreted to mean Coolidge economy
and that we mustn't run through our money too fast . . .
I enclose the Quakers' announcement of a talk for next
week. I'm so sick of the "Women of Persia" I could scream
(N.B. this was the title many groups chose to have me
speak on, while allowing me the privilege of speaking of the
Cause as well), but it may be a way of establishing cordial
relations with the Quakers. I've been to see them and bor-
rowed two enormous books on their history and war-time
activity. (N.B. The Quakers in Vienna were especially cordial to us and to Martha Root.) If people hear the words
"women" and "Persia" they usually gallop to the lecture,
and spend the hour regretting their rash act and getting back
at the lecturer by loud, unpleasant creaks. If it's on politics
or something you can always pound the table at them, but
if it's on religion you have to let them creak . . .

Nov. 8, 1932

. . . Now really you must stop worrying every time you
hear there's a plague or a hurricane somewhere or we'll start
worrying about your living in the midst of gangsters and
bootleggers. Some poor chaps . . . were beaten up . . . at
the university, but the government has placed guards
around and says it will never happen again. We didn't know
a thing about it until long after. Austria is so dependent on
students and tourists that they do everything to take care of
us.

November 10, 1932

. . . The Austrian voting question is interesting: some of it is compulsory, but they have secret ballot, so at least you're free to vote for whom you please, and one man wrote, "I vote for Jesus Christ."

. . . The maid question is frightfully interesting. We're on our fifth maid since arriving. They're all named Mitzi. The last permanent one stayed about a week – she was pretty and I foresaw trouble. The morning she left she came in for a farewell look at our stove, and sure enough told us young X was "too fresh," hence her departure (although the Madam, as Howard insists on calling her, gave other reasons). We're sorry she went because we'd taught her to knock, which didn't help much, though, because she'd always barge right in immediately after knocking, no matter how many languages we'd yell at her in to stay out. When one maid goes the lady advertises in a paper and about sixty appear. It's like Ziegfeld choosing a chorus. Then the one who is ugliest and seems to have a glimmer of intelligence is selected. Their duties include everything from around six in the morning to ten at night.

Vienna
November 18, 1932

Dear Family,

. . . Apparently everything's going well with you, except for Margery's cold in the head – which I trust has long since been passed on to somebody else. (It's always been my conviction that there's only one cold in the world and only one yawn.) . . . We continue our two English meetings a week at the Bahá'í room. Last night the place was full and after the talk a lady came and asked me to talk at her house – she's a poet and it might be interesting – that was the first Bahá'í meeting she'd ever been to. I'm darned if I know whether the audience understands a word I say . . . Everyone knows English but only artificially – they don't know the values of the words. Of course the Bahá'ís understand because they already know the teachings in German. But as for the others – for instance they never do learn how to use the tenses; they'll look at you and say, "Are you playing the piano?" – and of course you're not doing anything – you're just sitting there.

Vienna
Thanksgiving Day

Dear Family,

. . . I've been exchanging English for Esperanto with the Bahá'í secretary – he's a very earnest young chap, just beginning to realize that Howard and I don't always mean what we say. He was here for tea, and Howard started conversing in his usual broken English, and when I explained that Howard's English wasn't correct he looked so sympathetic that we both got hysterical and I had to leave . . .

Vienna
December 16, 1932

Dear Family,

. . . We do think times are dreadful, and long to reach Persia and start functioning. Trouble is one can't get there during winter – we'd die on the way, which would be a discouraging start in life (besides I've been sort of keeping myself for the Truman Mortuary). Anyhow, it won't be so long now, and I feel sure that once we reach there everything will be all right . . .

We've had a fine letter from Martha Root – she's thrilled about our going by way of the Balkans – she says Sofia has a fine climate, and thinks we could live there very inexpensively. That is where we'd make our longest stop, after Vienna.

The weather's not bad at all – sun was out this morning, a remarkable event. The beggars are everywhere – Mr Lamb left three schillings change which I was to collect for him, and I've been giving it to beggars for over a month, and still there's a lot left. It's awful trying to keep their account straight – I keep borrowing car-fare from them and forgetting to pay it back. Tonight I have to speak to a student forum at the Quakers' rooms – on Persia, of course. We all have our cross to bear – mine seems to be a crescent.

19

Vienna, undated

Dear Family,

. . . The enclosed pictures of the Temple were made by a young Viennese woman. In Chicago she was attracted by the Temple and made a special trip to see it – is not a Bahá'í but knows a little about the Cause. Last week at her house there were several Chicago people, and they all spoke of the Temple very possessively, and told us all about it. One said the aviators use it as a landmark and call it "the thimble" . . . Well, people here think it's grand to collect some friends around a lot of food and have me speak to them, so I do what I can . . . people love lectures here – it's better than staying out in the snow . . .

Vienna
January 28, 1933

Dear Family,

I'm feeling jubilant this evening because my last lecture is over. It was on California (N.B. this time they had asked me not to refer to the Cause), very dull, and I had some views of Panama, contributed by a Viennese friend for use in case of need – Panama and California being all one over here. These last two lectures at Adult Education schools were arranged by a young woman who discovered our Bahá'í meetings a few weeks ago – she's very well-educated and enthusiastic, and will translate some of Martha's lectures. Martha's here – lovelier than ever, and so tired. She'll give eight lectures in six days – then we leave.

Beautiful weather today, almost spring-like - whereas yesterday my fingers were bent like tin, in spite of Viennese gloves. And I thought it was cold in San Francisco! They even have to disband the zoo during winter, and heaven knows what they do with the animals. Howard says they let them wander around, disguised as old army colonels. Poor boy, he used to be able to imitate a lion perfectly, and then one day we found he couldn't do it any more; he says all he needs is to hear another lion, but of course we're worried . . .

Vienna
February 3, 1933

Dear Family,
. . . We leave tomorrow, and are duly excited. We've been kissed and wept over – as for shaking the dust from off your feet I've collected everything from a Balkan jacket to a Bible . . .
We had an exciting moment the other night, getting Martha through a howling mob in front of the opera. Torchlight procession, trembling policemen, kicking horses, traffic jammed. The light flashed on a man they took for a Jew, and the mob yelled and snarled like animals. Howard as usual was the hero of the occasion, and got us through all right. I was scared to death . . . You could feel the thrill of hate in the crowd – at last I understood a little of how it was when they were killing Bahá'ís in Persia.

Sofia, Bulgaria
February 26, 1933

Dear Family,
It was fun to have the orgy of mail yesterday, though hard to extract the letters from the authorities, we being so swathed in red tape we can hardly move. They felt a lump in one letter, snarled and tore open the envelope, only to find the little blue hankie – were much disgruntled, and Howard couldn't help laughing. We live at the Elite Palace, because all the hotels here are palaces . . . So far we've eaten at an Armenian, a vegetarian and a German restaurant. (N.B. Early Bahá'í work in Bulgaria was often favored by contacts made in these restaurants.) The vegetarian one was of the "Tolstoi" persuasion, which goes so far as to allow cheese and eggs. They had a full-length picture of Tolstoi in his bare feet. Also two washbowls, because it's the thing in Bulgarian restaurants to wash right out in public. The pigeons make a racket all day, and newsboys yell, and there's a yellow palace with toy sentries, and snow-covered mountains . . .
As for Bahá'í news, there's tons of this, after being with Martha three weeks. In each town she goes to the most

21

important people and they do the rest – you should see people who aren't Bahá'ís translating the books, arranging lectures, being chairman at this and that function, studying the teachings. At lectures there are always people who come gradually to know about the Cause and after Martha has been in a place for a while she starts a study class.

Martha's method is straight-from-the-shoulder. She hasn't been with a person three minutes before she's given him a book or picture. In Belgrade we went to the American minister's, Martha was invited to tea with Prince Paul and Princess Olga (he represents the King – is most popular and influential), a bishop asked us to lunch but we couldn't go, several well-known professors were interested, and Martha arranged for the translation of the Serbian Esslemont. She also gave several lectures; made me chant at every function, e.g. at her university lecture, and then the audience wanted a translation. After traveling around we've come to two conclusions – one that those who stay at home have a harder time to interest people in the Cause but that their work and lives are tremendously important, because they're the people we tell the audiences about (a moving object naturally attracts more attention – but it's harder to be saintly when stationary), and the other is, that there should be more inter-assembly correspondence to stimulate the different centers.

Sofia, Bulgaria
March 10, 1933

Dear Family,

. . . We hear dreadful things of the dollar and everybody living on scrip. Of course it's hard to keep up with the news – no U.S. papers or magazines except the Paris Herald on occasion, and the English papers are too funny. (Of course there's the *Saturday Evening Post* at 40 cents and some *Ladies' Home Journals*.) Went to the market today. Lots of third-rate industrial products such as lilac cotton bloomers – a good deal of metalware left over from the Turks: bracelets and bangles, incense burners, a case with a little crank that had contained the Book of Esther (you turned the crank to unroll the manuscript), some peasant dresses and weaves, very uninteresting pottery à la five-and-ten – halva, hens, lambs and so on.

                                              Sofia, Bulgaria
                                              March 16, 1933
Dear Family,
    . . . We howled about the comments on whether or not
Martha likes wine-sauce. (I could tell more but Howard
promised Martha to keep a few things dark if she'd do the
same for us.)
    . . . As for Bahá'í news, there's plenty of it . . . The
main thing is we have a meeting every night in Miss Jack's
rooms at the hotel; people come and we talk – all four of us,
there being two German ladies here too. They come of their
own accord and stay for hours. The situation is complicated
by language difficulties – we don't even know how these
people react to us, or what their special problems are. I know if
the Cause didn't spread itself because it has a power in it, no
one could spread it; when you consider that it is all done
without material means, and often makes the person who
hears of it sacrifice some of his most cherished beliefs. A peace
worker in Budapest said he only reached people who were
already converted to his belief – but the Cause takes hold of
people who are opposed to it, and changes them, like Saul and
Paul. Anyhow, the whole town knows who we are, where
we're going, and in fact our every secret thought.
    . . . We've met a fascinating Armenian lady. She lives in an
enormous Turkish room at Miss Jack's hotel. She has silver
hair to her shoulders, endless eyebrows, and huge red-brown
eyes. She wears black velvet, a gray fox scarf and diamonds
that make you dizzy. Her heels are incredible, she speaks seven
languages, she's trying to reduce on lamb, fried potatoes and
Turkish delight . . . She asked Howard and me to dinner, and
I told him we'd have to follow Emerson's advice – at rich
men's tables eat bread and pulse – but there wasn't any pulse
(they never do serve any) . . . She comes to our talks and asks
many questions about the Cause . . .

Sofia, Bulgaria
March 27, 1933

Dear Family,

Just got your earthquake airmail letter – it took only twelve days to Vienna (sixteen to here). We felt sure that you would be protected so didn't worry. You've no idea how much we rely on your letters, so keep on sending nice fat ones – all the news interests us. We've been having a meeting every single night, except Sundays, and some in the afternoons – never talked so much in our lives. Miss Jack is dear to us – some of our friends want to know if we can't settle in Sofia! Vienna doesn't seem to have forgotten us yet – Professor X sent me two books – one his own French poems and the other a French anthology – was awfully thrilled to get them.

The enormous pink theater here is hung with crepe – famous actor dead. We saw his funeral the other day, from Miss Jack's window. First a silver coffin tilted in an open carriage (and held up by an uncomfortable-looking man seated under it) then the corpse himself, right out in the open, up to his neck in flowers and carried by a crowd of friends, then a battalion of priests in black and silver robes, then the empty hearse rattling along as an anti-climax – thousands of people, and chanting, and red student-caps . . .

[By Howard Carpenter]
Salonica, Greece
April 2, 1933

Dear Family,

We are progressing slowly, but not so surely. The trip from Sofia was a terrible experience. We came by automobile with a missionary family who had been many years in Bulgaria . . . They seemed to think it would be all right to come that way. The part of the trip that was in Bulgaria was very pleasant. We had a good car, the roads were fair and we saw lots of interesting scenery . . . But when we got to the frontier we had to wait three and a half hours for a car to come for us from Greece; finally two little cars with horrible old tires came . . . Before we started they took a tire off that had a huge bulging

24

hole in it and stuffed some old rubber tubing in it. There was no spare. Then for eight hours we travelled over the worst roads you can imagine. We were tossed and hurled around the car until we thought we could not stand it another minute. In the dark we went across country where there was practically no vestige of a road. Several times we were lost. The climax came about ten o'clock when both cars got stuck deep in the mud. Through some miracle one of them pulled out and pulled the other out. Strangely enough we had no tire trouble . . . Now it seems like a bad dream, but we still have plenty of aches and pains. Marzieh has a big black-and-blue spot in the middle of her back. *(I haven't seen it but Howard assures me it's there so I take it on faith – Marzieh.)*

. . . We had a grand send-off in Sofia with lots of gifts and messages. Miss Jack gave us a huge roasted chicken which we finally finished today.

[Postscript by Marzieh]
Really, you should have been on our trip. All crammed into a touring car with tons of luggage; then a hymn was sung, whereupon the tires flattened out. They were pumped up, and off we went – saw violets and snow mountains and trees full of storks. These are very aristocratic missionaries – good old families who've been here from about sixty years back . . .

Tirana, Albania
April 5, 1933

Dear Family,
Father Carpenter should come to live in Albania. In all the homes we've visited the men do the talking and the women just sit with folded hands, in the intervals when they aren't dragging in food. At the home we visited today – a professor's – the women didn't even eat. Of course I suppose they take it out on their husbands afterward, but then they do that in America too – here they at least declare a moratorium when guests are present.

If you're interested in Albania, read Martha Root's two

articles in *Stars*, 1928 or so. These days are the Muḥammadan feast of Bayram, when they sacrifice lambs, and there's plenty of baaing and trays of roast meat. The carriages are decorated with paper flowers. There are mosques and minarets, and a national costume running mostly to pants. A typical man's costume is black bolero jacket trimmed with black plush (anyhow it looks like plush), and short black sleeves with black plush pompoms, above long white sleeves; folded orange belt, black pantaloons, turn-up shoes, white felt hat à la inverted flower pot. Lots of people have their palms and finger tips dyed with henna. Everywhere you see Italian soldiers. A Catholic priest goes by, lifts his hat and discloses a magenta skullcap . . . Streets are rocky and dusty . . .

Salonica was the best town we've seen, since Budapest. The people said it was nothing to Athens – but it had lovely white buildings and a quiet harbor. The Greeks have a real sense of beauty – for instance in the market the fruits and vegetables are arranged to look beautiful and the meats have flowers on them. In Sofia, or here, similar shops are rather scrawny and unkempt. Our three days in Greece were remarkably interesting. At the Dean's house, Anatolia College, the students and professors kept me talking till I was hoarse, answering questions about the Cause . . . I'm afraid they'll wear out the Esslemont I gave them, in the scramble for it. We had several nice engagements and everyone was intensely interested in the Cause . . . We had time only for one editor. He'd never heard of the teachings, but said he'd do everything to help us, and next day printed an article I wrote for him in French, which he translated – on history and principles of the Cause. Howard's main joy in visiting Greece was that he could say everything was Greek to him. Americans abroad are the most comfortable people in the world. Their homes and schools are lovely.

Ṭihrán
Summer, 1934

Dear Family,

We don't have anything new to report, except heat as usual. Howard's . . . upset seems better . . . We miss you, and it's a great comfort to think of you living your well-ordered, scientific lives. We're going crazy, but trying to do so with dignity; every time we find a house, somebody rents it away; a friend of ours said that was nothing: every time he finds a girl she marries someone else. It's cloudy today, thank heaven. I'm trying to translate *The Raven* into Persian, but the Persians say that it isn't logical that a crow should come walking into one's room in the middle of the night . . .

Life is so intense and shaky and dramatic here – it's like living in a jungle with the lions, whereas in America you have them safe in a zoo and only visit them on Sundays. It takes a lot of guts to stand it, and I really think Howard is wonderful to have endured so much; you should be very proud of him, I think. Maybe our next letter will be more definite – who knows, we may actually find a place to hang the license in, and start work . . .

N.B. After a year of trouble, Howard had just obtained his license to practise medicine. For some strange reason, we were unable to find a house to live in, and shortly after this, he contracted the paralysis which led to his death.

III

AUTHOR'S NOTE

Shoghi Effendi, grandson of 'Abdu'l-Bahá and Guardian of the Bahá'í Faith for thirty-six years until he fell ill and died in London November 4, 1957, repeatedly exhorted the Bahá'ís to leave their homes and settle elsewhere as Bahá'í "pioneers" (teachers in areas where there were few or no Bahá'ís). He particularly emphasized the desirability of leaving heavily populated centers in the United States, and going to rural areas or smaller towns. Bahá'ís were urged to settle either in new places within their own country, or in other localities around the world, and their slogans became, "Pack your bags and go!" and "Go as far as you can, stay as long as you can!" Uprooting oneself to leave as a volunteer became the order of the day.

In 1954, only two years after Harold Gail had established a spring factory in Portland, Oregon, he and I decided to cable the Guardian and ask whether we should pioneer abroad or in a "goal town" outside Portland. The Guardian's immediate reply was: "Pioneer abroad more meritorious . . ." This was decades before Harold would be of retirement age. He is an extremely cautious individual, and knew the risks of living on capital and leaving one's means of livelihood behind. Nevertheless he somehow managed to pry himself loose from the American business scene, selling out to a national company, and we departed for Europe. I remember that we sailed from Quebec in an ancient tub that Lloyd's of London had reputedly refused to insure.

Once abroad, we heard from a number of other pioneers (including Mark Tobey, the artist, who telephoned us in London from Holland), asking us to join forces with them. After traveling about, and consultation with the European Teaching Committee, we arrived in Nice, where we happened to recall that Sara Kenny (the wife of Judge Robert Kenny, former Attorney General of California) and her mother Mrs Duffield were pioneers. At the request of these two, we stayed on, and with the arrival of other pioneers, and assistance from the Hands (pillars) of the Faith, the first Bahá'í Spiritual Assembly of Nice was formed in 1956. After two years in Nice, we were able to spend a total of six years in Salzburg, Austria, a year in Arnhem, Holland, with Edward and Mary Bode, and a number of months traveling to Italy,

31

England and Spain. Following some ten years abroad, we finally returned to the United States and settled in Keene, New Hampshire. The notes that follow were jotted down by me during our travels, and deal with our everyday experiences, rather than our Bahá'í teaching work. In the event, we felt greatly blessed, to have had the opportunity of responding to the Guardian's call during his lifetime. Our very last direct message from him was a cable in October, 1956, answering our request for guidance as to our next post: "Advise Salzburg . . ." We realized, after his passing, how necessary it was that the pioneers should have gone out when they did: otherwise, there could not possibly have been so many National Spiritual Assemblies, worldwide, on which the Universal House of Justice could be solidly established in 1963 (see Shoghi Effendi, *God Passes By*, pp. 331–2).

Siren on Monday

Portland is where you go if you don't have the money to get to Seattle if you're going north, or to San Francisco if you're going south.

Portland is not an aggressive city. Their "cloud-cover" (absent, often, in the beautiful, brief summer) protects them from everything. People slouch and slump and the women draw down their blinds, and age.

October 18, 1952 . . . Portlanders are in despair over the unaccustomed good weather.

The logs floating placidly in the Willamette River. Spang in the middle of our picture window, Mt Hood, and through the north window Mt St Helens, two double scoops of vanilla ice cream. Yellow logs in the blue river; rust-red roofs huddling down to the here dull green water. A rust-colored ship moored down by an orange hill of sawdust. Planes unseen purring . . . Robins liquidly singing in the trees where the lawn falls steeply away. I look out at the bend in the Willamette; nothing in life is like a river curving away from you. I know it goes to Oregon City and Oswego and the paper mills, but I think it goes to Oz or Cocaigne or the Rock Candy mountains.

July 10, 1954 . . . my kind of day . . . wind blowing, pink and white laundry blowing, way below our window in the yard where the rotted belvedere is, like shredded strips of paper on a string. Blue patches blowing across the sky and the sound of the wind and the robins eternally singing . . .

The mechanical surf of cars below through the trees, on Barbur Boulevard, a gray machine-age waste of concrete islands and billboards and ever-present red and ignominious, sprawled and disfigured and crumpled-up automobile death. The screech of tires through the day down there, and the nagging wail of sirens . . .

There is another kind of siren, Mondays in the center of Portland at 12:05: the great enveloping noise of doom. You walk in sound; some giggle nervously, strangers ask, "What's that?" and are quickly reassured; the more sophisticated pretend that nothing is happening. Afterward you are wrung dry. When you hear that, some day or night other than 12:05 on a Monday, it will be time to shake hands with eternity. I have long accustomed myself to the idea of dying ever since before I could read, with the teachings of the *Hidden Words*, and now through the making of several wills, and noticing how many old teachers and friends and public figures have vanished or now look like strangers to me. Nobody used to die in my life – it was remarkable and something to ponder if a person died; now everyone routinely dies and I read, every day, the prayer that says ". . . I am the one who is sure to perish; behold me clinging to Thy Name, the Imperishable." I used to love graveyards, and traveling would pass them with the startled recognition with which you happen upon old friends. So the climate of death will not bother me. As for terror, I have been frightened all my life long . . . There have been the horrors of love and sudden death and desertion and betrayal and mourning. There was the long terror of paralysis and poverty and morphine (not for me – I was given a pill once and vomited it back) and the shabby publicity that is the lot of the poor – when I was in Ṭihrán with Howard dying. So let the calamity come.

August 7, 1954 . . . Yesterday, nine years since Hiroshima . . . The Jehovah's Witnesses, all ages and sizes, throng the streets. They predict the end and pass out handbills to those who will take them.

The bomb was detonated at 8:15 A.M. and most of the town wiped out. A new town stands there now, filled with new people – because most of the people who were there that morning are not there any more, a point that is frequently overlooked.

Your dead are gone and yet you keep looking and listening around the world for them, peering at people, trying to see *them* again and finding for remembrance only a line here and there, a tone or a gesture. "My mother walked a little like *that*," you will say, watching at the window as an old woman goes by. Or: "Her hair was a little like *that*."

The Little Flag

When I was telling Horace Holley why we were going to live in Europe he laughed. "Reasons are never believable, Marzieh. Only excuses are plausible."

August 30, 1954 . . . The red barns and red-and-white clover, the water lilies and Queen Anne's lace; silos, rich moving fields under towering clouds – Michigan slipping by, slipping away . . .

Late afternoon . . . We just passed Sarnia and came under the British flag. A while ago a handsome man in uniform (all Eastern Canadian men are handsome; most of the women are not) poked his head in the compartment and asked a few quick questions: "Where is your home? Where were you born, Miss? Are you going straight through to England? Not leaving anything in Canada? Just carrying personal effects?" He was pleasant and got his business done fast and left. A moment later a brunette uniformed woman (post-maturely brown, I would think, and altogether the kind you would leave your husband with) popped in and asked the identical questions. No doubt her real function is to appraise the female passengers with an eye unclouded by emotion. They did not touch the luggage.

This train is a coal burner with a nostalgic whistle.

August 31, 1954 . . . Quebec. The Château Frontenac, seventh floor. Through the window a conventicle of copper-green, witch-hat roofs and the rain and the wind pushing and elbowing from the sea. (Hurricane Carol moving up the St Lawrence?) A shredded flag streaming. Below us, away from the hotel, a bit of grass or green park and a huddle of red buildings and still below that, the vague, storm-blotted water where we will disappear tomorrow. I think I feel this tower-room swaying but it must be the motion of all these days on the train from Oregon.

In our room one wall slants and there's oldish furniture and a genteel picture by Pilkington – lawn, laburnums and a garden gate – that couldn't offend anyone. Its appropriately lugubrious title: *The Passing of June* . . . You can hear the water sometimes, slithering against the outside wall. Always the wind, pushing, straining, muttering and yapping.

The long Terrace Room of the Château Frontenac. Hanging flower-baskets move in the wind. (In the writing room upstairs, water is gurgling in a window.) Gray glass walls show the wet, deserted Esplanade. Birds and leaves blow along it. Tree tops through the railing, their roots far below, writhe before wet deserted benches. The wind drum-beats continually. This great spooky hotel, dimly lighted, matches the hoot of the wind. Tourists submerge into the twilit dining room – they do not obtrude like American tourists. There is the town, straining at its anchors – a street globe blew away as Harold watched. Now the lights go out.

September 2 . . . Yesterday the storm was gone and our sailing was dull, or would have been but for the Catholic Church. Three priests perched flush with the top deck in an open, upper story of the pier. They wore long slim black dresses, belling out at the feet, and gestured bird-like with white fingers. One of these priests wore a beret, the other two, black priest-derbies. They darted and peered and gestured from their eyrie, each wearing a huge gold cross at his middle; one carried a Land camera and one kept twisting at binoculars and the third brandished a limp white handkerchief. A group of nuns in the alcove next to them gestured goodbye to nuns on the deck – over and over they formed the sign of the Cross, like deaf-and-dumb language. Ours beamed back out of white starch and their mourning robes.

On board the *Scythia* . . . "Owsie, owsie, I'm going to play," our British fellow passenger, the bus driver from Durham announced. Bingo? Or dalliance with a certain travelling blonde? He's returning to England from a construction job in Canada with plenty of LSD (pounds, shillings and pence, as we learned later). In six weeks he'll be eligible for benefits again and will receive absolutely free a 140-dollar set of lowers. It was from him that I first heard the word "pensionable" – i.e., old. He was nicely dressed in an aqua suit and gray shirt and gray tie with a section of red snake writhing across it. Two days and nights of sleeplessness had made him look like a nervous French intellectual when I first saw him – this is typical of my unerring judgments. I also categorized the handsome dark caracul and rice grower from Swaziland as a British college professor.

Since no one British, apparently, ever imparts his name on shipboard, you live in an anonymous world of vague descriptions – instead of Mr Smith from Milwaukee, whose biography you know only too well. At least, it stops name-dropping.

The class situation is summed up for us daily on each new "programme." A separate heading reads "Intermingling of Passengers." Under this is the following: "Passengers are requested to remain in the accommodation allocated to the class in which they have booked."

In time we learn that there are 92 in first class and 673 in tourist (the difference between the tickets is about 100 dollars a head). Apparently the whole trip is being managed for the benefit of these 92.

The firsts are completely sealed away from contamination by the tourists. Since they pay a great deal more they have to get something for their money: that something, and it is no trifle, is never to meet us. We do not ever see their passenger list and they would not care to see ours. Although this trip is pleasant I hope never again to travel tourist on an English ship. Everyone is friendly and we all get "our due" but there is an imposed acceptance of a class philosophy which is false. Their Customs Declaration form even makes you list what class you'll travel up to London in, after you land. The man from Durham felt it and exploded. "I hate it," he said, and told us that two women at the other end of the table belonged to the class he hates.

Later he changed his mind and got chummy with everyone. The real reason for his justified outburst was the empty chair beside him. An English girl of the "sweet" type, apparently a "lady," had sat in that chair through several meals, in a sequence of well-made sports shirts and slacks. Then she departed to return no more. H thinks what did it was a conversation (initiated, alas, by me) about "words we mustn't use in England." The bus driver then related his most embarrassing experience. He had requested his Canadian landlady to "knock him up" at six the next morning. "What kind of talk is that?" she had asked in a spasm of gentility.

"I blushed all over," the driver told us. "I sweat down to my waist. It'll be many years before I forget it. It's common in England. Isn't it common in England?" he asked the "lady" for corroboration. I didn't dare look at her; after all, I had brought this on.

"It's common in America too," I muttered to H.

"Especially in North Wales," he went on earnestly. "In the coal mines they have a regular bunch of 'knocker-uppers' who'll wake you up. They come down the street and knock at your door."

"Like our alarm clocks," I said, marveling. (I haven't yet learned to shut up about how *we* do things in America.)

Later we asked him about the ferry to Ireland. "Don't say ferry. Say boat. Say steamah. Otherwise they'll say, 'What do you think we've got here – a canoe?' "

My favorite rumor: Lloyd's of London refused to insure this ship; she's 33 and will be scrapped after one more voyage – to India.

Every day we look longingly at the big map with the steadily advancing little flag that shows our position. Every day the weather is reported somewhat ambiguously in this sentence: "Cloudy, fine and clear."

The world, I note, is full of unattractive, aging men, who go around hoping they look craggy. Whenever they see a desirable woman, they feel a quickening which blinds them to the woman's lack of interest in them, and keeps them obliviously cheerful. As I said to H, when you see a pie that you find attractive, you don't ask whether you are attractive to the pie.

When I was seven I had my only public school experience – since we were either tutored or sent to private schools and I never attended high school, passing on to the university without it. I curtsied to the teacher, that first day at public school, to the delight of the class, some of whom were ten years old. Feeling alien, I consoled myself with a wonderful plan: some day I would go up to the blackboard in front of the whole class and take a piece of chalk and write "knowledge" on the blackboard. Today my Arabic study was the same thing all over again. I was showing them. Later H and I played chess with a tiny traveling set and with some coaching from him, I won. So by afternoon, with the splendid mental exercise replacing all these months of physical things – selling furniture, moving, shopping – I felt almost in order again.

There is no shape. "What is shape?" I asked the bus driver from Durham. "There's no such thing," he said. No one else at the table had heard of this old standby dessert out of books on England. So it is like chop suey in China. I sighed. I felt as I had on learning that Mothersills was a mister. There is, however, something, still unidentified by me, called Bubble and Squeak (it's a mixture of cabbage and peas, the Durham man explained, and they serve it for breakfast). Then there is flan, a sort of pound cake for a half inch, surmounted by a helping of glue and topped off with a dab of artificial whipped cream – and there is trifle, a sponge for one eighth of an inch, on top of which is a gob of cornstarch-custard with fruit stuck into it.

The man from Durham likes the pleasant woman who sits beyond the now empty chair beside him and they have played

Owsie-Owsie together. After she'd left the table he joked about *her* accent. "I arst 'er where she was from. 'In-jaw,' she said. 'Injaw!' " Interested, I asked, "Where in India?" "Didn't arst 'er," he replied. "Didn't want a load of bull."

About another he commented: "That woman, she 'as a bell in every turret." I made him repeat this and he translated, "She talks too much." His pronunciation of *turret* was approximately *tort*. "I 'appen to know where she lives," he added contemptuously. "London N.W.1. A block of tenements, that is. Peabody Buildings, they call it." The voice of the offending old lady, two tables back from us, reverberates under the dining room dome and by some trick of sound is relayed loudly to him, coming disconcertingly enough under all the circumstances, as if from me, who sit across from him. He holds large groups of people in contempt.

"Did you go to Mass this morning?" I asked.

"Nothing would get me to Mass."

"What's your religion?"

"None."

"How about your wife?"

"The same. We don't go to church. We aren't *heathen*, though."

If what I hear through the partition is any criterion, British parents are stern disciplinarians. The other evening an indignant parental voice – male, too – was saying: "What's this? Pants off, underwear off, shoes still on! *You are seven years old*. You know how to undress!" It has been a long time since I've remembered the enormity of being seven years old. He said it much as an American father might say – in a far weaker, more tentative voice: "Well, son, your mother and I have seen you through college. From now on, you're on your own."

A sick child coughed batteringly in the bunk next to mine, in the next stateroom. I thought her lungs would explode. The mother wasn't there – at the cinema, no doubt – and she began to howl indignantly, "I want my mummy!" Neighbors, unable to sleep, finally rang for the steward. He came, surveyed the situation and told her calmly, "Crying won't get you nowheres. Climb back into your bed."

41

"I can't," the child said, "my bed is all fwowed up. I want my mummy."

"Crying won't get you nowheres," he reiterated. The statement obviously corroborated the child's past experience, because she stopped.

This morning, swaying along the corridors, I said to H, "Only two more days now." An old steward, overhearing, added quietly as he passed: "*All Being Well.*"

At dinner the driver from Durham said he laughed and laughed at the Danny Kaye movie, the way Danny took off the gentry. I had noticed, at the movie, that some raucous laughter did greet the episode, but at the same time from many viewers came an italicized silence. Later I spoke of world civilization and how the present world needs changing.

"It does me," he said. "I like it."

"But you want a better world, surely," I insisted. "Look how you're always criticizing the gentry."

"I like them too," he said.

I could see his point: they provide a familiar homey target for his aggressions. Their superiority is a necessity to him. They are one more stabilizing factor in Britain. All we have in the U.S.A. is ever-divorcing movie stars, constantly changing presidents and always toppling champions.

"Parting is such sweet sorrow," he said to the pretty Belgian as she rose to leave. "*Pardon?*" she replied in French. We laughed when she had gone: "To be or not to be, that is the question . . . 'Pardon?' " I said, and went on: "That's one thing that nothing can ever take away from the British people."

"Wot?" said he.

"Shakespeare," said I.

"Aah," he said, shaking his head in disgust.

"Don't you like him?" said I.

"He was nuts," said he.

"How many Shakespeare plays have you seen in your life?"

"None," he replied categorically. "I've been to 'is 'ome – I've been to the cottage where he died – but that's as far as I go."

"What *do* you like?"

"Mickey Spillane. He's very popular you know – proves there must be *something* to 'im – cawn't all be perverted."

Somewhere on the Atlantic . . . the *Scythia* is greeted by the *Saxonia* and the notice posted on the bulletin board reads:
"The new baby makes her curtsey to Granny Scythia and hopes to follow in the family tradition and attain the honourable age and reputation of said grandmere.

To Captain Armstrong, *Scythia*
From Captain Mackellar, *Saxonia*."

The other day the man from Durham saw a whale. Except for two or three passing boats, and a gull or two, there have been only these whales, recognized by their quickly blown-over spume. "I saw a whale, by golly," he exulted. " 'E wasn't arf shooting up too."

I was somewhat taken aback, when he was explaining English money to us, and held up a penny and remarked to the table how often it had been a real lifesaver to him. But later (confronted by British toilets) I thanked him in retrospect.

The British have half of something that doesn't exist: the crown. We have two, four and six times of a non-existent thing: the bit.

September 9, 1954 . . . At last the little flag made it. Watched daily by us, it had stumbled across the Atlantic from Canada to the British Isles.

London

When I first saw London I was surprised at two things: the city looked smaller, vertically speaking, than I had expected – it *is* small – seven or eight stories high for most parts of London; and I was surprised to find familiar buildings right here in London where I expected them. Big Ben, Westminster Abbey, the Houses of Parliament, Scotland Yard. It was like opening a Greek grammar and discovering you already knew a lot of the words.

We do not try to go on any conducted tours or to "do" London. We simply get lost and let things happen, or jump on a bus and discover ourselves in West Dulwich.

If only someone would keep the British off sauces, much would be gained. Even dramamine was barely proof against the egg sauces that all desserts swam in on the boat. They do have a good mint sauce for lamb, but most meat sauces are on a par with what you empty out of your galoshes.

The coffee looked all right and I took one gulp – my last. It had been many years since I'd tasted cascara.

The other twilight when all I wanted was a hot bath, H insisted on going to Evensong at Westminster Abbey. There were perhaps thirty-five of us in attendance, facing each other on narrow velvet-padded benches. As I looked up, high up to the red and blue stained-glass windows and shadowy roof, the Abbey won me over with its authentic nobility; it has a worth that no money could have supplied. Then the procession entered and twelve men in white surplices over scarlet robes divided themselves into two bands and sat facing each other with the aisle between them. Here was where I hit the ground with a thud – the faces of the twelve men. I was quite close or would not have noticed the boredom. The surreptitious grins at one another, the yawns and whisperings. A half hour of beautiful, mechanical performance, archaic and remote, unfolded. The men were all ages from young to balding. Several wore spectacles. They did not seem to believe in what they were doing; they were not having a religious experience, they were giving a performance. Very well they sang "The Lord is King, be the people never so impatient." Beautiful cultured English was let down to them from somewhere on high. The Queen was prayed for, and the clergy, and the people.

London at the moment is my favorite town. It's gusty and blowy and alive. The people are vigorous. I thought the men would be undersized and the women frumps; but the old style Englishwoman: brown felt pork-pie hat, brown oxfords, brown Harris tweed suit, stringy purple scarf, wisps of hair, reddish nose – has vanished. The shops bulge with good clothes and many girls look American. All have permanents, make-up, high heels.

The brown leaves fly. Fountains jet.

We get our bearings by such means as: It's over by George the Third. George is in front of Barclay's Bank (where the four thousand in crisp hundred-dollar bills we have been wearing stretched across our stomachs ever since Oregon now reside). Oddly, he is given a peanut head and a pillar which dwarfs even the shrunken figure they have given him. Lincoln, on the other hand, is a colossus; he stands before, never to sit down in, a colossal armchair that contrasts sharply with his small, narrow, horsehair-upholstered little rocking chair that I saw in his Springfield living room.

Much of the town is gaslit, and dark and mysterious by night. The streets curve and run irregularly. None of the deadly monotony of our rectangular and always contemporary and identical cities. The buildings pile up in strange scribblings and calligraphies along the sky, layers of old and new, dark and bright, this era, that era, all flung together. There is vista after vista so that the eye is always pleased. Low buildings mean more sky and the continued presence of the past.

Bristol . . . So far the English countryside is Oregon with people. Still, it's lovelier for having been cultivated longer.

Although not flat, Bristol is rather like New Orleans: the old, tobacco-stained houses and cathedral, flowers, fog, painted iron grillwork. It has steep hills and vistas and mottled moss; pink and stained walls. A Vermeer canal and two gold unicorns. As H said, you'd think it was somewhere in Europe. They make or have access to a wonderful sulphur-butter yellow brick. I'd like a living room walled with it and some kind of fawn-and-butter wood paneling. You'd never be unhappy in a room like that. Perhaps people should keep a room where sorrow would be forbidden and you'd not be allowed to bring grief in – you'd have to take it somewhere else.

The park at Bristol has a large sign reading, "No Carpet-Beating before 6 A.M. or after 9 P.M." Evidently the British wait to see what people will do anyhow, and then regulate it.

The Thos. Cook sold us tickets to Chester – for 2:05; information confided that the train would leave at 1:40.

"Chestah's *bean*," a lady flung at me over her shoulder at the Bristol station. All you can get is erroneous, incomprehensible information from fleeing passengers. Chester hadn't gone at all. It was waiting down one Alp of stairs and up another, and us on the wrong platform with no porter, six pieces of heavy luggage, coats and camera extra – to which we have "reduced down."

Rattling around in first class, a ghost car, nobody comes, not even for your ticket. You see a chance passenger sway past, you stick your head out into the corridor and scream as Americanly as possible, "Say, is this Chester?"

"I hope so," the passenger flings back.

"Is that a cemetery," Harold says, "or a parade?" We were by Old Dee Bridge at Chester. It was a cemetery down by the

46

river. Swans rocking, tilting in the water; the blue rustle of the water. Sunday at Chester – Sunday at Portland. Not one person in Chester was (a) mowing the lawn (b) edging the lawn (c) raking the lawn (d) clipping the lawn (e) weeding the lawn (f) re-sowing the lawn (g) shoveling man's best friend off the lawn (h) trimming the hedge (i) washing the windows (j) polishing the car (k) up on the roof fiddling with the TV aerial. Everyone was out with wife, dog, grandfather and child, relaxing in the sun. Signs advertised exciting doings: "Excursions to Blackpool. Illuminations."

We wandered hours along the top of the old wall. Set in the wall was a minuscule tea and postcard place. We ventured on the apple pie and regretted it. A squat pinkish tower rises out of the wall – between the East Gate and the North; worn, lopsided steps go up to it, and it bears this inscription:

> King Charles
> Stood on this tower
> Sept. 24, 1645 and saw
> His army defeated
> On Rowton Moor

A jet crashes by overhead as you read. Below the inscription is a sign:

> Admission 2d.
> Children 1d.

As usual we took a bus, climbed up top and rode off into the unknown. We didn't know till the following day that beyond the shipyards (the *Mauretania* was built around here) and the nondescript water, it was Liverpool we were looking at: an unlovely coal-filled town.

Liverpool . . . H saw his first traffic-directress – a skirted policewoman wearing those enormous white cuffs and directing with gusto. Why not? There's a stiff wind. I went into the Ladies' Waiting Room in the station only to find that all they do in there is wait.

The public buildings and Walker Art Gallery are coal-black, so that you don't want to go in them. They have a few good things in the gallery though – a magnificent head of Einstein by Epstein: a bewildered little German with his hair on end.

47

In the gallery there's also a good head of Rossetti by Watts. I could understand how Elizabeth Siddons used to feel, waiting and waiting for him, and he not coming. I repeated her verses:

> Leaving me empty of all love
> Like beaten corn of grain . . .

The Watts head is not up to the uncanny head by Van Dyck in the National. When I saw it looking at me I thought I'll say hullo to the man in the next world, and he'll say hullo, I saw you in the National Gallery. His face is fine, sensitive, harassed, torn – an uncertain twentieth-century face. He gazes at you – as alive as life.

Ultimately, most tragedy becomes a spectacle for the indifferent.

Boarding a bus yesterday we heard an anguished cry, "*Insoide*, Kathleen! Insoide!" Kathleen, pigtails and grubby face, determinedly scrambled ahead of us up top on the bus. Soon her slightly older brother rose into view.

"Mummy told us to stay *together*," he called.

"Then why cawn't you come up here?" she asked reasonably.

"Because Oi told yer to go *insoide*. Mummy told me to 'av chawge."

"She did not."

"She did."

"She didn't."

Kathleen went down fighting, like most relatives when tyrannized over. I have long wondered why we allow our kin to run us. Is it fear of a loud noise, which, with the fear of falling are supposedly our only two basic fears? Would we rather submit than be shouted at? Just what are we afraid of? If we disobey, will they blow us up? Will they turn us over to the police?

The British version of "*Insoide*, Kathleen": "ATTENTION – All persons who are not travelling are requested to proceed ashore immediately."

The British do have a sense of humor but they also have a

blind spot where some types of relationships are concerned, while much American humor deals with connections between disparate things. In Waterloo station, all by themselves, are two advertisements, one on top of the other; the top one said, "Virol: Health Vigour Happiness," while the bottom one was headed, "Funerals and Cremations."

The English were always very conscious of our being Americans, much like many white Americans when being polite to blacks. They couldn't let it alone. They never asked, "Are you Americans?" but "Are you Canadians?" They didn't want to insult us? They were always rather careful. You got the impression that each of them, just once in his life, had been punched in the nose for asking someone, "Are you an American?"

Old women do not seem shelved here. They have their place the same as everybody else. They do not look chronically peevish and indignant and seething. Everyone in England seems more completely a person than Americans do. A young girl is a complete girl. Granted they may be inferior in education to American girls, numerically speaking – but they stride boldly along – they have their place . . . A man is certainly more of a man. An American is a sketch for a portrait; an Englishman is a portrait.

Mme Tussaud's: the extraordinary part is not people looking at the wax figures but the wax figures looking at the people. The big shots are upstairs; the criminals in the "Chamber of Horrors" downstairs. A good many of those who are upstairs ought to be downstairs.
Anyone who has watched a dining-roomful of Britishers knows that Mme Tussaud's is really put on with live actors.

The British are obsessed by the U.S. They can't speak a paragraph without including "the States" or "the Americans."

Dublin

Dublin . . . H says all I require anywhere in the world is a hotel with private bath and a street of expensive shops.

Dublin air is two parts horse manure and one part alcohol. Everywhere, pubs and ads for the "Irish Sweep." Everywhere, the rosary-click of trotting horses. An "Irish car" is a man with a cap, in an open two-wheeled cart with two long shafts, drawn by a sturdy horse.

These two posters on the bridge this morning: "Immoral Foreign Papers must be kept out of Irish Homes." And, "The Foreign Press is a National Menace." They are quickly torn off.

Attached to lampposts here and there along the river, life preservers thoughtfully placed to impede suicides.

I'm told there are two classes of Irish: the rich and the poor.

Express, Dublin to Cork . . . Country ravishing – green and rolling, and cloudless sky. Just had tea on our table in the sunny first class compartment. Not much evidence of prosperity, luxurious farms, or such. Mostly isolated buildings, pasture land and a few cows. When a cow relaxes from its usual "activity" it simply slumps down like a sack of flour two-thirds empty. Brother, that's relaxing. Father told me he had a nervous breakdown once and the doctor ordered him to go and stay around cows for a while.

Cork all day . . . No "public conveniences," just like the U.S. – and cops exactly like those in New York, uniform and all. H has just pointed out the "Third Class Ladies' Waiting Room." We had an ocean of tea – good scones (look like U.S. biscuits and often are terrible – but these were made with light brown flour); wonderful fresh butter; beef-and-kidney pie sans kidney but at least a good crisp crust, not the usual slush; parsnips.

Cab drivers told us that September is usually dull and depressing and today's perfect Riviera weather is unusual. Cork tends to be a small Dublin, with flat lines of houses edging a flat river. In Dublin and Cork we have seen, not a few, but many men, women and children wearing clothes Americans wouldn't offer the Good Will and the Good Will wouldn't accept.

The Cork peasant women each had a wonderful, black, fringed, wool shawl, that covered them tent-wise or was gathered around their necks according to the weather.

Edinburgh

Edinburgh . . . Box in Edinburgh buses: "Uncollected Fares Please."

The Scots seem to go for one building-material and color and have every residence in town of that color so it all matches. Dismal gun-metal gray stucco in Glasgow – brownish stucco in a town we just passed through. Houses, as elsewhere in the Isles, two stories high and stuck together, marching up and down the narrow streets.

Edinburgh I would call a tall city – a tall angular heights-and-depths city. I would say of it what Mark Tobey said of San Francisco: it is a mineral city. Edinburgh is a stone – old dark-gray-stained stone – city. A polylithic city.

I feel as if I personally had to hold up all this stone. Identical is the word for the architecture. A new house goes up in exactly the same style.

The granite houses are timeless. We saw (from the bus) Raeburn's studio, A. Conan Doyle's birthplace, all timeless stone. An American town is in a constant state of being put up and torn down.

Edinburgh sports beautiful sunsets and at night, down beyond the end of Princes Street, Kremlinesque towers show black against the heather sky.

The mountains are like our own Far West, almost – even to a tall bluff. But gray is the predominant color. Heavy oatmeal gray. You feel that everything *weighs* a lot and is heavy and permanent. You scream inside for a French meringue, or a floating seed pod or a bubble.

On a church wall:

> Tak Tent o' Time
> Ere
> Time Be Tint

Walking somewhere near the University we saw this sign on a door:

> If the Lord will
> The Word of God
> Will be preached here
> Every Lord's Day
> at 6:30 P.M.

We stroll down Middle Meadow Walk and note Jawbone Walk. Mist covers the wide green meadow. This is my season. I find again the tea-rose chrysanthemums, mists and changing leaves, the lapis-lazuli asters, the constant downward drift. "Your season has no future," Harold says. His season is spring. I always dread spring. I was born then. It happens again every April; somehow I've managed to bury myself over the winter, and then the grave is ripped off me in spring. I am exposed and public and harassed and separated, in spring.

Perhaps a man's psychic map is determined by the shape of his native land, so that each Britisher is a tight little island. Meals are an especially isolated time; the food, of course, is baked meats, the flowers floral tributes – you look for a ribbon with Mother written across it – the diners and especially the breakfasters are mourners. There is no unseemly levity. Nothing breaks the silence except the Thank you Sir, Thank you Madam, Thank you very much Sir, of the uniformed waiter or waitress, repeated as the prunes, cold toast, fatty bacon, midget tomato are served and withdrawn (often pretty much intact).

Disregarding uncordiality, restaurant managers at resorts insist on seating one couple with another. Each couple sits hating the other through the remainder of the meal. All communication is reduced to a few murmurs. Eyes stare into nothingness. The tablecloth is, as usual, dirty; as usual there are no napkins. This situation obtains – as with us yesterday – even when the dining room is half empty. The only time the man of the other couple broke the silence was to whisper to the waitress to withdraw a collection of mouldy scones that, placed on a sort of croquet wicket fitted with saucers at four levels, had no doubt been occupying the center of the small table since the height of the tourist season. She removed the offending pastry without comment, leaving the rest of the collection untouched.

This brings me to the one supreme annoyance: the table must at all costs be cluttered with heterogeneous cups, plates, silver, platters of scones, cakes and cookies which, God forbid, you are not going to eat (if you do, you must make a full confession at the end) and so on.

H points out a number of tiny museum-piece steam engines still doing duty in the train yards as we travelled. Scotch thrift.

Britain offers you far too many services and far too few goods.

There are more redheads in Scotland than in Ireland. All over the British Isles, less baldness among the men than in the U.S.A., it seems to me. Gallup might not approve of my method of gathering statistics, which is simply to look around. I do this, and see more hair.

In Aberdeen banks the man stands at an open counter surrounded by stacks of money – no grille, glass or other barrier.

The dogs do not look like American dogs. They're like the dogs on old tapestries and Books of Hours – except of course the plump self-satisfied dachshunds.

A Wee Chappie?

Aberdeen is a city of tall tombstones, the large economy size, perhaps to compete with the tall gray towers and spires. The buildings are mostly gray granite. There is the same identicalness and lack of variety and originality in architecture. Frank Lloyd Wright might never have been born. As usual, new buildings are barracks-type and tend to be identical in color. And new, single houses are simply separated duplexes.

The Scotch are brisk and brusque, more energetic I'd say than the rest of the British (the maids run around the hotel, shaking the building down), less cosmopolitan, more independent, perhaps with less charm, less differentiation.

H says they deal out stamps at the P.O. as if they were on piece-work.

The Scotch are more sanitary than the English and their food has originality – not just the inferior copy of a bad English original, as is the Irish.

Montrose. Pretty Scotch Venice. Overhead, a shimmering wishbone in the sky: ducks flying south. Here they say a "skein" of geese flying.

Here in Aberdeen (as in Edinburgh) we are near the railway tracks and the trains squeak and gibber and shriek, and puff white ghostly smoke. It matches the stone spires. Out of the stone forest come the clanging chimes. They sound not progressive but repetitive.

A sequence of horizontal blue and yellow moons loom into our long windows from the dark spires.

All yesterday we planned to leave for Nice, and today – this is the way we do business – H sits with me by the shilling-in-the-slot heater with two tickets to the Shetland

Islands. At noon he flatly refused to go to the Orkneys, much less the Shetlands. I said nothing. Here he is with the tickets, which we bought from an unenthusiastic man at Thos. Cook's. The one hotel he knew of, closes tomorrow. The boat – *St Magnus* – leaves at 5 P.M. from St Matthew's Quay; when I asked about her arrival in the Shetlands the Cook's man said they refused to commit themselves; theoretically, Saturday eve at eight.

Our shilling-in-the-slot is used up and the heater goes out. H deposits another shilling and it glows again. You can't trust it; it's a friend that turns cold when your money's gone.

St Matthew's Quay, Aberdeen, twenty to five . . . Slate water. Four soaring black cranes. Two black cranes on the black coal-loader. Wet slate roofs beyond the cranes. Dark sky low over the water. Black hull. Rust hull. Low green hill. Gray gull low over the slate water.

All day we had slip-slopped around. I have on open-toed, nylon mesh and patent leather (now cracked) shoes. Other shoes, rubbers, in Edinburgh and London. Mournfullest of all mournful things, shopping in a strange wet town for overboots.

The *St Magnus* is narrower than an old San Francisco ferry but a bit longer and far more graceful. We sit here comfortably in the first-class cabin.

The next morning about seven or eight we got off the boat at Kirkwall in the Orkneys. We walked into a diminutive story-book town with unstudied charm that Provincetown and Monterey would give their eye-teeth for. Hardly anyone was up. The streets were covered with oblong flagstones – and wound and angled – and there were no sidewalks. A red-cheeked, blue-eyed man in a cap came by going along Albert Street. "We're looking for Charles Dunning," H said. "I know him," said the man, lowering his hand palm down. "A wee chappie. Up there past the Boots, before you get to the butcher, there's a close. It's at the end." We started down the alley by the pharmacy, got lost, wandered back up and saw a tall young man in the butcher shop. Still not quite sure, we asked him, "Do you know Charles Dunning?" He started making the gesture with his hand – "That's him," we said,

56

never having seen Charles in our life. The butcher walked out of his shop, leaving his bleeding hunks of red meat spread out, and pointed down the "close" with an obliging cleaver. We went down again, rang a door bell. No answer at all. That is how we got our walk in the country. We bathed in the quiet, the slowness, the animal sounds and cock-crowing, walking along past the little granite-block or gray stucco houses and looking beyond, out over the hills. There were romaine and butter lettuces in the fertile little gardens. Sometimes there was peat – dark brown, limp, homemade fudge, with straw in it, cut fairly thin and stuck together in a mound.

Back in town a wee chappie in a brown suit came toward us. He had a voice big enough for six-foot-five. "They wrote me you were coming," he said. (We hadn't known it ourselves.) "But they wrote not to worry; you would stay at a hotel."

He is sixty-eight, tough as nails, strong muscles, knows jujitsu, corresponds with people in many parts of the world. He soon produced a letter from a newspaper, thanking him for his valuable contribution on the color-bar. He'd read that some immigrant East Indians had complained that they weren't being gathered to English bosoms, and he'd answered that Bahá'ís everywhere receive them with open arms.

He pays $8.50 a week for half a room, four meals a day and his washing. That leaves him ten shillings ($1.40) to spend out of his monthly pension. He also sells sheets and pillowcases but right now has a surplus of twenty double sheets because the man should have sent flannelettes at this season. He knows everyone, goes out and consorts with the gypsies, knows all the children and so on. "These footsteps I make all over the islands," he said, "they can never be erased. These children will grow up and somebody will come to the islands and ask, 'Did ye know Charles – ?' 'Sure we knowed him,' they'll answer."

Charles became a Bahá'í shortly after meeting Isobel Locke. He also told us of a big tall woman from America in a big tall hat; she was a Pankhurst feminist, he said. "I dug it out of her. Mildred Nichols, her name was." He told about Mario-Hofman's [Marion Hofman's] wonderful personality.

I said that in part I had come here because the Guardian had asked Ramona Brown to, and she was laid up in Rome.

Charles had phoned the highest official on the islands and asked for an interview. He wouldn't grant it. "He said I had nothing to tell him," Charles reported cheerfully. We recognize here the lifelong inequality that comes, in Britain, from having the wrong accent. But then there is the other relationship, that of the lady of the manor and the villagers, from which both classes seem to benefit. "His wife was beautiful to me over the telephone," said Charles. "So happy when she heard I knew her grandfather the hearl of . . . Came from the same village . . ."

The Knights of Bahá'u'lláh were a small and precious group of men and women who opened up virgin areas of the globe to the Bahá'í Faith. Their missions were vital; they were 'spiritual conquerors', and their names were inscribed for all time, in the Guardian's own hand, on an illuminated Roll of Honor – a treasure of the Bahá'í world. Charles was one of this company. Considered not worthy to enter the presence of a now forgotten bureaucrat, he enjoys a rank that is the envy of all Bahá'ís. We often think of how that official rejected him, ignored a telephone call that could have brought him a gift beyond price. Charles explained to us: "The Guardian said that I, and the girl in the Shetlands, were like points of light radiating over the islands." His voice was hushed when he said this. He had no vanity, only awe at the mystery of it.

Charles' landlady didn't like our visiting her in the morning, though she shook hands cordially enough. Charles sat me down by a stove and produced a bushel of snapshots for me to look at. The landlady left potatoes simmering on another stove and disappeared. Her son-in-law, big and ruddy and friendly, disappeared. Her brunette fourteen-year-old daughter sat to watch. My stove was a coal or wood burner set in a niche lined with a strip of green tiles. We sampled a bit of the local cheese H had bought. It had no taste, was white and looked like Monterey jack cheese.

Charles took us out to an old grassy grave-mound which

reminded me of Margaret Murray's *The God of the Witches*. "Four thousand years old," he told us. He said that under the ground there, are tiny stone caskets holding the ashes of early people. All houses had to be built facing this mound, he said solemnly. So they'd bear death in mind. "There's a strange power here. You'll feel it."

A guide sprouted out of the ground. He had a lamp and Charles seized it and hurried down into the mound, to show me the corridor leading to the underground pillars and little caskets. I followed gingerly; it was wet, muddy and claustrophobic. "Dates from three hundred years before Christ," the guide said. "Don't believe what *that* old fellow says. How'd ye find *him*?" "Oh, we know friends of his in Edinburgh," I said.

Charles saw us off at the pier. We each kissed him and felt lonesome after we'd waved goodbye to the little Barry Fitzgerald man. He was tousling the head of one of the blooming island boys. "He'll be one of ours," Charles called up to us from the quay. Half a room to his name – and the brown suit he bought eight years ago – some work clothes – his dark blue "Dunlops" with thick crepe soles.

"Do you ride a bike?" we called.

"Don't like 'em. You miss too much going by on a bike. I like foot-sloggin' "

"Do you fish?"

"Can't fish – makes me too nervous."

"But people fish to quiet their nerves," I say.

"I don't want mine quieted," he booms back.

The man who has the other half of his room gets drunk about every three months. "I'm not scared of him," said Charles. "I put him to bed. He seed yer goin' by this morning. He was weighin' yer up."

The Old Days in Paris

France has a characteristic which reminds me of nature: it goes on its way regardless of man. Set off a bomb and destroy everything in sight and still a blade of grass will pigheadedly push up, ignoring you and your works. Destroy France and it will pigheadedly return, ignoring you. It has survived wars and occupations and wave upon wave of tourists and the battering of every philosophical concept and its own self, and still it goes on, sure it is right, regardless.

October 10, 1954. Paris . . . How wonderful to eliminate the Channel by taking the Night Ferry to Paris. Comfortable, luxurious, antique sleepers – mine sounds like an old denture.

Disappointed in the Champs-Élysées – had remembered it from long ago: hoop rolling and carousel and Punch and Judy. Today – no champs and very little élysée.

These seem to stir the French most – not necessarily in this order:

L'amour	Love
La mort	Death
La patrie	France
Le pays	Your home turf
L'amour des bêtes	Love of animals
La famille	The family
Les illustres	The great
Les mendiants	Beggars
Le repentir	Repentance
La rétribution	Retribution (for others)
L'individualisme	The right to be yourself
La méfiance de l'étranger	Distrust of foreigners
Les causes célèbres	Endless broils, like the Dreyfus case.

French news vendors hide their headlines. They don't want you to get anything for free. English news vendors put their headline topics on placards.

Paris smells of urine. On the quays along the Seine – in the expensive restaurant last midnight, in all subway approaches, at street corners – it smells of thirty-five years' worth more urine than when I lived here before.

At intervals from some man or woman in the pack-jammed streets floats back a tide of heavenly perfume. It seems logical to me that a people which likes and produces the worst smells should also like and produce the best.

The usual French way of asking a question is more logical than the English, giving the listener time to think of his answer in relation to the real subject of the question – the primary subject.

"The man who came here yesterday, what is his name?" instead of "What was the name of the man who came here yesterday?"

H says the reason they devised the continental breakfast is that, before, too many tourists didn't last long enough to pay their bill.

I never ask a French man or woman storekeeper anything unless we have a money transaction going, and in fact often make a small purchase to entitle myself to one question.

Our going to the Louvre: as usual, H was the indefatigable tourist, while I was defatigable (and had to go to the WC). We trudged past acres of treasures, listened to and misunderstood a few words that reached us for free from a guided tour (Swedish). My feeling about the Louvre is that it should be taken in small doses, at rare intervals throughout life. I always visit the Venus de Milo – on her pedestal, set with unerring French taste at the far end of a long gallery. Afterward we climbed the steps to the great (however Pyrrhic) Victory of Samothrace. The sun came out and threw a sequence of ogival yellow window-shapes. A long line of satyrs, centaurs and Dianas stood blackly in the yellow shapes. As always I visited the Mona Lisa.

We finally discovered the WC. A lady was presiding there at a table, she with a saucer of coins before her. I added my ten francs' worth.

"My three cubicles are occupied," she said.

I waited patiently.

"Was that your husband with you?" she asked.

Bewildered, I said yes.

"Then you can go in there too," she insisted, almost forcibly persuading me in through the door, and I found myself in the men's. We hurried past H himself in an unfamiliar pose. Afterward he told me he'd heard women's voices and had asked himself, "Good heavens, are the walls *that* thin?"

She shut me in a cubicle, cried "*Vite! Vite!*" and left me. It was bad enough being in the john with H, worse when I realized that other males, to whom I had never even been introduced, might materialize at any moment.

Messages chalked or painted on the walls: *NON au réarmement allemand. Vive la paix.* U.S. Go Home. Sometimes only a big *NON* remains. Chalked on a wall near a schoolhouse, my favorite: *Vive moi, à-bas les autres.* (Hooray for me, down with everybody else.)

The endless beauty of the shops and the women. The total fierce concentration on the things of this world. Sunday I saw the crowds and asked myself, where is everybody? These were not the French I once knew – ebullient, laughing, crying, fighting in the streets, staring – if you poked a finger at the sky a crowd gathered. These were stern, serious, almost English-sober (but not at all blossoming like the London crowds). They were pale, pasty, preoccupied, even in the Bois, and contrasted queerly with the people we had just left in the Shetland Islands, with red flags in their cheeks. I had glimpsed Paris as the center of the planet, with crowned and deposed kings going by (many of them long dead now). At the Meurice yesterday, we talked with Edna True and Honor Kempton – in that same stately hotel where we had once met the Sháh of Persia (Aḥmad). At the close of our audience I had stuck out my hand and after a moment he had gravely taken it; although our interview was in his suite, and he was bareheaded, his own hands were carefully protected by brown kid gloves.

When I was a child in Paris, we lived for a time at 4 avenue de Breteuil, by the Invalides. I can still see the gold cupid in the middle of the ceiling, holding down the light. And underneath, Father in his elegant Paris clothes and Persian *'abá* writing letters, the paper on the palm of his left hand, Persian style. The fold of his *'abá* lay flat on the floor, and our gray velvet cat would curl asleep on this fold.

Before this we had lived in Passy, where I can nostalgically remember us as a not too unhappy family. It was one of their big years, Father a delegate to the Versailles Conference, Mother going in to dinner on the arm of Orlando (one of the "Big Four"), the two visiting President Wilson's box at the Opera, the great banquet Father and Mother gave at the Ritz. My actual memories of that time are mostly guests and dresses, a harp arriving for Mother's at-home, Isadora Duncan coming to say hullo – all this was in the rue Colonel Bonnet – "She was in and out," I told Mother. "It was 'Where do we go from here, boys?' "

Walking along Passy looking for a memory. Something to return to in a world that, personally and intimately speaking, gets increasingly lonely. There is almost no one to go back with; and there are fewer and fewer things to go back to – as sorrow obliterates the memory areas that surround it.

Now, memories of this quarter begin to return. We had been to the florist's (Father said Mother ordered so many flowers the man added an annex) and I had caught sight of myself in a glass door – blue coat, sheaf of white flowers, red cheeks. Our hands were kissed, we knew ministers of foreign affairs; an ambassador who later became Premier brought us so many chocolates I've never eaten them since. I remember our comfortable-looking cook, Marie – and our black-haired maid. Anyhow, I walked along Passy and suddenly a street sign meant something to me: rue Singer. Then the next moment, another sign: ave du Colonel Bonnet. And that was where we had lived. We had fed the birds on one of these second-floor balconies. I remember the fashionable mother, all in black, who rented us the apartment – and all the mementoes of her son, killed in the war. And now she is dead too, surely, and all her sorrow with her, and all the mementoes in his little bachelor's room scattered, and nobody left to mourn either of them.

I walked through the liquid air that seemed about to burst into rain. All was dark gray as usual. I had gotten the subway to the Étoile, and stood looking at its soft brown mottlings in the gray light. The Étoile is all stained, soft browns and yellows running down; Paris has taken over, the way grass does. Paris has a way of taking monuments and people, clouds and trees and streets to itself and brushing them with its own patina. For example the Eiffel Tower should be hideous, and in America it would be; there would be workmen in paint-spattered white overalls swarming over it at all times, perpetually painting it orange and bright silver. No, here it is aloof and undisturbed and eternal, a perfect, fragile spire of brown lace.

Looking at it is one thing, but I hope never to go up in the Eiffel Tower again. In a series of elevators, you pass up and up into the top; the elevator is a spider dragging you slowly up to your death through a brown spider web; it is not like going up in a building or tower or plane – there is nothing around you but wisps of brown steel, and a microscopic Paris spins below.

My main memory of this place is that years and years back, walking beneath the tower with my mother, we came upon Shoghi Effendi (destined to be Guardian of the Bahá'í Faith), having a lonely walk. He wore the now famous trench coat and Persian hat of those days, and we chatted and arranged to meet. In all the years I have never forgotten him as he walked beneath the tower.

There is a photograph showing 'Abdu'l-Bahá with His suite, beneath this same tower, not many years before that day; and I wonder now if the Guardian wasn't walking there because the Master had.

Palace of the Popes

October 13, 1954 . . . Gare de Lyon . . . Many things have happened in layers. Little could be written down and now I suppose it's all gone together like the successive paintings of the Last Supper. It seems that experts can separate them: I can't.

Rain, like Roentgen rays, is cumulative in the system. After two years of Portland I cry when I see a cloud. Now today, heading south, I wallow in the sun. There are many people who are immune to weather – probably the same ones who wall out the view and put a picture-window facing the traffic.

When we got off the Paris train at Avignon we had glasses of tea at an outdoor café and plastered ourselves with sun. We noted the high, fourteenth-century city walls and for some reason thought, this is not France, this is an Arab town. Spotted plane trees lined the sunny streets. There were rapid, sprightly crowds and modern-looking shops.

Toward evening we walked along the shiny, black-swirling Rhône. An ice-cube planet floated in the claret pink sunset. There were posts at intervals along the deserted bank, for mooring boats.

We were able to lose all consciousness at the auberge that night, and were not awakened until loud lamentations burst forth, to the accompaniment of running feet in the hallway, on the following morning. "*Oh, les salauds, les salauds!*" (*Oh, the filthy beasts!*) a voice was crying. I raised up on one arm to listen. A busload of American tourists had just left, it developed, containing yet one more American tourist who had not been instructed about the bidet.

High up above the great fourteenth-century city wall, between two TV aerials, queening it over the Palace of the Popes stands Our Lady of the Lords. No use trying to take a photograph unless you wanted the aerials, and in any case she stands too far up in the sky from the river. We worked our way into a road that follows the inside of the wall. This is a place where tourists seldom come; very different from the "Little Paris" of the main streets, and the prosperous villas. A wine truck lumbered by us. Across the road from the old ramparts, battered and discolored houses. On one house wall, up in a niche, a small gray stone Virgin and baby. Beside us, through dark window-panes, past bits of torn lace curtains, people moving. A guessed-at housewife washing up, releasing dishwater through a hole in the wall, the water running out to an open gutter at our feet. Discolored laundry whipping at upper windows. The narrow sidewalk between the houses and the gutter is perhaps a foot wide, too small even for one person, and the dogs have been there first.

We walked up ruined steps, through crumbling remains of the old Jewish quarter, that clustered for protection close to the Popes. Ragged children, with red-rimmed eyes, dusty hair, scalp sores, thin bodies, run past us, leading a dog on a string. The loose-bodied, dusty dog has an anything-goes look; too old for the game, he is nevertheless evading the city dog's enemy number one: boredom. After ringing around us briefly to beg – the spokesman, whining with a professional technique reserved for tourists, but forgetting his magnificent, half-chewed crescent roll in one grimy hand – the tattered caravan struggles hurriedly on, keeping out of the blue shadows, staying in the warm patches of sun. It is hard to see how, even six hundred years back, Avignon's children would have looked any poorer. Yet the town itself is not poor; the tourist river must leave a rich silt. When you sit, not many steps from here, in a glassed-in dining room, eating your *cervelle d'agneau aux câpres*, your *coeur de fenouil* and your *langouste truffé*, a small, dirty, imploring face and dirty cupped hand suddenly appear through the pane, between the window boxes. These shapeless, mottled houses, mixed in with the ruins, are where such children live. We give the houses an absent-minded glance and go away for ever; but this is where these children live, every day and night.

"It remains for me to wish you, above all, fair weather," the guide said to us, bored, but as usual, polite. We straggled out of the Palace of the Popes, beaten down with information, wondering why we resent information, deciding: because it makes us feel inferior.

"There's a book there," Harold said as we emerged.

"Not for me," I answered.

I was wrong.

The grocery lady provided us with an assorted lunch: two crescents, two brioches, roquefort cheese, a litre of milk (we should return the bottle and get back the deposit; if she was still away for her three-to-four-hour midday closing, we could leave the bottle by the door and she would pay us back the next time – there always have to be negotiations). We also bought two rolls with chocolate inside, and two green chocolate frogs; they are a speciality of Avignon: the chocolate is light green and the frogs have dots of brown chocolate for eyes. Loaded down, we walked precariously away to a bench in the bare little park.

On the next bench was a lumpy tortoiseshell cat, about to have a numerous family. Cat today was a collective noun. Out of chivalry, H hollowed out the seal of the milk bottle for a saucer, put it down and poured her some milk. She came heavily down, sniffed, and leaped back on her bench. She addressed us a look of indignation.

After a while we wandered away. We passed through a hodge-podge of medieval streets. Dark gray walls; high, carved wooden doors; foot-wide sidewalks: a glimpse of old courtyards; arches, tunnels, a gray canal running along.

We drifted down a street of plane trees to the Gate of Saint-Roch, near where the Black Plague victims had been buried in 1348, in the Champ Fleury. We came to a slaughter-house that has animals' heads on it. A ram's head with curving horns, a bull, a cow, carved in relief, and with them, tools carved: a sledge-hammer, long saws and knives, a kind of halberd for chopping. French, and sad: we kill you, yes; but what a send-off. Across the street, which is the rue de la Velouterie, we saw a cream-colored house with bands of ceramic flowers across it.

"I'd like to buy a house here in Avignon," I said.

"You always want to buy a house, everywhere we go," said H. "The first thing you say in any town is: 'I want to buy a house here.' And the second is, 'When's the next bus?' "

"People are always making trouble for me," I answered. "They quote my words in context."

A tour took us out to Daudet's windmill – he and Don Quixote will for ever be associated with windmills. I asked whether his room was in the mill. "No, he didn't write here, just made notes," the guide said, explaining the process of literary creation. "He used to walk over here from his uncle's neighboring château," the guide went on. Daudet lost me at that moment: I had thought he was poor, like D. H. Lawrence. H comments lugubriously, "Maybe he *was* poor; after all, I had a rich uncle."

Everywhere, it is not the places that count – it is the writers, the poets, who have created the places. Even the events do not count until some writer gets hold of them. Musicians and painters can for all I care demur. They themselves have to be gotten hold of by some writer, and put into words. It is only words that are not put into words. The Prophet of God is the Word, not the Note, not the Brush Stroke.

In the little nameless Arab villages we pass, always the Crucifix. Is it from love of the Crucified, or hate of the crucifiers, that they have stared at the agonizing Body two thousand years? Is it the "pleasure in displeasure" idea? Napoleon is remembered on a horse, not dying of cancer. Lincoln is not habitually shown collapsed in a theater box, nor Joan of Arc at the stake, nor Socrates drinking the hemlock. When you love someone, you hate and hide his suffering.

"I have suffered much in my life," said Monsieur Sandobal, the factotum at the Auberge de France in Avignon. "I am sixty-two years old, but I have only had my papers for two months and a half. I was born in Barcelona. My parents brought me here when I was one. I fought in the First War, in Morocco. You see how I am crippled. I have only one lung. An Arab cut the other out."

Monsieur Sandobal made a crescent-shaped swathe under his left arm. I could see the moon shining on a curved blade, and hear the swift blood thudding.

"That was a different war, our war in Morocco, Madame. They came at you with their daggers in their teeth. But you see how I can carry baggage up and down these stairs. I can stand up to any man of thirty."

He looked at you out of his direct, sad brown eyes. You would always believe this man, trust him with anything.

"I know six languages, Madame. Enough English and German for my work; then very good Portuguese, Spanish and French. Some Swedish. But I have suffered much in my life, Madame, without my papers. I have been married twenty-nine years; there is a daughter in Paris and grandchildren; but I was legally married only two months ago and a half. After many years and much money, I have my papers. They were all destroyed in Spain. My kin were all gone. Here we found six witnesses to swear they remembered me when I was a baby, one year old."

We were silent, already dimly aware of what life is to a European without papers. We knew what had befallen a certain Madame Marceline. When a woman's body was pulled out of the Seine, Madame's concierge, her brother, her sister and others, identified it as that of Madame Marceline, dead at last of often-threatened suicide on account of a broken heart. The body was released for burial. One hour before the interment, a Guardian of the Peace – read cop – recognized Madame Marceline in the Bois.

"They're burying you," he told her. "You'd better hurry if you want to attend your funeral."

The policeman, however, did not manage to stop Madame Marceline's obsequies, which went forward with due French solemnity. And Madame was stupefied to learn that she was now dead and would have to undertake a long and costly lawsuit to prove any different.

Papers. You could paraphrase that old saying about death:

the young may die, the old must. An American may have papers; a European must.

"Now I am Spanish," Monsieur Sandobal went on. "But I have all a Frenchman's rights, because I fought in the war. You know what I will do, Madame? I will get a job in Barcelona, for I have never, since when I was a baby, set foot in Spain."

"Then this is your honeymoon," I said.

"Oh, my honeymoon is long passed," he said. "When I stood before the Mayor with my wife to be married, I wept."

With brown fingers, he traced the remembered tears down his cheeks.

"And why do you want to go to Spain after sixty-one years?" I asked.

"Because I want to die there," he said. "You know, Madame: *la patrie.*"

Across from the auberge, the old town clock strikes the hour twice. That way, when you've lost count you can check again. It has an old, tinny sound, like banging on a metal tray.

Today in the white sun, on a bench with a wall back of us, we sit and have lunch out of the slashing wind. Outwitting the restaurants, with their interminable meals, and almost permanent waits for the bill, we arrived here with a litre of milk from the Bon Lait, a large triangle of Brie, and two petits-suisses – which are plump soft cylinders of white cheese – besides the usual croissants and other rolls. Each of us lunched grand luxe for about forty cents. Somewhat regret-fully, at dessert time we remembered a box just mailed away to friends: in a small basket of osier, it contained uncannily perfect dead fish, clams, and slices of lemon, all made of candy.

We were high up in one of the world's loveliest and perhaps least known little parks, the Garden of the Rock at Avignon. Across and down from us, was the Palace of the Popes. In the sky over us, the Queen of Heaven stood on a great block of a tower, drawing up to herself, culminating and dominating the town. Peacocks walked here, and there were two swans with orange-sherbet beaks that looked exactly like the swans painted in the fourteenth century on the study wall of Pope

Clement VI in the Palace across from us. The few people about us were having their quiet two hours for lunch. A French family: grandparents, child, then mother and father swinging a rose-cretonne-covered baby basket between them, climbed past us to the *pique-nique* still higher, to where they could look down a sheer cliff and see the ferry crossing the curve of the Rhône. Where we were, the old pines leaned on tall wooden crutches, and along the walls the vagrant but discreetly behaved – at first glance almost house-bred – cats of Avignon were lightly festooned; infinite fur beads, a fur chaplet on an invisible string.

Fighting the wind, we went on up to the cliff's edge and watched the cable ferry far below. Hours later, still fascinated by the river, we were beside the Rhône again, watching long, low barges shove against the current. Walking on, past the utilitarian bridge, we passed by the broken-off span of Saint-Bénézet's, rounded the bend and came to the *bac-à-traille*. The dark, swirling water was already stained with sunset colors, and although business had been quiet, as we knew from our observations in the Garden of the Rock, the boatman was not happy to see us. He was a man like so many older Frenchmen, made up of circles: round cap, round cheeks, round trunk with comfortable curving arms, round legs. Believing that the French will not do anything because it is their job, but only if you enlist their sympathy on some personal basis, we parleyed. He finally admitted that he would take us across, if we promised to return by six o'clock.

We stepped into the long, flat *bac* and sat gingerly on a bench that ran around the sides. A horseshoe, painted light green, was stuck inside the prow to remind all comers not to trifle with the Rhône: uncaringly, the muscular black river could choke the life out of us as it hurried on.

Our man stood up in the stern and manipulated the long-handled rudder, laying it against the current so that we were twisted out into the river; after a while he stuck the rudder handle in a rope sling. High above us a cable was stretched across the river; our boat cable, fastened up near the prow, was hitched up there on to two small pulleys that slid, barely visible in the twilight, along the sky cable as our rudder moved us into the current. The current pushed us across, the cable tethered us, so that we could not be whirled away downstream, to possible panic and death.

The other side was nowhere in particular, just a way to somewhere. We walked for a while in the damp and twilight along the river. There was nothing to see, except, rising among low trees, a rusty metal Christ and crucifix of considerable beauty.

You Can Buy the Furniture, Too

We are now in that period that follows arrival and precedes settling down. We would like privacy and food of our own choosing at hours that seem reasonable to us, and we tramp the streets, so far avoiding the real estate agencies because it has been drummed into us by a native that if you rent you have to pay them blackmail every month for as long as you stay.

There are no For Rent signs anywhere, however. Finally one day, wandering along, we saw a real estate place and went in and talked to the man.

"Anything to rent?"

"Absolutely nothing. What do you want?"

"Can we buy a pied-à-terre for one million ($3,000)?"

"It would be very difficult."

When you approach a French person about anything, it would always be very difficult.

Come to find out he did have a place in mind for us: a house with six rooms, of which two were occupied. No bathroom, but a WC that he said connected with a sewer. We were worried about the two occupied rooms. We already knew that according to French law no tenant could be put out of a house for from three to four years and a half, depending on your informant. Even then no one could be put out, because at the end of that time the case would go to court and that interminable procedure, normally dragging out many years, might only result in a decision for the tenant – if he were old, or had a small child or almost any other excuse. It was obvious why there were no For Rent signs.

"I warn you," said the man, "don't ever rent a place to anyone. He will promise to leave at the stipulated time. Then he won't go, and there's nothing you can do about it. I would accompany you to the notary about the sale," he added, "because you are strangers here and I don't want you to have any surprises." He had all the dewy candor of a three-hundred-year-old carp.

"Come tomorrow," he said. The French always ask you to go away and come back.

We arrived at his agency the next morning. A shiny blue car stood in front of the door and we headed toward it – only to stop in mid-career as the agent unhitched a bicycle from the curb and began pushing it along ahead of us.

"I know Avignon like my own pocket," he said, leading us through the dark, narrow streets of the ancient quarter.

"How old is the house?" I asked, aware that with a house as with a woman, you don't expect the right answer.

"It will be here a hundred years after you are dead," he reassured me.

We stopped at a door in a dark green wall. A Madame Tropez, supposedly the current owner, let us in. She was plump and powdered, in a house-dress, her brown hair ringletted, her eyebrows plucked to thin arcs. She had the trick of talking friendlily right into your face.

"The house is sold," she announced.

"The gentleman is American," said the agent.

At this Madame Tropez decided the house wasn't quite sold after all.

"Please keep your voices down," she said; "the neighbors hear everything."

Once inside, she whispered loudly to the agent that she'd sold the house for 900,000 francs, then turned to us and said the price was one million two. The agent explained that the first buyer had put down 100,000 francs' deposit, and that the lady would, if we bought, have to give him back double this amount, according to French law. The extra 100,000 was of course because the gentleman was an American.

The house had indeed six rooms, two per floor, and a little courtyard in back, complete with the famed WC.

"You have to think of a room in a new house as 500,000 francs," the agent said.

The rooms were tiny and black-dark, though the day was dazzling.

"A typical southern interior," the man said, indicating beams in the ceiling and the floor of red tiles.

Madame Tropez's taste ran to frills and flounces and decorative dolls. Tarnished brass bedsteads and tall, dangerously tilting armoires crammed the little rooms.

"Far cry from what Americans call French Provincial," was H's contribution.

There was no bathroom.

We climbed to the floor above but here we were stopped. We had to buy the rest of the house unseen.

"Why?"

"Because there are tenants on the next floor."

"Tenants?"

"Two Italians," Madame Tropez said friendlily, into my face. "*She*'s just back from the hospital – only weighs 29 kilos." Multiply by two-point-two, I told myself, and came up with 64 pounds.

"Doomed," she went on. "And he's sixty-eight. You'll never see him. You can get rid of him *easily*. He pays 1,000 francs ($3.00) a month. Won't live long anyway."

"Oh, you can get rid of *him*, all right, once you're in," the agent airily abetted, forgetting what he had told us the day before. He made a gesture with his thumb and forefinger, counting out money: a thousand francs a month. I began to feel like Lady Macbeth.

We looked up at the silent ceiling. Two old people, up there quietly dying of poverty and disease, not even eligible for French pensions, and somehow producing three dollars rent a month. We wondered how they ever climbed the stairs, and where they went to the toilet. The WC in the courtyard was the only "facility." It was damp and dark, inside the house here and outside in the narrow medieval lane, despite the golden sky everywhere else.

"You can buy the furniture, too," offered Madame Tropez.

The Bulls at Nîmes

"The French love animals," we start to write, and then we remember the bulls at Nîmes.

We are still in Avignon. Last night we had been much impressed by a French crowd's reaction to an American film. It was a Western which the audience had watched quite placidly while both white and red protagonists bit the dust. Suddenly in the melee a dog was shot. The house started to rise as one. Loud exclamations burst out. For a moment we thought mass action would be taken. It was all right to kill people, apparently, especially foreigners, but an animal is something else again.

Glad to have pinned down a fact, we wandered out of the auberge the next morning and sat in the little park, back of what the Avignonese call the Protestant Temple. It is a park peopled by a few sleeping statues, a covey of black-clad old ladies (black in France is age's proper uniform) and a streaming cat-colony to which the old ladies bring bits of fish or chicken-skin in newspaper. An old lady with a greasy newspaper cat-treat rolled up, came and sat on the bench beside us, questioning the air.

"Where is he, the little black one?" she asked. "No, not you – not you," she said to two advancing tabbies, who certainly looked peaked enough to qualify for a lunch. "The little black one."

Touched by her interest in the animal kingdom, I tried to help. "He was here half an hour ago," I told her.

The fact remained that H was even then carrying two tickets in his wallet for the bullfight at Nîmes. It was to be a charity affair, and had the Church's blessing. Proceeds were to succor the "sinistered" French inhabitants of a distant city. They

76

were sinistered indeed, made homeless and destitute by an earthquake.

"A Grand Taurine Festival," announced the red-edged tickets, which showed a bull-fighter in his gold suit-of-lights and pink stockings, standing triumphant over a prone, lavishly bleeding bull, stuck with tasteful *banderillas*, its legs stiff in the air.

The small black cat had not turned up when it came time to leave our bench, walk out beyond the fourteenth-century city walls and get on the bus for Nîmes.

For an hour or so we watched the countryside, lapped in beauty. Old walls, black cypresses, gray bamboo fences, delicate white roads curving – all dreaming in the clear Provençal light, cradled in the thirty-two regional winds. But the beauty abated somewhat around Nîmes, which is just another inert, provincial town, of awnings, of huddled café chairs and tables encroaching on the streets, and dust clouds rising from bare, unplanted parks. Today the streets of Nîmes were empty, with everyone drained into the big Roman amphitheater, that Christians once died in, and that Charles the Hammer set fire to in 737, to drive the "Barbarians" (the far more civilized Muslims) out.

Present-day, undistinguished crowds, with bare arms, thin shirts and dresses, were chattering around the great circle in the hot sun. There was a brisk trade going in huge, conical hats: purple straw ones with appliquéed roses, green ones made of paper, with wide paper brims. In constant motion, sweating and fanning themselves, these moderns probably did not match up to many a sumptuous crowd of other days, long gone.

At last a windy little band struck up, and the parade into the arena began. The *toreros* did not at all resemble the splendid matador on our tickets. These were little men dressed in browns and grays, accompanied by nondescript attendants and a few ailing horses. French thrift had obviously prevailed. After ritual bows before the President's box, the arena was cleared, a gate swung open, and a bull burst in. He had a familiar look; he was pretty much like any bull down on the farm.

77

There was the opening work with the cape, watched mostly by the matador, and then he made a few passes of his own. Now the picador's spindly horse tottered over, wearing a red blindfold. We had the feeling its rider was holding it erect by the reins. Quivering, it was ridden over to the bull. Near the barrier, the bull found the horse, and gored it repeatedly under its quilt-like coverings, finally throwing it, all in its blindness, to the ground, as the picador slid away. He then came back on another horse, and this time plunged his lance deep into the bull, badly damaging the bull so the fight began leaking out of him too fast. Meanwhile the new horse braced itself and refused to go down and the bull banged it against the barrier; then, losing interest, turned aimlessly to worry the magenta and yellow cape now lying on the sand. From across the arena, the matador summoned the tiring bull, and standing tall, on tiptoe, in two separate, interrupted gestures, went about plunging in two pairs of pink and yellow banderillas, which hung from the bull's hide like paper streamers off the deck of a ship.

Time was clearly running out. The matador hurried his business with the red muleta, the fighting cape. He went quickly back to the barrier, changed swords, advanced to the bull and suddenly thrust his blade deep between the heaving shoulders.

The bull, alone with his enemy in the middle of the arena, stood braced. Twice, he moaned. He looked around as if he were trying to remember something. Suddenly he urinated long and copiously in the place where he was dying. The crowd laughed and applauded. The bull stood swaying, back and forth, back and forth; he lurched, he refused to go down; he collapsed at last to loud applause and disapproving whistles. An official voice rang out over the loudspeaker: "The Presidency accords one ear." The crowd whistled again as the bull was dragged away by galloping dray horses, a man running behind the carcass, cracking a long whip to speed the ignominious dead.

The next fighter faced a small but wild, black animal who charged into the arena, already maddened, with the red and green ribbons flowing from the barbs in his hide. "*Olé!*"

uncertainly roared the French crowd. After the first passes, *da capo*, along came the picador on his moribund horse in its red blindfold, and muffled in its quilt. For a moment, man, bull and horse rocked together against the barrier, while, to frenzied applause, the pic was plunged in. After more passes by the matador he crossed the arena, called the bull to him, stood on tiptoe and stuck in two peppermint-green banderillas, then saw fit to run off. Again, he gave a voice-summons to the bull, stood high, and placed two orange-sherbet ones. Swaying ludicrously awry, all four banderillas stuck out here and there from the bull. A broad red smear of blood plastered the bull's heart-side and glistened in the sun. Saliva dripped from its mouth. The matador's magenta butterfly-cape flashed gracefully, leading the animal on, wearing down the ebbing life. But the bull still lived; he seemed drunk and unsure with his dying and the matador's helpers jumped warily out of the way. The muleta came now, like a flag sideways on a handle, concealing the sword. The matador's Spanish bullfighter's hat lay on the ground, a jet spot on the gold sand. He held out the red muleta. He shouted at the now dancing bull.

"*Musique!*" someone called. The tinny band played. Somebody cried, "Oh, he is formidable, terrific, this bull!" There was crazy applause. Stock-still now, the bull looked around as if for help. There was no help. Only the unexplained enemy before him, and circling him, the screaming, jeering crowd. One banderilla dropped from his hide. The matador picked it up and tossed it contemptuously aside, but then hastily saw fit to run. He dropped the muleta as he went, while his assistants diverted the charging bull. The fighter then turned his back on the bull – he almost had to after running away – walked to the barrier, changed swords, was back with the bull again, and plunged the blade deep in. It fell out of the over-large wound and lay on the glaring sand. There were thick red stripes of blood on the blade. The bull, his tongue loosely out, lunged and charged. The matador retrieved the sword, placed it deep into the great shoulder and ran out of the arena, dropping the muleta again. Assistants with magenta-and-yellow butterfly-shaped capes lured the bull and spun him round. The cape of one of them caught onto the deep-planted sword and pulled it out. Paint-red blood flowed; blood, too, from the bull's mouth, and the bright red tongue hung out. Experimentally, the returned matador reached out and touched the bull's nose with his sword-tip. The bull, standing in his place, jumped; above one ear, ridiculous, caught on a banderilla, hung a yellow and magenta cape. The matador raised his sword and thrust it in deep, near the base of the animal's brain. The bull jumped again, started, refused to die, and the two assistants caped him this way and that under the hot sun. The banderillas, one green and two orange, were still in his hide when, all flags flying, the bull at last bowed down, his nose bending to the sand and the paint-red slick of his blood. He toppled, to tired applause; his legs still moved in the air as he was horsewhipped out. The matador was accorded one ear. In tribute, a woman flung down her green leather handbag; he caught it and hurled it back. An attendant came in and sprinkled the sand.

Against a new man, a new bull exploded into the arena, brown this one, sporting red and green ribbons stuck in its back. This bull cried out repeatedly in a high falsetto. It was somehow horrifying; it was a protest, not gentlemanly and not playing the game. There is no free speech for bulls. The new bull skidded on the wet sand. Brandishing his horns, he almost lifted the picador's horse off the ground. He skidded and stumbled, and speared the horse again. The crowd whistled. At intervals, the tinny band played. They led the shivering, blindfolded horse away. With two banderillas stuck into him, the bull gave a high shriek, a hopeless soprano shriek like a train at a crossing in the night. Near us in the always moving, uncoordinated crowd a man yawned. A woman close by us hummed to herself. The bull shrieked again. The crowd laughed. The bull banged his nose into the barrier and shrieked. The crowd was chuckling. The matador worked very close. He shook the muleta, he shouted at the bull and turned his back on him, dragging the muleta in the sand. There was applause. The bull stared, charged, shrieked, charged again, dipped low on the wet sand, recovered. Suddenly he tossed the man up on his horn, so the man was

briefly riding the horn – then the man was off somehow; he
may have been gored; he limped away to the barrier. Here he
changed his sword for the kill. He returned to face the bull. He
danced and the bull danced and the bull shrieked. The man
turned his back, dragged the muleta. He went back to the
barrier for another sword. He was a graceful brown man in a
dark suit made like a Spanish dancer's, with high, tight pants
and a short jacket cut away. By now the bull was plastered
with blood. It shrieked. It charged the man again and again. A
banderilla fell off in the sand. The man held his sword out
level. The bull stood, his monstrous sides moving in and out.
Without warning he charged, and at that moment the man
placed the sword. The bull shrieked. Attendants ran to the bull
and caped him away. He stumbled dizzily from one to the
other, and the sword fell out of him. The man retrieved it, and
punched it in again, to death at last, and silence. There was
nothing to be seen here at Nîmes of that most magnificent
gesture, when the matador raises his right arm, his hand
spread in goodbye above the kneeling, finished bull, and
exchanges one knowing look with him, and wordlessly
commands him to die. Having butchered, the torero now
walked around the ring, holding up the cut-off ear he was
awarded, pausing to fling back the hats, caps, and other
tributes that were admiringly hurled down at him.

Memories of a bullfight in Mexico City came back to mind.
There, it was a religious rite, and the crowd moved as one
with traditional responses and cries. To occasional celestial
music, the gorgeous drama had unfolded, for the most part a
deadly serious matter, and in the end evil was destroyed, and
the exhausted watchers were drained and at peace. Here in the
Nîmes arena you were at the butcher shop. Here was no
integrated response, no give-and-take between the crowd and
the business before them, no desperate need. Only constant
squirming, laughs and chatter. Was it the relatively domestic
look of the bulls, which, though much touted beforehand,
were after all mostly cattle, homely and familiar? Or was it the
rummage-sale look of the show, the brown or gray suits, the
matchstick horses? Does this performance require beautiful
trappings, as concealment?

There was still one more bull to go. This one pawed, backed, lowered his nose to the ground. His hide proved too tough for the picador; the pic would not puncture it and the crowd booed. *"Musique!"* The little band struck up in sympathy; and heartened, the picador plunged in his lance. Too deep. He tried and failed to recover his lance from the wound. The bull was bleeding away in streams. Too hastily, the banderillas were stuck in. The bull looked like a birthday cake with candles awry. Already, far too soon, the red muleta appeared. But the people were absentminded now. They were sated. They were wondering about unscrambling their cars before everybody else, or finding places on the packjammed buses and going home, to thick bread, and good soup. Tediously, the last bull backed, pawed, gored the red cloth, taking the muleta and not the man for his enemy. He dragged his nose along the ground, and pawed. The man talked to the bull; he emitted little shouts. The bull charged. He came close, very close, to the man; pass, repass, pass, repass. *"Musique!"* called the crowd. Bursts of hasty applause for the man. Assistants diverted the bull. The matador held out his blade. The time had not come, however; tongue lolling, nose down, still; and irrelevantly, the bull charged. These interactions seemed to go on forever. The man plunged in his sword. His assistants spun the bull. At last the animal slumped along the barrier and went down. As his two ears were graciously ordered cut off by *la Présidence* and bestowed on the matador, the crowd piled from their seats.

Not long after, we spotted a letter from a well-meaning society in the London *Observer*. It stated that the fans at Nîmes had been complaining because not enough horses were killed at the bullfights. Accordingly, the letter went on, the authorities had reduced the weight of the horses' protective caparisons from ninety-six to fifty-seven pounds. To this, the letter continued, only one protest had been raised. It was from the man who supplied the horses. His complaint was that now he didn't get to use the horses over again.

We thought it all over. We remembered the animal, fictitiously assassinated in the film, and the crowd's indignation. We remembered birds singing at French windows, in little wooden cages. We remembered, also, the old lady who had brought a picnic to the park for one special cat, and other old ladies, companionably waddling beside equally waddling old-lady dogs. "The French are a highly subjective people," we decided to write. "They have to have a personal, not a general, relation to things. They love the animals they personally know."

Settling in Nice

October 30, 1954. Nice . . . If Persians are the French of Asia, the French are the Chinese of Europe. Everything is squeeze here. They discover whatever is essential to you and slap a price on it. We are sitting in two pale aqua wooden armchairs in the park at Nice. They are not free. We call the chair woman The Vulture – she swoops down, all in black, and collects. At ten to two we got here and saw no vulture. "She'll be here at two," prophesied H. "She's out for her two-hour lunch." Promptly at two, when we were craning toward her usual ambush and planning to be off in a trice if she emerged, she bore down from the opposite direction and triumphantly collected sixteen francs. She even knew how to say it in English.

This is France's fourth or fifth largest city. Considered a paradise and yet every other commercial establishment is a travel bureau to take you away. Except for the bakers, most of the remaining businesses seem to be real estate agencies, and how they live I don't know – there are more agencies than places to buy or rent.

It is typically French to kill the goose that lays the golden egg, and make *foie gras*.

Rainy Sunday

Late November, 1954. Nice. We have rented a bachelor apartment (known here as a *garçonnière*) near the sea, which sounds romantic; but in point of fact we are living in a burrow in a black rabbit-warren, the magnificent name of which we will conceal, where the dazzling Mediterranean sun never comes, and Indochinese tenants fill the air with exotic messes never smelled before. These odors wedge themselves into the dark, stained, crumbling halls where, when you punch on the light that immediately turns itself off – a triumph of French ingenuity – there is, we know from memory, a large clock that doesn't run, and a sign warning you, if you can speed-read, to shut your radio off at ten P.M. This is a supposedly reputable establishment located one block from the world-famed Promenade des Anglais.

For 15,000 francs a month we get a bathroom, and one all-purpose room with a single window opening on the rush of noisy traffic along the rue de France. This room contains a wardrobe, several hand-me-down chairs, and for kitchenette, a gas plate on a table. It has a three-quarter-size bed that can be slid part way into a sort of bookcase-cum-china closet, so that by day the bed masquerades as a divan, not very successfully. On our second day in the *garçonnière*, noticing that we have come out all over with red spots, we fumigate the bed and all its appurtenances in a fog of DDT.

The bathroom deserves a word. It boasts a white enamel bidet on a wire stand, and a washbasin with the usual dripping faucets. Between this and the back of the toilet are intertwined coils of lead pipe, obviously discards from a sausage factory. Thumb-tacked next to the improvised shower, a sign assures us that there will be hot water (read tepid) every Wednesday and Sunday from eight till noon, and all the rest of the week from eight to ten A.M.

The days go by and the rains come. We have had due warning: last week, on the street, a tightly wrapped old lady blew past us, muttering, to us or herself or the world: "Ça commence . . ." We do not walk out now and get wet, for fear the coats will never dry, although since November 15 there have certainly been two warmish pipes in our room and a radiator that does dry bathtowels in the course of time.

Every morning H darts across the street and brings back four crescent rolls for breakfast, and the pastry lady has gotten to know him. He feels stupid and inferior (being a perfection-ist and always having to be better than everyone else) on account of his French, which he is really acquiring quite rapidly, in spite of having studied it in college.

This particular morning, Black Sunday, the pastry lady said to him, *Comment allez-vous?* And H answered: *Quatre croissants.*

He came home furious with himself. His mood worsened. By mid-afternoon, although we had not gotten around to discussing methods, we were both suicidal. The cold little shuttered room was in awful disorder – garments piled everywhere, and we sitting there, contemplating each other, in our overcoats.

It was pouring, but with death so near anyhow I thought we might as well go out and walk along the Promenade des Anglais by the sea. My principal objection to suicide is that then you miss what is coming next; I feel, too, that if you no longer choose to live, you might as well have some fun, relax and do a few of the things you've always wanted to; enjoy the liberty which belongs to whoever has slipped the leash of his life. There is another side to it, too, which I learned in Persia: I was told by an eminent Bahá'í, a one-time mujtahid, Jináb-i-Fáḍil, who said he could not vouch for it, that after Nabíl had drowned himself in the Mediterranean Sea, 'Abdu'l-Bahá was deeply saddened, and said: "Why did he not tell me that he wished to die? I could have sent him into Afghanistan, where he could have died for the Faith."

Well, we went. And there in the rain that slashed across us

like sword blades, that choked us and plastered our hair and clothes, we found unearthly beauty with no one to look at it. Palms wrenching, writhing in the sky and the mirroring streets; a few raincoated people blowing, as if put there to illustrate the size of the storm; and then the great, pale brown waves revolving, and all the forepart of the water muddied and brown where the earth had run in, passing way out to a demarcation line where the sea turned peacock green. All the crazy sea chopping and writhing and revolving, against the static curve of buildings along the Promenade, everything dim, obliterated in the rain and leaping spray.

On the walk, against the brown sea, a big black poodle, flat as a cut-out. Quite naked, no raincoat, no collar, he pranced and whirled. This same poodle I had seen once before on the Boulevard, grandly doing a Pavlova ballet-kick with his hind legs, majestically and thoroughly cleaning up behind himself on the clean pavement, several yards from the place where he had obviously stopped. He now loomed big and black on the Promenade des Anglais against the pale brown convolving waters, and he danced in time to the storm.

We walked till we were drowned. Then we struggled to the pastry lady's and bought cakes. Then we had a big tea, Earl Grey tea made exactly the way it says to on the Twining's box. Afterward we spent the hours peacefully drying out.

Reminiscing, I tell H that when I was a child the Nice *nuits* or galas – an interminable series of which draws tourists, God knows why, into the awful weather of the Nice winter – were splendid affairs, or so I thought. The wobbly floats were gigantic then, when I was smaller. (Some are huge to this day, and parts of them are artistically of a high order, the faces and figures wisely made – although mechanically the floats are still amateurish.) I tell him I'm sure these present carriages, decked with faded flowers and soiled paper decorations, are the same as they were then, and that I recognize a good many of the horses. He says glumly, "I believe you. The same girls, too."

The people then ran wild with an awakened bawdiness noticeable even to a child. The whole town was caught up in it. Along with that, the Carnival – farewell to meat – had a religious meaning in those days, not present now. The great masses and the *congés payés* (paid vacations) hadn't been born then, and there were world-famed people on the Promenade of a morning. Nice was big enough for its visitors then – you could walk along the narrow sidewalks without eternally bumping and dodging; the town was not, in those days, a tourist slum. Cars were fewer, you could breathe then – take in the orange-scented air. You could breakfast in peace on a hotel balcony facing the sea. Cimiez was far off, no longer Victoria's leisure abode, and belonged mostly to boarding-house British. Its mimosa dripped liquid gold under the hot sky.

Although I hated Nice and had the measles there and was furious with the town for not letting me into the gambling casinos because I wasn't eighteen, I knew it was beautiful. The art shops today are repetitions of what they were then, the canvases as bad as then: but that perennial still life of the bubbling gold mimosa in the peacock blue vase I worshipped then.

Besides, in those days Nice was studded with small turquoise domes, now vanished.

A Beautiful Old Age

December 24, 1954 . . . Today we had an ugly lesson in economics, but we could not learn it – it eludes us. We went to Hyères and saw the Bahá'í couple, Monsieur and Madame Acard. She is fifty-seven, her husband sixty-eight. They live in one or two well-heated little rooms with their brown velvet dog, Dick. They started to talk of figures and that is where the lesson began. Their dream is to move to Nice but the prices there make it impossible. I told them, to show how simply we shall be living, that our rent at the villa will be 18,500 francs (about $55) a month. Their jaws dropped. They muttered excitedly to each other. The sum, smaller than anything else we could find and way below a figure the agencies would even consider, appears to them princely. It was all they could do to afford his bronchitis: 6,000 francs ($18).

Their second great dream, failing the first, is to move beyond the hill to the HLM – the *Habitations à Loyer Modéré* (low-cost housing), where they would, if they could somehow raise it, pay the equivalent of $15 per month (we think roughly of 1,000 francs as three dollars).

She put on her brown woolen cape with the buttons in front and the monk's cowl, her aqua wool headscarf shaped to a becoming peak, and we walked along the road in the hurtling traffic toward the town, she on the way pointing out the castle where "Meese War-ton" (we recognized Edith Wharton) wrote her books. The weather was cold and sunny, the sky autumnal blue, the Mistral blowing. We went up dark, tiled steps, two flights in the dark, into one of those plush, overstuffed, too-full-of-photographs that no longer resemble their originals, museum rooms where very old ladies are apt to end their days. The fumes from the kerosene stove choked us. After a time Mademoiselle Toussaint stood in the door; inch by inch she advanced, leaning on a steel tube crutch. "Her heart and liver are good," Madame Acard evaluated. "It is her legs." Mademoiselle Toussaint inched along. Eventually she reached an upholstered chair; eventually she sat. She had a round pink face, round globular blue eyes, round felt-shod feet. Her blue eyes looked out dim but intelligent, toward the afternoon sun slanting in. "That's what they tell me," she said, "that I look well." She seemed almost impatient about this. She asked Madame Acard to do the honors. Madame Acard passed us the plate of *calissons*, a local pastry, diamond-shaped and made of almond paste and honey.

The two ladies spoke of the fanaticism of local Christians. "We were praying," they said, "and we told our friend, 'Surely you can remain while we pray; surely there is no harm in a prayer.' 'Oh, no harm at all,' our friend said, and then when she thought we were not looking, she quickly made the sign of the cross."

Madame Acard has been denounced by the local curé from his pulpit. "There is a stout woman hereabouts," he said, "who is passing out prayers. Beware – beware of this woman . . ."

Later I saw a statue in the public square, where there are palms and century plants and eucalyptus and magnolia, just like in Southern California, so that to her disappointment she had nothing new to show us. "Whose statue?" I asked. "Why, it is the duc de . . . the duc de . . . I cannot remember," she said. "Anyhow, he's lucky to be in stone, because if he'd been in bronze, the Nazis would have melted him down like the others." We crossed over and read: "The duc d'Anjou, the brother of Saint Louis" (who died in 1270). "Whenever I see it," she said, "I remember how, during the war, the mother of one of our Bahá'ís kept her little supply of money hidden beneath it."

Tactlessly, I asked Monsieur Acard (once we were back at their house) why the French suffer so much from liver trouble. "I will tell you why," he said. "It is because we almost starved to death during the war. My wife and I, between us we lost the equivalent of a man like your husband. I lost seventy pounds." He brought out the album and showed us how he had looked.

"There was nothing to eat," Madame Acard said, counting off on her fingers all the nonexistent things. "Nothing. I refused to budge from this house. When the battle came, they fought it around us. They dragged cannon past that window. There was a machine gun by that post. They stationed black troops from the colonies across the road there. And oh, the dead were everywhere. Oh, the dead. If another war comes, we shall not be able to bear it. We have already borne all we could bear."

A Christmas card had been sent them from Dallas, Texas, from their ward, a Jewish girl whom they had looked after as their own for two of the war years. They had mislaid the card, and when Madame Acard refused to look carefully for it, Monsieur Acard, who wanted us to translate the English part for him, sulked and went into the other room to go to bed. "Just like a child," Madame Acard said. She went to the cupboard and looked carefully. "I've found it," she called. Back came Monsieur Acard and drew up a chair beside me. They must have printed a billion cards exactly like this one, I thought to myself. Monsieur Acard concentrated on the picture. "It shows a Christmas tree," I said. "In America each family has a tree, and then, out in the public square, each town has a tree, a community tree." Monsieur Acard was fascinated. I understand that even Nice has sported public Christmas trees for only two or three years now.

"A movie came to Hyères called 'Dallas,' " he said. "My wife and I, we hurried to see this movie. We wanted to see Dallas. But it was only in the title. It *was* Dallas, but a hundred years ago, in the time of the Indians."

We do not know, and cannot ask, how these people live. Mademoiselle Toussaint has *une belle vieillesse*, "a beautiful old age," Madame Acard told us. She gets 10,000 francs a month from the government, 2,000 from a nephew who paints pictures here and goes away to North Africa and sells every one, and then 6,000 francs from an annuity. We added it all up mentally and it came to about fifty-four dollars.

Later Madame Acard took us straight up the hill into the old town and we looked down over the naked coast. "The Nazis stripped it," she said. "They cut down all the trees. You see, there on that plain is where they expected the Allies to land."

Villa Christiane

Villa Christiane, 32 boulevard de l'Observatoire, Nice . . .
The gold lights of the city move and palpitate like bees on a
hive. They are not many-colored like the Berkeley, California, city lights (night lights that used to be repeated on the wet
grass blades in the morning sunlight so we had topaz and
amber and zircon and emerald drops, by night and by day).
They are soft yellow lights, and of streets, not of houses, since
these are boxed up back of their wooden blinds. Mornings
when haze holds the town in the bowl below, columns of
smoke rise part way through, and then, as if held in aspic,
bend over instead of escaping up and out.

Across from our kitchen window, the layers of mountains
form a distant wall, and on sunny mornings the light climbs
down them from the top as it rises over the rim behind us. We
breakfast, watching out the window to see the lights shifting
down.

We have the whole top floor and the owner is in French
Guinea, which is one basic reason why I wanted to rent here;
for after investigating the ways of French proprietors for the
past three months, I now know at least as much about the
French as Secretary of State John Foster Dulles.

It is now something over a week since we moved in. Our ad
in the *Nice-Matin* brought five answers, four of them offering
accommodation that made our garçonnière *grand luxe* by
comparison. In one, the kitchen consisted of a board placed
across the bathtub, and on the board a two-burner gas plate.

After endless negotiations with M. Murat, *agent* and *avocat*,
and many trips up here on foot, we signed a sheaf of
documents, duly became renters, and are now adding to the
furniture. Easy to say, but each expedition requires miles of

foot-slogging up and down our hill and along the flat of Nice's business district.

January 5, 1955 . . . Tonight the radio-phonograph came. Fortunately it works, even on the uncertain electricity here at the villa. It is a Pathé-Marconi and cost about 61,000 francs ($183), plus two long-play records at $7.80 each. We sit in the dark light of the coal fire and the shimmering lights of Nice down the hill; the sagging clouds in the upper two-thirds of the window are smeared over with moonlight. We have our wicker chairs from the Galeries Lafayette; our Indianesque cushions (the material is really Provençal, specifically from Valence, near Lyon) that I have personally stuffed with kapok; our Arab brass bowl from the flea market; and a grate that began by costing us three dollars, and now, since the *fonderie* has sawn and welded it down to size, has cost nine dollars in all. We turn off the light and sit in the dull rumble of the coal fire and listen to Kathleen Ferrier singing Handel's hymn to the Glory of God. "Return, O God, return," the dead woman sings.

Our good piece of furniture we bought at a modern shop – a long, low, tweedy-looking black-iron-legged sofa that makes up into a bed. It cost about $165 altogether. Our tile floors have an ancient look with their eight-pointed star design, the points alternating black and rust. The sofa sports a violently modern lemon-yellow cushion.

Today when we were downtown we had this conversation:
ME: Is that bus full of mourners or are they tourists?
H: They must be tourists. They're too miserable to be mourners.

93

An Italian Matriarch

Madame Socorro below us is an Italian matriarch, cousin of a general who won't have anything to do with her because she is poor. She is a gallant old woman – only sixty-five but that's old here – raises her family and descendants, battles their tuberculosis (two are in heaven, having given up the fight), cooks luscious rabbit stew, brings us gifts of fruit, flowers and vegetables that people up the mountain give her: slim courgettes (a kind of pornographic zucchini) pale green with a brash yellow flower, Spanish broom, figs. She cleans the steps for us, runs errands, helps carry luggage, addresses me in the third person – in exchange for small sums. Her drunken husband died way back. Now she has a drunken son. She kicked him out when he drank up his board and rent money and then he slept in a cellar. "He could be sleeping here in his room like a king," she told me in one of her rare weeping spells. His dark little room has a brass bed, neat patched coverlet on flattened mattress and full-length photographs of the two who are in paradise, stiff in their first communion outfits, sagging from the stained walls. "I nursed him six years and cured his tuberculosis," she said. "*Ce salaud.*" She did not use the word tuberculosis. She says as a rule that the children are "*fatigué.*" Through her I see how much aid is given the French poor: summer camps (*la colonie*) for the small children; clinics for the sick; pensions for the mutilated, blind and old. She had a bad time finding it, but at last located a faded snapshot – a group of employees – which proved her unlamented had worked for a certain firm; this proof made her eligible for a widow's pension. Tiny sums but they add up. "To think that I carried wood on my head while I was expecting him," she said of the drunken son. "I had never done that work before. It was in Italy and my neck hurt so. And then six years I nursed him. And now – just like his father." He's thirty-nine and unmarried.

"He needs a new interest," I said, after trying to tell her about Alcoholics Anonymous.

"I can't sleep with him," she said.

The man under Madame Socorro is "*un sauvage*." Her definition of a *sauvage* seems to be a man who won't talk over his affairs in the neighborhood. His son, back from the wars and married last Tuesday, is *un sauvage* also, and "probably a lunger" – *poitrinaire*. I gathered that the man, a widower, hadn't shown the proper neighborly interest. "He's a factory worker down the hill. Earns next to nothing. Walks up here and cooks some kind of *cochonnerie* (mess) for his lunch. Has a bit of soup for his dinner." She sniffed to convey the quality of the soup.

About this time the *sauvage* sent me, through Madame, a dainty frilly white paper bag with gold letters on it saying "*Mariage*." Inside were the ubiquitous white-coated almonds.

This morning Madame Socorro had it out with the rat, on her terrace. Counting his tail, she said, he was almost as long as her forearm. She had spent 500 francs for two batches of poison. He would always carefully pick out the food and leave the poison behind. Finally she invested in a trap. When she looked out on the dark terrace this early morning, there he was on his hind legs, holding onto his bleeding muzzle which he had managed to extricate from the trap.

She ran to old M. Morand up the street for help. He told her he was busy (he has done nothing except chop a bit of wood in the year we have been here), and to beat the rat to death.

Sickened, she ran back and threw blocks of wood at the rat. He danced around the terrace. He tried to force himself down the hole for the outside water pipe. She got a broom handle, and beat on his head. He fell, and lay dead. Then he suddenly leaped up, and she came down again and again on him with her handle, and at the end she threw the wet, pulpy mass into the yard where the *sauvage* found it and buried it when he came home for lunch.

"That swine – he has hands of gold," Madame Socorro says

about her son who drinks. "He made the cabinet that seals off the door to the terrace. He and I could live here like kings – if he didn't drink. In general I have noticed," she adds, "woodworkers either drink or are crazy. Once I went into his room and he was sleeping with the sheet over his face. 'Hold, even in this he is like that drunken father of his,' I said to myself. I drew away the sheet and there on his forehead was a big purple bruise. He had gotten drunk again, taken to fighting. Did you read about that drunk who was found dead outside the bistro? He had put his chair out in the rain to take a shower – red liquid inside him and white without – and they found him dead. *He* says all his friends at the hospital are dead and *they* didn't drink – they all died from their lungs. What is he alive for? he says. I pray to his sister every night."

After Madame Socorro had nursed her now thirty-nine-year-old son from tuberculosis to health, he became an incurable alcoholic and finally drank himself back to suicide and the Pasteur Hospital. He had been caught naked, trying to run into the sea down opposite the big hotels on the Promenade des Anglais. As usual, of course, the police knew better, and saved him. "Nothing to live for," he had said, "and I've seen so many of my comrades die of TB."

This suicide attempt was precipitated by the doctor who examines the men where he works: "If you go on like this, I give you three months."

We went up to see him at Pasteur – many old buildings swarming with marine-blue outfitted inmates (the women wear ugly gray) – it takes up a group of hills in the sun. One or two handsome new buildings (solid, well-designed, with elevators that work) were, we understand, put up by the Americans for German prisoners of war. At least so the inmates say, and add: "The American guard watching over the prisoners was always drunk, so they had to put a German prisoner in his place."

They were giving Jules, virtually free, all the latest TB drugs (from America mostly – that is where French doctors and dentists turn) and he was in a fine, light ward, only four other beds, facing the distant Mediterranean. As he walked us up through the sunlit grounds, he kept pointing here and there around the hills of Nice: "That is a cemetery," he would point out, "and see, over there, that is a cemetery. And that is a cemetery."

A few years later someone sent us a clipping about his death. He had died under a staircase in the hallway of some building.

Leisure Hours at the Post Office

When the French get their hands on any legal or bureaucratic matter they are carried away by their impassioned love of detail, of innumerable petty regulations, carbon copies and rubber stamps. For example our mail often comes back from the Post Office because it infringes some tiny invisible regulation.

Example (a): We asked the P.O. clerk to weigh an important registered letter, already stamped. She did so, calculated, and sold us what she called the necessary extra amount of stamps. These were duly affixed. Then she carried the letter over to another weighing machine and weighed it with the new stamps and made us buy more stamps to take care of the added weight.

Example (b): Today at the cable office an Englishman was trying to send a cable to Benghazi, and I volunteered to interpret. At the end of interminable complications while a patient line gathered, he handed over the money and said he also wanted to prepay the reply. The clerk, a deep frown between his handsome brows, rocked in his chair. The added request opened up a whole new avenue of bureaucratic procedure. The line back of me breathlessly watched the two principals. The clerk half rose to go and get the additional forms.

"Oh, never mind," said the Englishman.

"He says never mind," I said. "He doesn't want to bother you."

"It wouldn't bother me," said the clerk crossly.

"You know," said the Englishman to me, "it would take a week. They have fifteen different ways of doing the simplest thing. At the end of the year," he said, as the clerk gave out

with that most joyous, most desired of all French sounds –
dearer than the first murmurings of love, dearer than the first
cry of a new child: three solid final thumps with a rubber
stamp – "at the end of the year the amount of completed paper
work they have accumulated must be simply fantastic."

"Who reads it?" said I.

"Nobody," said he; "at the end of the year they have a
bonfire. Well, *au revoir*," he added as he moved away from the
wicket.

"He says what?" the clerk asked suspiciously.

"He says never mind," I soothed.

All this time I had been waiting – having walked half across
town for it – to pick up Ramona's* cable from Palma. The
clerk eventually, with magnificent deliberation, brought it
forth. "How much?" I asked – because nothing in France is
free, not even a prepaid cable. "Two hundred francs," said he.
I paid and signed the name on the cable: Harold Gail.
"Harold?" he caught me up. "That isn't you, is it?" I had a
vision of endless new forms, not getting the cable, and maybe
jail for forgery. "It's my husband, sitting over there," said I.
"I often sign for him." (Not strictly true, as in America you
generally append your own initials.) "We write pretty much
the same." (Not strictly true either – but to a Frenchman both
our hands look equally foreign and queer.)

With a liberal sprinkling of thanks, I edged out of his
purview.

* Ramona Allen Brown, noted Bahá'í pioneer and author of *Memories of
'Abdu'l-Bahá*.

Language and Other Barriers

"You don't say thirty, you say thurdy," Mademoiselle Premetz told us at tea. Ever since, I have been thinking about this. I, who was excused from the required speech course at Vassar because they said I didn't need it, say thurdy. The awful thing is, she was right. "Thurdy days hath September . . ."

The French distinguish between English and American. They band into different clubs according to which they want to learn. A book will say on it, "Translated from the American." I remember how I nearly got myself chucked out of Persia, trying not to laugh after a Persian general in a position of great authority remarked solemnly to me: "You speak English. Do you also speak American?"

"What animal goes *meu-meu-eu?*" a mother, passing by, asked her small, brown, red-suited boy, leaping and squirming at the end of her arm. "*La vache!*" he cried in triumph. French cows do not say moo.

In Berkeley, California, H would double-park outside the laundry, run in, they would shove our package of clean laundry at him, he would shove the money at them and run out. Maximum time elapsed: two minutes.

The other day, although it was already 12:10 and every day here, from twelve to indefinite, is Sunday, we decided to collect our laundry. The door was open a crack and we pushed in to the steamy, chicken-broth air. The dog, cranky with age, who because of deafness snarls and barks abnormally loudly at each customer, lay stiffly under the ironing table, almost filling up the space. I winced back at each bark. From steps leading down into a dark inner room, the laundress came. She recognized us and brought out two large bundles of assorted bits of paper, and began to look through them for the scrap on which we had written our list. The old yellow-white dog lurched stiffly to the door and asked, not really caring, to be let out; she let him out. A sporty-looking girl in large checks with two men to match came in. They and the laundress had a long business chat. She showed them out and went back to pawing through the scraps of paper in the paper bundles, now lying open on the ironing table. The dog asked to be let in and she let him in. A man came up from the dark room at the back and went out. The laundress triumphantly fished up our scrap of paper from the heap of other scraps and brandished it. The man came back in with a bottle of wine and went down the dark steps. The dog barked abnormally loudly from under the ironing table and I winced back. He asked to be let out. The laundress let him out. She began to collect our laundry from various parts of the establishment. I studied the wall-calendar, calculating how long it would be till Christmas. Down in the dark inner room, at a dark table, an old woman all in black with a round black kerchief, waited for the laundress and lunch.

The laundress looked for and found a big piece of wrapping paper, almost new. She looked for and found a pin. She piled our laundry neatly on the paper and brought up the sides to where they overlapped and pinned them together, leaving the ends open. H got out his money. She charges forty-five cents for a shirt and he produced 5,000 francs, say fifteen dollars. She couldn't make change. Finally she could make change. He laboriously wadded up the large, torn, pin-holed bills and put his billfold away. The laundress laid the laundry flat on his outstretched arms. She let us out. Time elapsed: twenty-two minutes.

Afterward, at the Ruhl kiosk, I bought a suspense novel and discovered it was splattered with real blood. H, who hates my low reading tastes, said, "All right, this time. But don't bring one home tipped with curare."

The Gunny Sacks

February, 1955. Marseilles. I was warm for the first time in three months. There was a red wall-to-wall carpet. There was a big bathroom and I had had a real tub bath for the first time in three months – I had now had three baths in a row. The talk, in French, was over, my mind was free at last. The Bristol is a good hotel and our bill was all paid up till noon. I looked forward to a leisurely breakfast, a leisurely fourth bath, and maybe a short walk to the shops. But then matrimony stepped in. H awoke at four, and tossed. By six he had rooted me out. No breakfast in the hotel at that hour, so we blew through the night and the glacial Mistral and crossed the street to a bar.

A man and an old woman were sweeping the floors against the day and taking down chairs stacked on tables. He said yes we could have tea and croissants and cleared us chairs and a table in the rubbish under the dim lights. The old lady swept vigorously around us. I compared her with her peevish and powdered bridge-playing contemporaries in America. Fifteen minutes went by in the dusty cold. I was not speaking to H. At last I said to the old lady, "Madame, we have to take the bus to Digne." (The side-trip was H's idea, not mine.) At once everything changed. "If you had only *told* me you had to take the bus to Digne," the man said. Apparently he had thought we were sitting there for pleasure. Immediately the old lady produced crackling new croissants; the man poured scalding tea. I lived again. We left with tips and compliments, H pointedly handing a special tip to the old lady.

Just outside as we left, warmed and fed, was a doorway in the windy dark and in the doorway on the ground was a bundle of gunny sacks. We saw a vast hairy head in the sackings. H produced money and no sound came, but the money was taken and two blackened fingers came up and touched the head. Now when I'm worn out and don't feel like doing all this work in French, I do it for that pile of sacks.

I wished my notebook was handy, as the bus pulled out for Digne. One thing I'll always thank the French for: they never bore you. Sit on a bus with a notebook and write down what you see of all the human dramas going by. This does not seem to be the case, in most other countries where I've lived.

Another thing to remember is all those French firsts. I kept a list of them once, but lost the list. Most are genuine too (even if they conveniently forget to teach their schoolchildren about the Wright Brothers – whom friends told me not to bring up in my talks).

Wherever you go, the French have already been there – been there and gone. I open my Brother Lawrence and am reminded that he was Nicolas Herman of Lorraine, a lay brother, member of the discalced Carmelite order of Paris, and that *The Practice of the Presence of God* was translated from the French.

Enjoying Lawrence, my English version, for the tenth time, it occurred to me that the bare winter tree, the sight of which converted him, was really a promise of the new Day. I thought too how a bare tree was enough for him, but Newton had to have an apple.

The Port at Twilight

My two favorite places in Nice are the English graveyard and the Port at twilight. In the latter place one can find a few moments of true peace. The prematurely old, sun-faded buildings border the long rectangle of water. I wish I were washed up out of the Mediterranean in a rowboat and were entering this haven for the first time, because I would be dumbfounded by the dim grandeur at the city end of the Port. The two long pink buildings, taking up most of that vast end of the Port, with their jade shutters above their colonnades, and between these two the Greek-looking, columned church with the dim Greek-looking figure surmounting it, gesturing down with outstretched hands. Rising back of the church to the right, a square clock tower and in the far back, against the sky, soft and gold now like pale fruit, the delicate blue line of the hills and the pinnacle of the highest one, a bald mountain. All down through the big rectangle of water, the moiré sunset colors, and rising black along the left (northwest) side, cemetery hill, that shuts off the tourist world of the Promenade des Anglais and has at its summit the ruins of a twelfth- (?) century castle.

We have thought of acquiring a rowboat, since we have already been down the coast and up, and inland, and only the sea, out there beyond the breakwater, remains. Yachts and rowboats and a white *bateau mouche* are here, and a black liner that goes to Corsica. Rowboats freshly painted dry on a tiny artificial beach. One of these was marked for sale. Boat people are always polishing, cleaning, painting. The long low stone wall that rises from this beach is daubed like a palette. I asked an old sailor if it is dangerous here. "Oh no," he answered. "Those who go out always come back." I asked another sailor (their faces are like boat people's everywhere – the sea is all one nationality) about the rowboat. It must have belonged to an enemy because he sneered, "He wants 30,000 for it. I hate to see people buy a boat to drown in. It leaks. You'd be bailing the whole time. See where he's nailed this copper, at the prow and down across the back – that's where the leaks are. It won't even sit straight in the water. That other one anchored out there, the green one, belongs to my brother. It's all mahogany, carpenter-built. I saw it building and I know. That's a fine little craft – and only 25,000. I'll look around for you. Just ask over at the *Café Escale* (Port of call) for the proprietor of the *Grand Frisson*, that's me."

Another boat drying there was called the *Mektoub* ("It is written"), which H did not think reassuring.

Permis de Séjour

Sara, who has been here almost a year, was convoked the other day. She went to the police station. "Have you a piece of paper?" said the man. He told her where to go and buy it. She wandered around; several paper stores were closed, but at last she discovered one that was open. She returned to the police with a package of fifty sheets of paper. "Here," she said grandly, handing it to the man. "Here is a present for you and for the *entire* Department." "Oh no," he said, perfectly serious. "Only *one* sheet." And with all solemnity returned the other forty-nine.

"Don't you want a convocation dress?" I asked Sara, using French governmentese.

"This is my second convocation," she said. "It's tin, I believe."

The Consulate had warned us that there is an enormous fine to pay unless after your three months as a tourist are over you apply for your sojourn permit – *permis de séjour*. Yesterday morning accordingly, easing under the awnings and arcades to avoid the rain, we got ourselves over to the police station on avenue Maréchal Foch. After asking three people we came to a room in which were a permanent-looking man and woman. They both had that gray, held-in-aspic look acquired by so many people who work in government offices. "Have you each a piece of paper?" asked the man. Too late, I remembered about Sara. "What kind of paper?" "Ordinary white paper," said he. "No," I said. "Then you must go out the front door, turn to your left and find a paper store on the corner."

We went back into the rain, groped to the right store and eventually returned with fifty sheets of paper. "One each is sufficient," said the man. He consulted our passports again, wrote down various data, we signed something and that was the end of session one. "In two or three days you will receive a letter by which you will be convoked upstairs to the first floor," said the man. "We are anxious about it because the tenth is approaching and our three months will be up then," I said. "You have nothing to fear," he said.

Walking back to the bus in the rain I realized we had no tangible proof that we had paid this call to the police station. I consoled myself, however, remembering the matter of the inventory.

We had rented for some weeks a cold, dark, one-room apartment near the Promenade des Anglais, and had spent half a day with the owner, going over and checking off every object on her inventory. There was virtually nothing of value in the place and the long inventory listed such items as the electric company's meter and two empty jam jars. On surrendering the apartment another half-day had to be devoted to rechecking the inventory, our copy of which we had kept during our tenure and now ceremoniously handed back to the proprietor, she having at last been persuaded that every item – except a copper band which she maintained had encircled a cracked, flowered ornamental vase on our taking the apartment and now was missing – was present and accounted for. The substantial rent had been paid in full in advance, and the owner was eloquently explaining why she had to keep the equally substantial deposit we had given her to cover loss or damage, when we realized we had no proof of having paid her anything at all. Could you give us a receipt? I asked, not understanding at that time that the French, for the purpose of income tax avoidance, will never sign their name to any such financial commitment. "But you have no need of a receipt!" she said in astonishment. "Then how can we prove we paid?" I asked helplessly. "*Du moment que vous n'avez plus l'inventaire!*" she said pityingly. ("Why, your proof is that you no longer have the inventory!")

Scene II of the *permis de séjour*: We found a notice in our mail box "convoking" us to the police station, to appear at 10 A.M. yesterday. We were somewhat frightened. "Don't worry," Sara said. "The same thing happened to me. My landlady said it isn't important. They naturally have to put *some* hour and date on the notice, she says."

We got ourselves off our hill, boulevard de l'Observatoire, and down there on Maréchal Foch about twenty-four hours late. We found a typical government roomful of battered tables and about seven young men. The talk was lively, and the room was warm – all French bureaucrats manage to keep warm. A dark young man in blue serge, with a light-blue shirt and subdued green, small-patterned tie and a wedding ring and his fingers stained with tobacco, took charge. "Where are you born?" he said to me in English. He wore, for professional purposes, an unconvincing, pseudo-Anglo-Saxon phlegmatic scowl, but would burst into genuine French smiles when I would smile at him in my efforts to look like a good person to admit.

I had my usual panic when we got to such questions as my father's name and my own *nom de jeune fille*. Almost every tourist has something queer about him which does not fit the form, and the difference between his reality and the forms can cause a situation verging on hysteria. Take my father's simple enough name: Mirza Ali-Kuli Khan-Nabil. I never have time to explain about Persian nomenclature to whoever is filling out the form. Mírzá isn't a name, I think in terror; at the end of a name it means Prince; at the beginning, the way it is in my father's name, it means, or used to mean, something like a gentleman and a scholar. 'Alí-Kulí means servant of 'Alí; 'Alí is the First Imám; Kulí is Turkish for servant; yes, I know he isn't Turkish – he's Persian; no, I don't know why he has a Turkish section to his name. Anyhow, the whole thing is only his *first* name; it's only like John, I mean Jean. Then we come to <u>Kh</u>án. <u>Kh</u>án isn't a name. It's an old Mogul title as in <u>Ch</u>angíz <u>Kh</u>án; The Grand Chan was the Great <u>Kh</u>án. No, he isn't a Mongol. He's a Persian, an Aryan with some Arab blood from the Prophet, through his mother <u>Kh</u>adíjih <u>Kh</u>ánum of Ká<u>sh</u>án, who was (silent conciliatory laughter to placate a receding audience) what they call a descendant of the Prophet on Friday eves – I mean she was only partly descended from Muḥammad. I know that practically every-one is called <u>Kh</u>án nowadays, just as a courtesy, but it used to be a title, and it was hereditary in my father's family. Then of course his name Nabíl – well, that isn't really a name, you know. It was a title given him by Aḥmad Sháh Qájár (whose dynasty ended in 1925): Nabíli'd-Dawlih. And you see, as children of titled Persians often did, I took that name – Nabíl – as *my* last name when the government passed a law that people *had* to have last names, because you see . . .

At this point I remember school teachers who knew me, when I started going to private school at three and a half, as Marzieh Khánum, Khánum being the feminine of Khán, and I expect them to materialize and call me a liar, and I hear myself explaining the whole thing to them all over again.

No wonder the dark curly-haired young man looked quizzically at me from behind his Underwood typewriter. "Your profession is you are writing?" "When I do," I deprecated, although I have a lump on my middle finger from writing all these years. My passport was in the man's hands. He knew my age. With perfect tact he eliminated this question, contenting himself with asking how much money I have. "None," I said. "Ask my husband." H figured away on the back of an envelope and as usual with all the impromptu mathematics I have ever watched unfolding, he got the answer wrong. Instead of three or four hundred dollars a month from our stocks, he said we have 12,000 francs – say about $36. The man dutifully tapped away. Later H corrected himself but the man didn't seem to care and said it was of no moment. We had not learned then, that while the document is all-important its contents mean nothing. The French feel that one may swear to anything one likes in a legal paper, and all is well so long as the paper is correctly drawn up and has the right number of stamps on it.

"And you are here for *Tourisme*? Work? Health?" the man asked us next. "We're here because we like it," I answered. He also wanted to know if I know French, I having followed my usual rule with any French person who knows more than three words of English: let them practise it – that is their heart's desire.

He turned to H. "You are born in Kay–no–*sha*?" he said. The most abstruse French sometimes proves to be an

American place name. Recognizing American place names in French mouths requires a straighter face than mine. "I have a friend in O–ee–oo," a French person will tell you. H had all his answers, father's name, mother's maiden name and so forth down pat and the young man was soon through with him. "In twenty days," he closed mysteriously, "you will be convoked again." What will happen during the next twenty days? No doubt the police of two continents will go over our records. I feel like an international diamond smuggler in E. Phillips Oppenheim.

We reluctantly went away from the gaily chattering young men in the warm room out into the chill January morning.

February 21, 1955 . . . A guard stood in the lee of the Salad Basket, the Black Maria, outside the police station which is down toward the center of Nice. I waited so as not to interrupt the spit he was about to have and then waved our paper at him. "Where is the Préfecture?" I asked. "I am going to explain this to you," he said, wiping his chin. "Go right. Then go left. Then, outside a big building, you will see a Guardian of the Peace, just like me. It is there."

Room No. 3 of the Préfecture proved to be large, light and well-heated, with a red tile floor. It gave onto the park, where for once during this long, cold, dark winter, all the fault of the American atomic tests in Nevada say the French, the sun and wind sparkled in the palm trees. Ahead of me at the counter stood a leathery woman in a rubbed-off muskrat (rat of America, they call them here) coat and with bird's nest hair and a rough male voice. Like all those who stand ahead of H or me in a line of this sort, she was working on an impossibly complicated project. We refer to these people, whom we attract and cannot fight or protest against because they are in our life and part of the pattern, by the generic term "Outer Mongolia" because one crowded noon in San Francisco when H had only ten minutes for lunch and had parked by a fire hydrant to get a letter registered at the Post Office, the man ahead of him at the window was trying to mail a package to Outer Mongolia, that improbable locality. Today, this woman wanted to take innumerable, intermittent trips to Italy, back and forth, back and forth over the border. The lady clerk had burnt-orange hair with an inch of gray at the roots. In France, so long as you have made the attempt to dye your hair and part of the dye shows, the rest does not matter; you have achieved the symbol of youthfulness and good grooming. French hair colors are more varied than American and are not required to imitate nature or to be renewed at frequent intervals. A red rose color is much in favor, also a pinkish copper and a light blue. She wore a gold ring embedded in a plump white finger, and peeling pink nail enamel. Her black dress, which had probably been made for her, fitted better than a mass-produced American equivalent; the skirt hung open in a wrap-over fold in back, to prevent sagging, wrinkling and wear caused by strain.

I showed her our convocation notice and she gave us each a blue form to fill out. Name, address, all the usual round, which makes one wish he were somebody else just to get a change of data. The questions on the reverse looked complicated. One was: "Alleged motive for remaining in France." I asked the clerk about this section and she said, "Oh, don't answer those. They have nothing to do with your case." With that, she took away our passports and gave us two small slips and told us to carry them upstairs to room No. 162.

Now we were denuded. In all these months we had never been without our passports. We were persons without a country. We trudged wearily upstairs and along a dark corridor, into the unknown, with no passports and two incomprehensible bits of paper.

Room 162 proved to be the cashier's. Here, without warning, we were presented with a bill. "That will be 7,000 francs," the woman said from her cage. "In all?" I asked. "Total," she said. It was a crisis. We had brought no money. Where to get twenty-one dollars quickly, before everything in Nice shut down for the inexorable daily holiday, several hours long. "Madame," I said, "our bank is nearby, may we go to our bank and come back?" "If it is before twelve," she agreed. "We'll never make it," H said to me. However, I now remembered some bills which I had worn so long in case of emergency that they had become as routine as lingerie and I no longer thought of them as legal tender. On our way along the corridors I had noticed a door marked WC. These are often coeducational in France and afford little privacy of any kind. Remembering our experience with other French johns, we didn't think the door would lead to a private enough place to get at our money belts (true, the other day at the Lycée when I was substituting for Mrs Sprague I went to the toilet and on that occasion found only one man in it and he didn't stay – but luck like that is unusual).

Anyhow I pushed into the WC and it led to another door and I pushed through into one of those flat-on-the-floor tile toilets. Nobody was there, so I unzipped my belt and drew out a 10,000 franc note and threw it on the floor. Wonder what would happen if I flushed it down? I thought gleefully.

Zipping up, I was careful not to catch the edge of any of the bills. These French bills are of many sizes, some almost as large as a man's handkerchief. They generally have holes in them from being pinned together at the bank. They come in pastel colors and bear – unless it's the Victor Hugo, all-time favorite – Greek-looking men and women, festooned with fruits and vegetables indicative of plenty. It's an inconvenient money to wear, being apt to rustle. Not infrequently a bill is held together only with scotch tape or glued brown paper.

Almost at once I was back at the cashier's, triumphantly waving a bill for 10,000 francs. This denomination shows a blonde in a lavender dress, with a large book and an olive or laurel sprig in her hands, a light-blue globe behind her, proliferating foliage, two objects sticking out of the foliage that look like hose-nozzles but may be cannon, and so on. A French counterfeiter would die of overwork.

The cashier started when she saw us. She decided the bank must be awfully close by.

We were now provided with two stamped receipts and were instructed to go back downstairs to Room No. 3. The orange-headed clerk received us and our receipts without enthusiasm; she responded better, I noticed, when I addressed her as Mademoiselle instead of Madame. "Come back in fifteen minutes," she said.

I tried to make some phone calls at the bus station – spotting public phones is one of your problems here. For reasons too complicated to list, I got neither number (life here is a continual eroding process of tiny frustrations) and collapsed outside on a park bench, but it was windy, which was why the fairly sunny bench had been empty. By then the fifteen minutes were up so we returned to the now hideously familiar Room 3. This time the clerk was back at her table and we got a man who started asking questions all over again, having come into the case late. What is your address? Where is your convocation slip? I knew the address but H had lost the slip and started searching through his clothes. Finally the woman deigned to give some directions to the man and he fished out our two passports which were right in front of him under the counter. It had taken fifteen minutes to staple our cash receipts to our passports. "Now what?" said I. "*Now* you go to the police over on Avenue Foch," he said. Since we must have our residence permit number to send to the French Consul in San Francisco (in order to clear our household goods through French Customs) and the typed letter to the Consul was waiting in H's pocket for the permit number, we in our innocence, hoping to expedite matters, took a taxi in order to get over to the police before closing time at twelve. Alas for the 270 francs . . . Same man we'd seen way back at the beginning. "Nothing for you here. Return tomorrow at 9:30."

Next day . . . He was just leaving as we arrived, at about 10:15 today. He escorted us to another room – large, warm, giving on to a sunny back yard, KLM calendar showing a happy family of travellers. At another table a well-entrenched-looking blonde in glasses and a black smock. "There's a *type* waiting for you," she reported to our escort, who left to interview the *type*. The blonde went over and stood in the sun by the window a while then decided it was warmer back in the corner with her rear to the radiator. A man acquaintance smoking a cigarette came in and stood beside her for a friendly chat the rest of the twenty-five minutes we were there.

Meanwhile, our man, a pleasant individual in a checked suit and the usual wedding ring, plus a diagonal mourning band across the left lapel, asked us if we each had a white sheet of paper. We didn't. Nobody had told us we'd need *another* sheet

113

of white paper. We did have the six hideous right profile photographs as required, but no sheet of paper. As a special concession this man rummaged in a desk drawer, found two old sheets of paper and trimmed what were priceless notations off the tops. Then he got to work with paste and scissors and four photos (snipping and pasting). Then he began asking us all the same questions we had answered long before in another office of this same building, and copying down the answers in endless longhand pen and ink ("What, no quill?" said H).

After a long time he told us, "Now you go to the Wilson Post Office and pay 300 francs each and bring me back the receipts. Then it will be finished," he added.

It was almost a quarter to eleven and fortunately not raining, and not windy, and in fact perfect. We started out and trudged dutifully across town to the Wilson Post Office and found wicket No. 4 and paid not six hundred francs but six hundred and fifty-two (the extra is inevitable – it's always for mysterious stamps or God knows what) and got the receipts and walked back and then it was maybe 11:10 and the blonde and her friend were still chatting. We handed our receipts to the man and he got busy with his paste again and finally handed us two formidable documents. "So these are our identity cards," we said. "No," he said, "they are not, but they have the same validity as if they were. They are provisional; in two weeks you will get your convocation and . . ." "Please tell us what our sojourn permit number is," I asked, "so we can send it to the French Consul in San Francisco so he can send us the documents we need to get our household goods out of the Customs." "Oh, for that you must go to the Préfecture," he began.

I could ask no more; we rose and said goodbye and went out past the blond who was still chatting with her friend and sought refuge in the Scotch Tea House where they serve real buttered toast.

Not for Cowards

Leon, who is afraid of nothing, has decided to get married in France to a girl from America. We went over to Monsieur Iques, plump and virtually bald, at the U.S. Consulate and listened while he told Leon what he must do.

One. He must have proof that he has been, for one month, a resident of the town where he will marry (Saint-Paul de Vence).

Two. "Are you trying a second experience?" asked Monsieur Iques. "You should read the works of 'Umar Khayyám. In any case you must produce a copy of your divorce certificate, translated into French by a sworn translator. Why don't you go to the city hall at Saint-Paul and ask them for a list of the documents you need?"

"Because they don't know," said Leon. "I went there and they asked if she was coming over by boat, and then they said she might fall for someone else on the boat and then they would have had all that work for nothing. They said I must have a certificate showing *three* months residence . . ."

Monsieur Iques said, "They know in Nice and Villefranche; in Cannes they are beginning to know; in Saint-Paul they don't know."

"How will they find out?" Leon asked.

"Tell them to phone *me*," Iques replied. "Now let's see. When your complete dossier has been accumulated, your banns must be posted outside the *mairie*. They must be posted for ten days, including two Sundays."

Three. "Have you a birth certificate? No? Then you must produce an affidavit. In Nice, there would be no discussion about this. In Saint-Paul, there will be discussion."

Four. "Then you must have a *certificat de coutumes* –

115

certificate of customs. In the case of every country in the world that certificate is handed to you by the consulate, but there is one exception: the United States. In the United States you have forty-eight different codes of law, so we never deliver a certificate of customs to you. You have to obtain one from an American lawyer. There is only one American lawyer in this part of the country. He lives on the sixth floor of a building that is divided into two halves, so when you call there, take the lift on the *left* side; otherwise you will find yourself on the wrong half. Both you and the young lady should be present at the time. You see, French civil marriage is valid in the United States so France has to be sure you could legally marry in your particular state. The lawyer will declare that you could."

Five. "Have you an identity card?"

"I have this pink card," Leon said.

"It's no good," said Iques. "You have to plan to be a resident for a year and a day, if you're going to get married, and this only permits you to stay a year. Besides, this permits you to live in Paris, but you will have to apply to the Prefect – say this is requirement Number Six – for permission to reside in the Alpes Maritimes, the department in which Saint-Paul is located. Then, Number Seven, the two of you must come to this consulate with your passports and the secretary will give you an application addressed to the Prefect of this District for permission to get married. This permission is always granted.

"By the way, if you're planning to stay here with your bride for some time, remember that she can only be counted as a tourist for three months, at the end of which time she must either apply for a residence permit or be heavily fined. However, to avoid all that, just take her down to San Remo for lunch and be sure they put an official stamp on her passport at the Italian frontier. This automatically renews her tourist status for another three months. Oh, it's not legal, but it's accepted all over France. And lastly, of course, you each have to take a medical examination."

Leon was quite happy as we went down the front steps.

"I'm so relieved," he said. "I'd thought there'd be a lot of red tape."

You Get It Back When You Leave

Gray and cold . . . As we eat our veal and zucchini I say, "I don't believe in these exhaustive modern biographies. You get to know too much about the person. Here is what Elizabeth Barrett wrote to Robert Browning, before they had met: 'Winters shut me up as they do a dormouse's eyes . . .' "
"Don't," says H. "I'm eating."
I go on about *The Immortal Lovers* by Frances Winwar. "Anyhow it's more readable than Maurois' *The Edwardians*," I say. We look at each other. Although indoors, we are fully clothed for the street, I in my light-blue, imported British cloth coat, H in the suède, cat's-eye button vest he bought against the blasts of Edinburgh, worn under his Irish tweed jacket bought against those of Dublin. None of our garments are proof against French *chauffage central*. I shiver. "*Tout confort*," I mutter.
One of Maurois' rare dull books, I go on to say. Imagine leaving out the Jersey Lily. A very old gentleman told me that when she came to America her admirers provided her with a champagne bath; when they bottled up the champagne afterward, he maintained, there was a quart extra. I rose to carry my plate out into our slice of kitchen. "With gages from a hundred brighter eyes," I say, scraping off the plate into the Paris Herald Tribune, "than tears even can make mine." I still know that a few of her lines are as durable as Sappho's. That one goes: "And death must dig the level where these agree." And that other: "Beholding, besides love, the end of love/ Hearing oblivion beyond memory."
It all comes from our discovering a door in a wall at 12 rue de France, with a sign saying that an English-American Library was behind it with 9,000 books. (The labels on the

books themselves say, founded in 1863, and 10,000 volumes
on open shelves. The selling phrase is that "on open shelves."
It's like "the open sea"; suddenly you feel rich and unat-
tached.) You pass through the door and find yourself in a
corner of the English graveyard, whose two main attractions
prove to be the slab of the author of "Abide with me," and a
black cat, non-Manx, with no tail. Many lesser cats slip like
shadows over the old graves here, and there is a direct
connection between them and the all-healing cat-furs, to be
worn across breast, back or stomach, which one sees so
abundantly displayed in neighboring pharmacies. Then you
go up steps, and if you can push through the blast of escaping
gas from the heater and get through the library door, you
arrive at a desk manned by obvious volunteers, who sit
protectively walled around by shelves labeled: B – Biography;
P – Poetry; S – Science. In the back section, isolated by tall
bookcases and giving on the rue de France, is a round table
loaded with magazines apparently contributed by friends of
the Library who are more generous than prompt, and
surrounded by exiles English and American, mutually as
non-fused but amicable as dogs and fish in the same living
room. While all is silent here, a permanent conversation, loud
and worried, is carried on back at the desk, between the
volunteers, the borrowers and the returners. The books
include many titles I traded in long ago at San Francisco
secondhand stores. At last, said H when we first saw them, we
have the opportunity to read Ouida. We were able right off,
however, to grab Elliot Paul, and disappeared into *Linden on
the Saugus Branch*, at a time when I was supposed to be
teaching French out of *La Chèvre de Monsieur Séguin*.

Vindictively, I now read this about the Brownings' married
life to H, who deigns to interrupt his reading for it:

"After three o'clock dinner he would wheel a comfortable
chair into the dressing room, the coolest in the house, and
make her sit in it. Then he poured *eau de cologne* into her palms
and on her forehead, and fanned her till her eyes closed of
themselves for the siesta."

H simply grinned.

"Damn you," I said.

I read him one more sentence from the book, the place on page 258 where the Brownings go to see George Sand: "She was sitting by the fire, warming her feet quietly." "What does that mean?" I ask him.

"It means she wasn't cracking her toes, like the Fox sisters," said H disgustedly, trying to stay back in Linden.

"Anyhow," I muse, "Elizabeth Barrett must have loved Browning. She certainly presented him with enough miscarriages. Do you know what I think?" I conclude, "I think sufficient has been done about the Brownings."

With that unerring protection vouchsafed by life to the defective (what does Darwin mean when he says beneficial changes are preserved and the fit survive? Nothing, for example, is so immortal as a sick old lady) the English-American Library triumphed over the Second World War.

When the Nazis came they, in all seriousness, wrapped each of the 10,000 volumes up separately and shipped them home to the Fatherland. *Tish, When Patty Went to College, Elizabeth and Her German Garden, Lorna Doone, Your Friend the Pomeranian* and the *Memoirs of Lord Birkenhead*, were presumably swept away from Nice forever. Not so – as a philosopher might have predicted. The whole lot got sidetracked in Grenoble. When the war was over the word came through: We have a pile of books here. Do you want them back? Of course Nice wanted them back.

The other afternoon a voice from behind the tall shelves where the magazine table is, suddenly proclaimed: "Murder is a crime against God!"

No one seemed to be paying much attention. I thought possibly the remark was a criticism of my favourite reading material, of which the Library does have a few English examples: *The Moonstone*, etc.

A loud and acrid debate, however, ensued on the Sir Jack Drummond murders. The farmer Gaston Dominici, on whose land the Drummonds had, in their innocence, camped, had just been convicted.

France, incidentally, takes a detached view of such English tourists as are, now and again, murdered on her soil. The French ask: "The Drummonds were rich, weren't they? Why didn't they go to a hotel?" Or "The schoolteacher? Those English women come over here to have themselves a time."

"Perhaps they do," comments H, "but why should getting murdered be the alternative?"

The sun is one's main occupation in Nice. No sun – nothing to do. I wondered how the bad weather would affect the Library.

Around the cluttered table in back, lumps of damp refugees; not a chair without its exile, mostly hatted and coated, smelling of wet sheep, isolated in the greasy, gray light, no smile among the lot, just private, hopeless dreams of tea.

The desk was as hysterical as ever.

"Good-*bye*, Eugenia," a gentleman habitué called back from the door to the current volunteer, all but blowing a kiss her way. The door closed behind him.

"Mr Brown is such a sweet person," the volunteer announced to whom it might concern. It is customary at the Library to make some personal comment on each one who exits.

A woman in the elaborate black clothes of another era came in and hovered. She wasn't sure she wanted to join.

"Will you be in Nice six months?" Eugenia asked. We all waited, wherever we were. Six months. What stamina.

The woman wasn't sure.

"*Three* months?" said Eugenia. Then she broke the news about the deposit you have to give the Library along with your registration fee and added immediately, running all the information brightly together: "But-you-get-it-back-when-you-leave."

The woman would have the right to take out two books, Eugenia said. But the woman wasn't sure she wanted to take any books out *today*. "I'm not sure I could get the two books back to the hotel in the taxi," she explained.

The exiles turned this over in their damp, unheated minds and gave up. The old newspapers and magazines they held were worn too limp to rustle.

The Demonstration

Twenty minutes ago I never thought to see this corner of the sofa again. We were on the steep curves of the Grande Corniche, having a pearl-gray Citroën demonstrated.

In France you never do business with the man you start out with. Yesterday the very slow, dogmatic, down-to-earth salesman said, "I will give you a demonstration tomorrow," and so we should not have been surprised to see the totally different man who showed up this morning, a handsome Italian called Massone. "This is *my* territory," he explained.

A year ago, someone at the U.S. Consulate told us, "Whatever you do, don't buy a Citroën. They're going to change the model. One tourist here is losing a thousand dollars on his resale." For a year now, Citroën owners and salesmen have scoffed to us that Citroën will *not* change its model. "The motor, yes, but not the *carrosserie* (body). We are showing this car at the Salon the first of October to prove that we are keeping on with the same model." (It looks like an old Lincoln Continental – which H says was probably copied from the Citroën – and hasn't been changed in twenty years.)

Anyhow we had gone downstairs to our rocky and littered lane, that is covered with cats, babies and refuse, lined with an occasional parked car, and blocked by a pile of sand at the hairpin turn, where workers are forever putting up a house. In the economical French tradition of naming segments of streets, our end of the road is called avenue Fracchia and the other end is called avenue du Caroubier, for an old carob tree, long gone, but remembered. Meanwhile our address mysteriously remains 32 boulevard de l'Observatoire – along with several other neighboring houses which are also 32. This whole quarter, aged as it looks, can't be over forty years old, since only yesterday the hill used to be empty and below us, way down on the flat, there used to be orange groves.

Monsieur Massone installed us in the car, he driving, H beside him, I with the empty back seat to bounce around in. He reached the acute angle where our street gives on to the Grande Corniche and turned right up the famous road that runs like a cornice along the hilltops. We lurched up the hill in second, horn illegally sounding and tires screeching. We would all but plough into the back of a truck and then stop; then pull out, always on a blind curve, and pass. A wandering horse, mostly skeleton, managed to avoid us by shrinking against a wall; children and mothers at the roadside went on about their business, paying no mind to the sudden death one hair away; the landscape veered around us, sweeping by on one plane after another, nothing in its right place. (I rub the still deep mark on my shin where I had it permanently braced against the seat ahead.) There was no strap to cling to so I held on to the upholstery. Monsieur Massone maintained a steady flow of talk, head turned sideways to H, as trucks, cars, bicycles, motorbikes and pedestrians flew by.

The Corniche is a two-lane highway suspended in sky. If you pull out to pass on a curve and you meet something coming your way, you have had it. "This is it," I would say to myself at each bend. "Poor Nice Bahá'ís, having to sort out the chaos of my papers . . . Are French plastic surgeons any better than their doctors? . . . You could duck down there back of the seat," I advise myself . . . I tried to pray, but was laughing too hard to myself at the notion of selling a car by murdering the buyer, and also afraid M. Massone would see me in the mirror. Furthermore, always a poor sailor, I was getting queasy. The driver lurched happily on, stopping suddenly in mid-Corniche, jerking forward again, slithering around the curves. "How it holds the road! How it slides! Security, security!" He wasn't demonstrating the car, he was testing it. When I decently could, I suggested we had now got the idea and he could turn back as soon as he wished. H did not demur. I only had to say this a couple of times as we catapulted on. When he swerved off the road to turn, it was I, not he, who looked back to see if something was coming. Something was.

The return, with the slopes of the mountains rushing up at us, was of course far worse than the ascent. "It's a pleasure to drive!" he cried joyfully, rocking the car from side to side and sounding the horn. An old Citroën, black and dirty like most of them, but obviously considering itself to be the kind that gets you there and brings you back, defiantly sounded its horn at him as it climbed toward us. Exultant, he honked back. "You can do all sorts of acrobatics with this car," he shouted redundantly. We steered to the edge of the chasm, turned sharply right across the road toward the rock wall, veered back, avoided the bony old horse, avoided the laboring truck piled with gravel, lurched past the children, skidded to a stop, jerked forward, changed speeds from third to second in full career. H seemed imperturbable; now admits he was paralyzed.

Monsieur Massone is obviously a frustrated jet pilot. The motor smelt as if it were burning up. "Just a few drops of gasoline from the carburetor dropping onto this hot pan," he assured us. "Perfectly normal."

We finally went down town and bought a Simca *Aronde* (old name for swallow) that nobody demonstrated. And sure enough, Citroën changed their model that very year.

Oh God, Save Whom?

April 21, 1956 . . . Yesterday, to narrow things down, we counted all the items that have gone wrong in the new bathroom, installed in this house just before our tenure. The painter broke one of the windows prior to our moving in – that's in the inventory. His fresh-cream-colored paint curdled into orange droplets all over the walls and ceiling. (He himself isn't doing too well either. At work he is a mass of whitish substance inside and out. He disdains to take any precautions, as to not breathing in plaster dust and paint fumes, and when asked why he didn't wear a mask, replied that he had been in the business thirty years.) The shower never has let out a drop. The small "demountable" (in case of trouble) water-heater, too-firmly anchored, had to be virtually torn away from the wall and carted off to the factory when it went wrong; now it still heats water instantaneously, after only one preliminary explosion, but it showers blue-green flakes of corroded copper on anything placed beneath it – which notably includes the towel rack. The wash basin, contrary to the supposedly removable heater which wouldn't come loose, is so casually rooted that we don't dare forget and lean against it. The fluorescent roll of light over the basin won't stay turned on, giving up soon after you push the button. So much for just one room of the house.

Or you could take the "attic." When we came, H asked why he could see no chimney over the fireplace. The agent said the smoke went through a long horizontal pipe and came out at a corner of the roof. Sure enough there was an outlet up there, and smoke undeniably issued from it. The pipe was probably French thrift, we supposed – to get extra good out of the heat.

So we enjoyed about a full year out of the fireplace, often

using up highly inflammable materials, like excelsior, out of our packing cases shipped from America. Then the rains came, the roof sprang a leak, and we sent for the mason-engineer-electrician down the street. (He refuses to work for the owner of this house, as doesn't like him, but says he likes us and will work for us.) Apparently a trained gymnast, he climbed on a table, swung himself up through the trap door and wriggled into the attic space.

Immediately, we heard an anguished cry: "Put out the fire! *Vite! Vite!*"

We doused the fire, wondering what the emergency was.

"Your attic is full of smoke," he called down. "Your beams are all charred."

Obviously the portly agent had never seen the attic. There was no long horizontal pipe. According to all logic, the villa should have caught fire long since. We were retrospectively alarmed, but would have been more so had we known of a certain French law: if a fire breaks out, the owner of the house does not pay for the damage. His tenant does.

The other day as we drove away from our parking place beside the villa, we felt a sudden bump. H, cautious as always, got out to investigate. Mysteriously, a deep hole had opened up in the road under the car. We had just escaped sinking in. Examination showed a sort of cave under the macadam of the roadway, the thin layer of which had apparently been undermined by recent rains.

"Oh, that cave – that was the former owner's bomb shelter," explained Madame Socorro from downstairs. "She was a great big woman and there was just room in there for her and her husband. The bombs would drop and she would scuttle in there, crying, 'Oh God, save me! Oh God, save me!' 'Save you?' the neighbors would say. 'And how about the rest of us?' But she never prayed for anyone but herself," Madame concluded.

As for us, we have taken the necessary steps. We telephoned to, and then called on, the lawyer who is the present (absent) owner's agent. He got in touch with the *mairie* (city hall), and they said: "That is a national road. It has nothing to do with us." He then entered into negotiations with the

Ponts et Chaussées (Bridges and Roadways), and they said: "That is a private road. The hole must be filled by the co-proprietors."

Since then, nothing has happened, except that the cave is growing steadily larger and that we have found no childproof way of marking the spot. Perhaps if some car, truck or dignitary falls in, action will result.

The hole continued. A generous section of the roadway is now broken through, threatening the house as well as the passersby. Someone – the city perhaps – filled in the top of it with gravel but did not think to plug up the bottom, and the gravel has leaked away. Our mason came and looked at the hole for a while but refused to take action because the owner hasn't yet paid him for his work on the bathroom in the autumn of 1954.

The city or the water department or possibly the *Ponts et Chaussées* did write a letter to the lawyer to report that all is well: that a sign saying DANGER has been erected over the hole. As a California friend of mine likes to remark, nothing could be f. from the t. They must mean some other hole. This hole, unmarked, yawns for victims.

"Tell the proprietor's cousin," advised Madame Socorro. "It is the proprietor who must pay if anyone falls in."

In spite of all that happened at the Villa Christiane, when the agent completed his final tour of inspection and we surrendered its numerous medieval keys, he told us it was in better shape than when we came.

We did not think it pertinent to mention the wood-borers. They had been there long before we had. Early on, I had pleaded their case with H.

"They have rights too. After all, this is their home," I told him.

"I know who pays the rent," he said.

This brings me to how H improved our central heating system.

Up under the kitchen ceiling, and clamped to the wall in a metal frame, was a large hot water tank, its water heated through a pipe from the stove. From this tank an octopus of other pipes reached out to the various radiators in the villa, and even kept them close on to lukewarm.

Well, H noticed that the tank, through its outlet, was leaking hot water into the street. Why heat the street, he thought to himself. He decided to close a certain mysterious valve, thus keeping all the warmth indoors, and sure enough it worked. The radiators grew warm, later even hot. The rooms got virtually livable.

Some time afterward he chanced to look up at the kitchen tank. He blinked. He looked again. Why was the tank bulging? Then he knew. By closing the outlet valve, he had turned our hot water system to steam, and the tank couldn't take it. So that was how H almost blew up the villa.

The Exotic Garden

We are at Èze, where Dante passed, and was inspired with the Purgatorio – Èze where Nietzsche wrote a large part of the *Zarathustra* – at its very top, in the shell of the one-time castle, surrounded by the "Exotic Garden" ("Cactus," H the Californian says disdainfully). We are above the town that fans briefly below us – apricot tile roofs, ridges of tiles like fans, each roof on a long thin house of stone. As usual, the blaze of blue and gold sea and sun all around, and the dank, dark streets. Here and there in the alleys, the usual tourist traps – but the bit of laundry strung out must mean some real life goes on here. Off on the misty blue horizon, a long shape. A nearby French family of three, mother, wife and husband (the wife in the usual black patent leather high-heeled pumps and curly bowl-shaped bob) ask a man who is sweeping up: "What is that?" "That's Corsica," he told them, leaning on the handle of his broom of rough twigs. "They say it means bad weather when you can see Corsica. They say it means rain, three days afterward." "We'll pretend we haven't seen it," said the husband.

At Èze, the lithe brown girl in a yellow sweater set and a brown skirt and yellow socks. She spoke, casually and well, both French and English. From somewhere in Africa, I decided. She was with a big loose-limbed white man in a raincoat, camera and beret. He knew no French and she translated for him, airily, a bit here and there. The man carried a brown canvas bag. He had with him an off-white bathmat dog named Dima. After complications at the ticket window (you have to pay to get into the "Exotic Garden"), the girl airily translating, the man methodically folding up endless French 100-franc bills – Dima disappeared. The man said to the girl, "We have to keep the dog in sight at all times. When I'm doing something else, *you* watch the dog."

The girl tripped lightly and independently ahead of the large, loose, balding man; lithely she climbed the vertical paths. She started to take a snapshot of the mountains into the sun. "You are only throwing away your film," the man said. Noncommittally, the girl desisted. She leaned down and pulled up her yellow socks. Dima had run off again, trailing his leash. Is she his ward? His wife? His mistress? I thought. Is he a missionary and she a convert? Is he conducting her somewhere? She had short hair and smooth red cheeks. Noncommittally, she tripped along, far ahead of the man. The man clutched his canvas bag. "At all times," he called, "we must watch the dog."

Yet another case, I thought, of tyrant and victim; and as usual the victim is wearing the tyrant away. Gaily, absent-mindedly, she is destroying him. The off-white dog had disappeared again through the cactus, trailing his leash.

American children, these days, are killing each other with space weapons. The little French boy at Èze did have a gun strapped to his back, but still, he went warring down the street with a bow and arrow . . .

The Gypsies and Me

My relationships with the gypsies of Nice are cloudy. A woman comes to the door. She has hollow cheeks, a beak, a cough, a fierce, intense look, a bramble of brownish hair, a chartreuse-colored rag around her throat, and long, limp, cast-off clothes. She has the usual basket containing, today, a catch of safety pins and some sewing tape, filched, possibly during the peak of the rush hour down at the Nice-Echo in the Place Garibaldi. It is cleaner than the lace she had last time, dirty tattered bands of lace which she assured me would bring me luck as it had been blessed at Saintes-Maries-de-la-Mer. Last time I had asked her name and the curtains had dropped in her eyes and she had said slyly, "Madame Dubois" (Mrs Jones, Mrs Smith). Again today she had a girl of about thirteen with her, a blonde child with a dirty face by Botticelli.

"Good-day, Madame Dubois," I said. "Is this your daughter?"

"My niece."

"Her name?"

Madame Dubois thought for a moment. "Marie," she answered. "Buy this tape," she said.

"I never sew," said I.

"Then buy these safety pins – only 100 francs the lot." She held out a gaggle. "These things will bring you luck," she added mechanically. "You are going to get good news from across the water."

I brushed this aside. "How do you say good-day in your language? *Lacho divvus?*" said I. The other time she had told me *Lacho rat* which proved to be good night.

"We say Lacho da-ov," she said.

"How do you say girl?" pointing to "Marie."

"*Tikini*," she said, adding an unintelligible sentence which no doubt damned me to hell, as Marie began to giggle.

"*Tikini*," said I, probably mispronouncing it, as Marie giggled. Sure enough, I found it later in Paspati: "Infant, young – *Tiknó* . . . Fem. *Tikní*." For a long time I've been trying to translate the Bahá'í Twelve Principles into Romany. Since the gypsies wash in with their own language whatever is the language of the country they are in, Borrow, Leland and Paspati's Romany sound as various as Spanish, English and Greek. I notice that this people, which the *Britannica* calls mentally ten years old, are always bilingual and manage to live as free human beings, without work, or at least drudgery, by duping us high I.Q.'d slaves.

Anyhow I said to Madame Dubois, "How do you say, 'Men and women are equals'?" I explained by drawing imaginary lines on the door – we were standing at the door, I more or less blocking it – what I meant. "Not man up *here*." She understood immediately.

"*Rom te Romni sun para*," she said. Marie giggled. I went in and got a hundred francs for the pins, which I did not want; I also brought out an old T sweater and contributed it. She began to cough tuberculously. We shook hands all around and parted with expressions of mutual esteem. As she turned I caught the word "Santa" (health?).

It is vastly exciting to have an untamed woman give you a word this way, and then to find it in gypsy texts compiled in other countries by long-dead scholars. The gypsies are walking glossaries.

June 8, 1956 . . . A while back, Madame Dubois, my gypsy friend (H always calls them disgustedly, "your friends") came to the door with another set of dirty children. (Either her family is inexhaustible or she is a part-time ambulating baby-sitter and borrows the babies to beg with. H maintains that every day she takes out a new class to learn the art.) I have always considered her to be in the last stages of consumption, and her coughing and spraying around does nothing to belie this. On that occasion, besides the walkers, she had an inert bundle laid over one arm. She pushed aside a rag and I saw what looked like a yellow stick of taffy warped over her arm in an embryonic sleep. "What's his name?"

"Jeannot."

I thought, I am looking at a dying baby. He can't live out the week . . .

Today, she came again and squatted on the porch, her bag of lace and sewing tape open before her, the baby at her surprisingly rounded breast. Her hollowed cheeks were browned by the sun and there was a reddish light in her shaggy hair, rough as a wild boar's. The baby was unmistakably alive and Jeannot. Still quiet and listless, but sucking. "Did you go to Saintes-Maries-de-la-Mer?" (This is the ancient town in the Camargue, where the gypsies have a shrine and foregather every year, to the trepidation of the shopkeepers.) "How was it?"

"Not so good," she answered.

I brought out a plastic handbag, and the brat with her – supposedly the absent Marie's sister, but one of those rapacious gypsy beggar types – perhaps nine – shrieked, "*Man-qui!*" and grabbed it.

"What does that mean?"

"*Pour moi,*" said Madame Dubois. (It is the Persian *man*, I or me – and naturally delighted me.)

"What is your name?"

"Angèle." I almost laughed at the inappropriateness.

She kept looking at me as if I were flotsam and jetsam, and pointing out in gypsy, objects of interest to (I suppose) her aunt. Mentally I reviewed my clothes and thought, I'm safe. Nothing on but a sweater and old skirt. But I had forgotten. "That ring!" she screamed.

"It is for my religion," I said. (Indeed, it was a Bahá'í ring given me by the daughter of Bahá'u'lláh – and I have worn it most of my life.)

"That pin!"

"A dear friend gave it to me."

"I want earrings!" she screamed, wriggling and jumping up and down and talking to me as if I were a tree with cherries on.

"I'll think about it," said I.

THE GYPSIES AND ME

Madame Dubois asked, "Does your husband have a *pantalon?*"

"He wears his," said I. This is certainly true. I never saw anyone whose clothes last the way H's do. "But I have a friend who collects clothes. I'll ask her tonight."

"Buy something from me," said Madame Dubois, picking up a length of cheap lace. "This is blest."

"I am not Catholic," I said. "I am Bahá'í. My religion is: one God (I pointed up) and one family (I made a circle) you – her – me – all one family." This seemed to please Madame Dubois. She nodded thoughtfully. A neighbor watched from a half-closed blind across the way. (The same neighbor whose roof is a sieve because the proprietor is letting the house fall in ruins in order to force out the old couple who live there and pay regularly the legal rent – an absurd sum, in accord with current French law. "We don't need a bathroom," her old husband laughs, "our bedroom is a shower bath.")

"Have you a *foularde* for the baby?" said Madame Dubois.

"Unfortunately I have no baby and no baby clothes." I managed to produce a green sweater, my size, from Berkeley, California (the destiny of clothes!) and handed it over. I had forgotten all my gypsy, so I asked her, "Say *bon jour.*"

"*Latürat,*" she answered.

"Say beautiful day today."

"*Kerla shooka djournada.*"

"Say how are you?"

"*Dyé la toké mish tòss?*"

Another day, this time in Avignon, weather overcast and cold, we were waiting outside the old walls, going to cross the river on a bus and pay a belated visit to Pope Innocent VI.

Two gypsy women came by, one offering our fortunes, the other a packet of needles. We refused both; we don't sew, and would rather be surprised. "Listen," we disarmed them, "we know ladies of your group who live on a lot in Nice. Where do you live?" They changed at once, no longer preying on us but friend to friend.

"Saintes-Maries-de-la-Mer," one of them said.

It was only here in Avignon, after years in France, that we learned why there is such an influx of gypsies annually at Saintes-Maries: it seems that the saintly ladies, Marie Jacobé the Virgin's sister, Marie Salomé mother of James and John, Marie Madeleine, and a Sainte-Marthe who paused to subdue the monstrous Tarasque in Tarascon (the personnel and details vary with the teller) had all been set adrift in an open boat by enemies in the Holy Land, and had been wafted to the Camargue. Among others in their party was Sara the Egyptian, their serving woman, and this Sara the gypsies hereabouts honor as their mother, although to outsiders they generally speak only of the Holy Maries.

"How far away from here?" we asked.

"About eighty-seven kilometres," was the view of the shorter, pock-marked one.

They both were healthier and broader and more Nordic-looking than most European gypsies; in fact, it was only by their method of approach and their rag-bag appearance (for they were in mufti) that we had recognized them.

"How's the climate here?" we asked, wanting the truth. Natives and the Syndicate of Initiative looked evasive when you produced this question.

"No good," they said categorically. "Always this wind . . ."

Another woman affirmed, "We froze this morning. It was minus two [Celsius], and I've already been three kilometres on a bicycle. It's the Bomb."

"They never say it's the Bomb when the sun shines," H grumbled.

The day was fresh all right, but just then there was no beating, battering wind. Yesterday we had forced ourselves up into the garden growing on the Rock, that hangs there high above the Rhône. The wind was strong enough to hurl a child over the cliff, which accounts for the sturdy railings everywhere. We had clung, slammed and buffeted, to the iron railing and looked down, way down at the Rhône; at the small open boat that slides across the river on wire, at the broken-off bridge, and the country laid out, like a picture in a Book of Hours, fresh and unchanged since Pope Clement V first saw it. The flat plains greening. Philip the Fair's toy tower, squarely facing the Pope's Palace from the other side of the river, where the Bridge used to reach. And further over on a low hill, the pale round towers of the Fort Saint-André, that was built by John the Good.

More women waited near us, watching for the bus.

"They cut off three fingers – then there was nothing more to do, they had to cut off the arm. Nothing saved his life except pills brought from some foreign country, I forget which, and now he can't get the pills any more – fifty-three years old, *vous vous rendez compte.*"

It is always the same; once love is gone, women want nothing to talk about except sickness, the more awful the better; disease is their drama. Well, Innocent is even worse off, we thought: dead six hundred years, and may not even be in his tomb.

We went over the ordinary, utilitarian bridge that actually spans the river; we passed a tufted green island, recent and alluvial perhaps, and came to the gray walls and white fruit blossoms of Villeneuve, and Philip's tower, set up at what was then the edge of Southern France. We found a thirteenth-century church, with a Virgin and Child in a high-up niche; there were good little shops, some even modern and elegant; a bird sang in its wooden cage, and as we passed an open doorway we heard a woman singing too, as often happens in the South. This town is still somebody; the winding old streets still have an air to them; it is not too hard to remember that this place once boasted many a sumptuous Cardinal's palace, or "livery" as the word then was.

As for Innocent, he was long gone from Villeneuve. There had been a contest over his remains and Villeneuve had lost. It was even a long time since a peasant had turned his tomb into a rabbit hutch.

The Tourmaline Pool

April, 1956 (A return to Avignon and the Petrarch country.)

Going to Vaucluse, the bus rumbles laboriously through scenery around Avignon that rests as gently on the eyes as the auberge dinners on the stomach. Here are the forked vine trunks like rows of cloves pricked in; the long gray walls, the windbreaks of black cypresses, the furrows neatly combed. Gray villages piled on rounded hills. Spanking new villas, stucco over cement blocks, painted pink or yellow, and with pistachio or turquoise blinds; under their orange-tiled roofs, a painted band around the walls, of fruit or flowers. A man, round and squat, moves by, all spheres, in a round beret and a round, purplish suit of clothes. Life goes on, ageless; soil being cultivated, children running, schools, hospitals, church buildings – all with orderly schedules, all going on whether there is or is not a new government, though there have been all the years of cruel, draining war. The gray road winds through battered, pastel villages that sink impressionistically into lights and shadows. Sweet France. Not America's magnificence – no Grand Canyon or Death Valley; not the ancient oil-painting backgrounds of high, symmetrical Italian villages under smooth blue sky, sunlit as if fixed in amber. Only a disarming gentleness and sweetness. A balance and a rightness. A "this is how things must be done."

Here where the willows are hung with green rosaries is Laura's country. Black, lacy high-tension towers, not of Petrarch's time, stand in the fields. A big sign by the road says *Miel*, and you add the thought of warm, slow honey.

The soft gray pigeon-wing sky brushes along. A line of white blossoming trees, full out, look like white peacocks spreading their tails in courting. Some Gaudi-like or Victorian houses pass. In villages, elegantly dressed girls promenading in Sunday best. Sedate children walking. Canals. Hitched outside an upper window, a bird cage. A village fair: carousel under its jade dome, grinding out mechanical music, presenting small sports cars, a red cow saddled, a jet-plane, a pink pig, a saddled rabbit, something for every six-year-old taste. Houses on the square at L'Ile-sur-Sorgue: pale green with burgundy shutters.

Woman on the bus: "My husband has lived forty-three years in Vaucluse and has never seen the Fountain." (The "Fountain" is really, as we were to discover, an infinite dark pool.) A polite tourist to old lady: "Madame, are you from here?" She: "I was born here." "In the Fountain?" "No," smiling; "I wouldn't have these wrinkles if it was in the Fountain . . . See the rock cliff way out there? The Fountain comes out of that."

The bus finally lands us in a village square, dwarfed under a high mountain semicircle of bare, gray rock. Almost everywhere, silent green water hurries. In the square a graceful, weathered granite column, raised to Petrarch in 1804.

Now begins the usual twentieth-century affront to the memory of great men: the open tables and booths and shopfuls of tourist commercial objects. Plastic birds, sandwiches, ceramic storks, small statuettes of people sitting on toilets, funny postcards, pennants, nut-crackers shaped like women's legs, key rings, cups with pictures on them, faked dog-excrement, ash trays. Candied nuts cooking. "Almonds and hazelnuts! Taste them, Madame!" WC signs much in evidence. On a flat terrace over the water is the "Café Pétrarque et Laure."

Above all this, detached, remote, the massive, bare-rock amphitheatre of a mountain, reaching into the sky. Sheer, gray cliffs. Caves in them, gouged out. Here, six hundred years is a breath.

To the right of the rising path, the hurrying water. It is deep green, and under it is a lighter green moss. Another café along the stream: "The Garden of Petrarch; Lunch, 1100 francs." The famous green of the water is a blend of many greens, and even dark blues. The river's sounds are gentle now, not booming as in the rainy season. It plunges down white as you climb higher. Trees along here are ivy-smothered. There are sleepy factory buildings along the stream, with a mosaic brick smokestack. The thousand inhabitants of the village earn their living in local paper mills, carpet and woolen coverlet factories. Petrarch had a garden around here once; white lilac grows here; on the rough hillside, H finds iris, and we speculate that these are descendants of his flowers. Old plane trees stand here. We climb upwards through the steep ravine. Over our heads the cliffs are eroded, crenelated. Near the top of the steep path, among enormous mossy boulders, separate rivulets of white plunge down.

H upbraids me because, down at the shops, I asked to see the guide book and then bought it. "A person can't let a book get in your hands —" "Well, you ought to know that, after all these years. Why not prevent me?"

The path suddenly ends. We are left on the edge of a great, circular pool, hollowed into sheer rock. Here is the mysterious source of the Sorgue. This is what they call the Fountain. The pool is a tourmaline color, a strange purple-blue-green. The drama is in the shape and color, and the cliff and tree reflections; it is in the contrast between the deep, still pool and the powerful torrent leaping away from its edge, down through the rocks. In the rainy season there is a universal drumming sound.

Tourists are skipping pebbles and chunking rocks into Petrarch's pool. "Everything in our day has to be spoiled," I say. "You can dive in a bikini and drink a Jumbo Malt at Walden Pond." "A hundred years ago you couldn't get there at all, or here either," says H. He is always so reasonable. We find two rocks off the path, and sit and eat our chocolate-filled rolls. As Petrarch did, I wash my hands in the cold water. At last the tourists are gone. "We are not tourists," I insist to H. "What are we then?" he wants to know. "Pilgrims," I sigh.

For a few minutes, we are alone here at the water that wells up from under the sheer, towering rock. Then more tourists. We start back down the path. "It always amuses me how French women tour in spiked heels." "I don't know why it should amuse *you*," says H, "because that's *your* favorite device." I point indignantly to my shoes with low cuban heels. "That's only today," he says, closing the subject.

Above us, the bare, bony mountains, with flute-holes drilled out. Before us the green pathway, and at our left, the hurrying white stream. Ahead and down, climbing a lesser hilltop, a Bishop's château in ruins, crumbling away, demolished, say locals, "by Richelieu on account of the Huguenots." Petrarch was often a guest there. It was the home of his friend, Philippe de Cabassoles.

We stop to read an unobtrusive stone plaque fastened to a rock and well written over with tourists' names: "To this shut valley, fleeing the pleasure of the age, came François Pétrarque, to shelter his meditations, in the autumn of the year 1337, faithful to his worship of Laura and to the study of antiquity. No place was dearer to his heart, nor more propitious to his fame. The city of Vaucluse, to its poet, August, 1937."

They showed us "Petrarch's house." Little whitewashed rooms with red tile floors. There is a wooden table "where he wrote," under a terra cotta bust of "Laura." There is a bunch of blackened laurels on the wall, "because he always went around crowned with laurel," explains the small, brown lady who keeps the house. There are pictures on the walls and papers and mementoes in cases. "Here is Laura's cap," she showed us; it looked suspiciously like an antique night-cap such as Persian bridegrooms used to wear. "And here is a portrait of Boccace; he was a little poet of long ago . . ." Having thus dismissed the author of the *Decameron*, she continued with a flourish: "And here is Laura." Laura de Noves, a problematical candidate at best, stared darkly at us from the wall.

What is real in this place is the still, gray light in the bare rooms, sleeping above their bit of lush green garden, along the hurrying stream.

To Live Happy . . .

"The only thing that keeps me from your Bahá'í belief is my little dog," the Frenchman said to us. We looked helplessly at the five-year-old fox terrier. Was it reincarnated or metempsychosed? Sara patted it. We are still trying to fathom the place of the dog in the French psyche. What is this unconditional worship?

The French do not talk of the future, a bigger and better France by 19—, the way Americans do. They seem like a people shocked into dreaminess, just wanting to live their traditional way of life, quietly eating, promenading, working only enough to get by, dressing up very beautifully on Sunday. The Nice people are well-dressed, not ragged like the Dubliners. "The Frenchman wants peace," a Frenchman said to us. "All he says is, '*Fichez-moi la paix.*'" Their proverb reads: *Pour vivre heureux vivons cachés.* ("To live happy, live hidden.")

We heard a local show-off sermonizing to friends, they on benches, he walking up and down before them, in the little park at the bus stop at St-Jean. "But we are immortal," he was saying to them. "The atom bombs? But they are caramels!"

Unlike the French

Italy. December 22, 1955 . . . Outside the Café Shelley by the sea wall at San Ferenzo. The Italians live more intimately with the sea than the southern French. Around Nice you are often frustrated, kept away from the sea by train tracks and rich men's villas, the latter of the old days. We hesitated to make this trip, thinking it would be just more Nice. But no, the air is different. We are glutted with beauty. The Romans are still road-builders, everywhere fine stone work, fine new apartments going up, bougainvillea vines trained up the stone walls; elaborate stone terraces. Forests of mimosa at this season. The French in comparison do only the adequate minimum whereas these people outdo themselves. San Remo is easily reachable from Nice, so we counted our trip as beginning from there. Genoa this morning proved a huge Italian Seattle and all we saw there was the traffic we fought – trucks (many huge, others small three-wheelers) hurtling through industrial sections that could have been in America. Of course the omnipresent Fiats, new, clean, glittering, are far smaller than present-day U.S. monsters. Genoa where I came with Howard [Carpenter] in 1932 at the beginning of life, foreseeing nothing. Great new apartments climb the busy hills and the Italians aren't afraid to use color – soft jade, pale strawberry.

Wonderful mountains around Rapallo, but the town itself – in spite of some splendid new housing, is shabby and nostalgic. I photographed the octopus fountain. The donkeys, sawn-off and run chiefly by vocabulary, wearing modish straw hats from which feathers explode, do a brisk business carting children up and down the promenade.

In the country, laundry is vigorously clothespinned to the

bushes. The hillside towns are longer than in France, more elaborate, more colored. Entering Massa where we now are (Thursday night), spectacular snow mountains.

Carrara . . . On the roads old women in black. Young women in red. Many men and women carrying huge loads of wood or branches on their heads. Many big people in Carrara, an old Book of Hours town, settled in a hollow among high mountains, some terraced, some bare, some wooded – and way above, one peak, on the way in, a sharp white snow peak. Everywhere here, marble. (Some emptied-out quarries on the way in from Massa.) The long blue buses angling, with their musical nervous trumpet. Marble in corners, lying about or lumbering by in horse-drawn carts, or piled in yards. Marble dust thick and white in one workshop. The workers living in this deadly Chavannes mist. A sculptor using an air chisel. Boys in newspaper hats. Saints and Christs and Madonnas lying stiffly around in various stages. In one workshop a man showed us Caesar in a crate. With my two or three words of Italian, bits of German and such, we learned that the column on its side was for a Church of Mary in Rome. The column here, and Mary lying on her side next door. In a "museum" the worker took out and held silently in his hands a slim polished stick of dark green marble. "Peru," he said.

Black accentuating cypresses; the flat, flat, two-dimensional churches in these flat, two-dimensional Book of Hours cities. In the shop, they were cutting slabs with carborundum – a wire does the cutting, worked by an old-fashioned wheel and pulley. Elsewhere we saw modern machines. Carrara has the most perfect house and garden walls I've seen – palimpsests: battered, runny yellow and pink and faded Pompeian – jade blinds, periwinkle blinds, everything stained, mottled, washed down by sun. At the bridge into Massa, the pale green water and above it the marble yard Ronchieri in magenta letters. A huge modern white crane – an enormous wheel in a red brick wall – factory buildings – in among the marble a worker in robin's egg blue.

In Carrara, lavish use of marble everywhere. The bandstand in the park is floored with it.

In Italy something vital is always going on at the top of everyone's lungs.

Italian sounds a lot easier than French, and the Italians do not make a cult of their language. I have never, repeat never, made a mistake in speaking French but what my interlocutor corrected me, not in so many words, but by using the term correctly in his next sentence or so. The Italians don't seem to care what you do to their language. We all talk pidgin together; I use nouns, God bless all nouns, and point. The language barrier is a relief to me here. English, French and Persian give me a guilt feeling; I have no right to do them wrong; I must forever look this up and look that up. But with Italian I am not supposed to know anything and it's a real joy.

Rome. December 28, 1955. The Pietà – done by Michelangelo when he was of the still-illusioned young. The Christ is wholesome, not emaciated, not racked – young and sleeping in the arms of the still young mother.

Rome. January 1, 1956 . . . Unlike the French, who are a reticulation of mutually exclusive, tiny family cells, these people seem to be clubby. Their club is the road. On a holiday you can't see the highway for the people. A left front door slams open across our right of way and the driver jumps out; four persons, arm in arm, like cut-outs, spread across your lane. We see city-dressed people in even the smallest hill villages, city-dressed and with many young men such as you seldom see in American small towns. The people promenade up and down the roads. A passing car on the highway means nothing to them. This is a point of psychology which we can't understand. We would even attribute it to communist doctrine if it weren't so universal. They don't seem to despise the car though – it isn't that. Then what is it? The little square Italian Fiats go hurtle-bong through the thick crowds, making a temporary passage that at once closes back. If you bong and don't hurtle, merely pushing along in low gear, they won't budge. A man pulls a girl in a red coat (the girls' favorite color) out of our path; she deliberately steps back in front of us again.

We're driving a French Simca which looks comparatively big and is seldom seen here, but can't possibly attract the hate, admiration and envy that the new U.S. cars do. It isn't that. It's almost as if your life as a motorist were completely outside their life in the sidewalk club, completely remote. Meanwhile you pray and curse and try to keep from killing them. I avoid a huge magenta balloon and its small rescuing owner. On the finally empty highway I avoid a galloping pig, and the car swerves horribly. Down near Naples, either side of the road is apt to be occupied by two-wheel, salmon-pink and ornamented carts; you try to pass a truck, wondering why it is so far out in the road: you find that it is trying to pass a roadside cart. Most horses' harnesses are surmounted at the shoulder by a tall brass sort of pommel with knobs on it. The horses and donkeys are carrying loads too heavy for them, I think – though H maintains that wicker baskets, hay or long twigs aren't heavy even in mountainous quantities. Cows, loose-jointed and uncorseted, were not planned as beasts of transport but the milk-white oxen are delightful in the role.

At Ostia, the cloudy Roman sunset under the umbrella pines. Eastward, the pale moon rising over the pale broken columns eternally supporting long-vanished roofs, and over the pale statues in their niches. The "*maison close*" with the bar in front beside the ticket-vendor's booth.

Again, unlike the French, Italians do not sit down to supper as to a sacrament; every supper is not their Last Supper. Their food is good, they feed you quickly, almost as fast as Americans, and get you out of the restaurant; they are, in this as well, unlike the French. French restaurants expect you to stay two hours.

The Italian *bars* – a word which I believe America has contributed – sell very little alcohol. Mario Fiorentino tells us alcohol is not an Italian problem. Over ninety per cent who go in the bars buy *caffe espresso capuchino* and take it standing or at a table, with pastry. The bar is a nice place to sit and be in – almost like the wonderful club-like atmosphere of the Vienna café where you can stay and read and be warm forever. People's café habits are evidently too intimately a phase of their national personality to cross frontiers. I can't imagine a

Viennese café in America, though I have often felt the need of one there; and I have not seen a real Italian "bar" in France.

The Italians differ from the French in this too; they are assiduous salesmen: they will go to any lengths for you; they will change all the furniture if you will rent the hotel bedroom; they will make over the blouse for you before sundown if you will buy it; they want you to bargain; they give you the store. In a handbag shop, I saw a bag at roughly $22. It never occurred to me to question the price. I simply remarked in tourist pidgin that my American bag had cost $20. In no time the Italian bag was down to $18. We began to wonder why we like the French. We decided it was because of their magnificent contempt for you. They don't care if you buy. They despise you the way a cat does, down from their empyrean isolation; their fort in the skies with nobody in it but *moi* and a few close, close relatives. A contempt that parallels and is not at all incompatible with their perfect politeness. I keep trying to relate Italians to Middle Easterners; they are European Persians and the French are European Chinese.

Looking for Pedro de Luna

Was I imagining it, or did the people in Spain, especially the cities, look cautious? Rather grave, melancholic, no brisk swinging along as you might see in London, say.

In the bookstores of Barcelona, they almost took cover when I asked for a life of Pope Benedict XIII. Either they had never heard of him, or they knew they shouldn't have. One clerk shook her head, as if reminiscently. "No, not any more," she said. We knew there were at least four in Spanish, available somewhere, but we finally gave it up. It began to seem as if I would have to write his life myself.★

Barcelona is like most of our dreadful post-automobile cities. Noise. Traffic. Rectangles for the proles. Giant cranes. At its best, a drab grandeur I try to find an adjective for: lonesome? The French word *morne*? Uncomforting, like the opposite of Austria? We should never travel without Roget.

We look briefly at a Gaudi temple, commemorating one of the great houses of Spain. It does make a statement: it is crawly, pullulating like a bad Rodin – but wins respect for daring to be horrible.

After a passing cop had fined us a dollar for going through a red light, and after an hour and a quarter of search, we found a parking space and went walking. "I am facing a Coca-Cola (tastes queer) in a hell-hole," my note says.

The museums, naturally, were all closed. They close automatically, as by electric beam, the world over, at our approach.

The Spaniards litter, not surreptitiously, but with a grand air. Restaurant floors proved well-strewn with match packs,

★ See my book, *The Three Popes*.

146

cigarette packs, paper napkins, old sales tickets. The people seem very clean, anyway. The proprietors of a small café let us use their toilet, and it was a revelation. It was spotless, with neat ragged sections of newspaper on a nail. But you went through their living quarters to get there, dampish, window-less boxes where cooking and ironing went on, and two tiny, spindly children were growing up.

So far as we could tell, the Spanish have two nights: twelve to four P.M., and three A.M. to seven. During those hours, even the men's loud conversation is heard no more.

At four that afternoon it stopped raining and the sun even came out. We got into the cathedral then and saw chapels with high railings, to some of which, wax figurines were fastened: babies, models of human organs – votive offerings to holy beings from grateful, rescued believers. The Virgin of Fatima had the best collection: on her railings we saw a wax leg, a foot, a hand, and a heart. The cathedral was pitch-dark, empty except for a tourist or so, an interchangeable, black-clothed old woman or two praying, another old woman sweeping up. High above us, an explosion of stained glass – and outside, a brooding Moorish courtyard, with palms, magnolias, and the patter of fountains. They did not allow us down in the crypt, to Saint Eulalia's bones. *Prohibido*, they said.

Is it the recent dead that make Barcelona so melancholy? Next day, in the countryside, it is joyous: we have pines, stone terraces, and the silver-green sea. We have drifting blossoms, and wind in the olives. Along the road are Persian earthen jars for sale, the same kind as in ʿUmar Khayyám.

Each day I keep finding traces of the almost eight centuries of Muslim involvement in Spain. Because after all, what with the spiritual power and the tolerance that Islám displayed at its peak, the philosophers, artists, scholars, drawn under its aegis, who were Jews, Christians, Persians, whatever – had combined there to shape a new world. And out of that world, as ʿAbduʾl-Bahá says, Europe was reborn.[1]

Oh, they were driven out afterward, their books were destroyed, their names blew away on the wind. But history is not mocked forever, and forgotten treasures will surface over time. There were those Spanish galleys, sailing the Mediterranean, that captured three Moorish vessels loaded with the priceless library of the Sulṭán of Morocco. And toward the close of the nineteenth century, there was that manuscript of a hundred and forty-nine of their ancient songs, that turned up in what was then St Petersburg.

"This was brought by the Arabs," I keep saying – "and that was Arab," *ad nauseam* to Harold, who bores easy. Today I comment on the opalescent mountains, bare and sharp and spotted with sunlight and shadow. "Brought by the Arabs, no doubt," says H.

Unfortunately, what modern times are doing to the country should be punishable by law. Le Corbusier's rectangles on stilts; American-type billboards, like, say, that one standing up stark and alone, in the shape of a huge yellow wine bottle; and fake Riviera-style villas, shutting out the sea. Modern traffic, it seemed to us, was especially hard on the locals with their two-wheeled carts – drawn by mule, donkey or stunted horse – and on the dog running along underneath.

On we go, following a stubborn old man with a stubbornness sometimes equal to his, and we pass many of the mules he was likened to, the mules of Aragon who personify self-will. To get close to him, we seek out the same things he experienced himself, when he was on earth, six centuries ago: he too smelled the woodsmoke, and skirted a wide, dry river; he looked at sea and mountains and turquoise sky, at branches bending in the wind, at the long road ahead, the far horizon.

He, Pedro de Luna, Benedict XIII, legally elected to the See of Saint Peter by the Cardinals of Pope Clement VII, if you count Clement VII as a valid Pope. On this issue, Western Christendom once split for close to forty years. Officially, but only officially, that Great Schism of the West, as the books call it, ended in 1417 – after it had divided families, had spelled torture and bloodshed, had set region against region, city against city.

Who was the true Pope? Pedro de Luna said he was, till he drew his last breath in 1423. Three successors followed after him. And even in 1431, her inquisitors asked Joan of Arc: "What say you of the Pope? Which do you hold for true?" Fighting for her life, nineteen years old, the Maid told them to pass on by. (A little while longer and they burned her alive.)

When he was on earth de Luna travelled from high place to high place, and following his steps we notice how topographical the old class distinctions can be: how hard it is to believe that the man down there in the plain is equal to the man up here on the summit.

Anyhow, we are arriving now at the last of his high places, to where, from the far-up top of Peñiscola, he could look out over the blue, unbroken miles of water, and wait for welcoming ships that never came. For that deep, violet line to the north is France, and he died here, defiantly facing France, ignoring the buffeting winds and the empty sea, sure of his right.

We leave the conspiratorially whispering, clerically lace-edged sand, and start the long climb along an ancient amber wall. A seated line of old men watch. An old woman, all in black, passes by, her primordial errands never done. Other old women are tying lobster nets. Another displays a live crayfish, like a huge gray shrimp, that she holds in a newspaper. The cats and dogs are thin. The children run, jump and call. There is Coca-Cola of sorts, and tourist *shlock*, and even, to our surprise, a French booklet about "le pape Luna."

This whole great rock is a kind of beehive, a village echoing with voices – people's, roosters', gulls' – especially today when the sea is too quiet to cannonade through its ancient vent in the rock, its *bufador*. At the top, over the castle entrance, is carved a forgotten coat-of-arms, a templar's, from before the days of Benedict. Now we are in the castle itself, with its sheer drops, its bare, vaulted chambers, its dizzy terraces where he must have paced so often over the long years, and gazed toward France.

We are in the chapel now, and something, or someone, is angrily tapping and tapping away. Is it an old man's peremptory cane, expressing a vast, fourteenth-century wrath that has never been stilled? Above us we see a loose sign, knocking in the wind. But we wonder, anyhow.

When, in 1923, he had been dead five hundred years, they (by "they" we mean the University of Zaragoza) put up a plaque for him here, where his body once lay, till it was carried back to the high place where he was born. Among other things, the marble tablet says: *Pedro de Luna, de vida limpia, austera, generosa, sacrificada por una idea del deber* ("Pedro de Luna, of a life pure, austere, high-minded, offered up for the concept of duty"). He may be forgotten now in the book-stores, and hushed up in the Avignon Palace of the Popes and in Perpignan, but they know him here.

Surely he felt safe on this rock, but he had his escape routes too. From what used to be his study, there is a flight of steps on the outside wall, steps so narrow you have to climb them sideways. And over the parapet, when you look so far down that a brown hawk floats way below you, you see, carved into foundation rock, another stair, that provided him with a getaway to the sea.

Everything about this old stronghold, with its towering heights, its thick walls, its slits for weapons, breathes security and protection. Yet what killed Pedro de Luna? Poison.

How much those medieval people travelled. Even with a modern car and a good road, this trip is wearying. No doubt Pope Benedict took it without hurry, and with relative ease, all his facilities, his kitchen, his toilet essentials, traveling along with him. Still, it is surprising how far he went. Following him from castle to castle, from high point to high point, gives one a sense of past time that is seldom found in the books.

We are not at our best. Yesterday evening in Zaragoza we found no place to stay. We caromed precariously through cars that were coming at us from all directions, saw no place to park, and were apparently wedged into the traffic for good and would have to be lifted out by crane. Meanwhile a "runner" kept pursuing us. "How can I shake this guy?" H asked me. "Give him a tip and say 'Adios,' " I told him. However (although like so many blessings impenetrably disguised), the man got us parked and led Harold off to a hotel. Harold was back like a shot. "How do they say

'impossible,' and 'house of assignation' in Spanish?" he asked
me. Luckily the man had another suggestion, and finally
settled us into a family hotel.

Here a vivid life was proceeding at all times. Through our
bathroom wall came, hour after hour, yells, cries, baby
howls, the slip-slap of shuffling feet, and even castanets. Well
played, too. Hard to do. I know. As a sophomore I signed up
for Spanish dancing, and after one attempt at swinging my
hips, and one try with the castanets, I dropped out.

As the hours wore on, we found that the relatively few
above noises did not exhaust the list. Besides the elevator's
continual bells, followed by its steady whine, there were
vague, horror-film groans and gurgles from the plumbing,
and we also seemed to be harboring a stranger gently snoring
away in our room. Upstairs, directly over our bed, there was a
family that were either running a bowling alley, or else they
were all weight-lifters, and butter-fingered.

At last our breakfast drink arrived. It was either instant
coffee or instant cocoa; we were not sure which, but were in
no mood to quibble.

Later, in the bookstore, we stood around till the lone
customer, a priest, had left, and asked our question: "Do you
have a life of Pedro de Luna?" "Not *us*," the man said, but then
he sent us on to another bookstore, a fine big one with a card
index – and here, yes, they had heard of Papa de Luna, but no,
they had no Life. We reflected that it was forty-one years since
this city's university had placed that marble commemorative
tablet in the chapel at Peñiscola. Things were different now.

Something pushes us on and on, to our goal, his birthplace,
Illueca. It is cold. No women today. The few men we see are
some in berets, some in soft, helmet-like caps, and they wrap a
highwayman sort of cloth – pink, white, even lavender –
around their mouths.

Empty hills, deep red and mustard earth, snowflakes poised
on blossoming trees, thousands of ballerina trees in their
spreading tutus, stepping mincingly among the vines. A gray
donkey loaded with a basket to each side kicked and danced
when he saw our car.

Sometimes the hilly road winds past a forlorn cluster of tiny, whitewashed houses, huddled beside an enormous earthen church. In one area we found the soil yellowish, the houses yellowish, a few lumpy sheep that looked like yellow rocks, and a flock of small, pale yellow birds.

Suddenly in the emptiness, swooping toward us on motorcycles, we saw what looked like two black crows, but we knew that these were birds of a different feather: these were the police. Had someone been on the telephone between the towns? We had heard of foreigners languishing in Spanish prisons, penned up on any excuse, or none. The two swerved alongside our car. We stopped.

They asked by gestures what Europe's police had already asked a number of times before: why did our car have no license plate *in front*, only *behind*? We conveyed the fact that in the state of Pennsylvania, where this Chevrolet wagon came from, you did not have a license plate *in front*. They looked dubious, and asked for our documents. All these, thank Heaven, were impeccable. But they still seemed to be wondering what to do with us – suspect foreigners, way off the beaten track in Franco's Spain. It happened that wedged into our glove compartment, we had a long sheaf of illegible German papers, in tiny print. Never read by either of us, these were the laborious accomplishment of an Austrian insurance company, and consisted of a virtually endless statement as to what the *Allgemeine . . . Versicherungsanstalt* undertook, or did not undertake, or in certain elaborately qualified conditions might or might not undertake, always provided that the insured parties had or had not done thus and so . . . until such time as the lapse of the policy would part the insurers and insured forevermore.

I extricated these and handed them to the cops. They considered them sombrely, and right side up. The papers might as well have been Dead Sea scrolls. Anyway, with documentation like this, we were obviously people of probity. The cops handed them back, waved us on our way, and continued on theirs.

Out of Azaila we saw a painted desert like America's Far West, shrimp-pink and orange. We passed the usual dry rivers. Out of Alcuñiz there was a vast, pale green lake with wavelets, and we thought maybe they'd dammed up the Rio Ebro, which begins way up north near Santander and empties at Amposta into the Mediterranean Sea. We found them growing corn hereabouts and saw the gold ears piled in their cribs.

"The rich are rich everywhere, and the poor are poor everywhere," a friend of ours has said. So are the powerful powerful everywhere. This Illueca is still, after all the endless years, a seat of power. As we neared here, and drove past the very olive trees Pedro de Luna must have seen himself, we looked upward toward the summit, and saw his home – a central point in the sky.

The great bare castle stands on a kind of plateau and reigns over all it surveys: the huddled village immediately below, the lesser hills, and the vast plain, through it running the River Jalon, stretching out to infinity before it. Perhaps when he walked the terraces of his last high place, and he gazed down over the sea on a rough day, it put him in mind of these tossed hills where he first saw the light.

A dark man in a beret attached himself to us as soon as we left the car in the tiny village square. The castle is a national monument, he said. He would lead us to the house of the official who had the key. This functionary, however, standing in his doorway, refused to let us see the place, except of course from the outside, which could hardly be concealed. He couldn't take the responsibility, he said. The castle was too ruined. Too *peligroso*. The Alcalde himself could not grant us permission. Only Zaragoza or maybe even only Madrid could let us in.

The man in the beret assured us we could drive up the narrow path to the summit, but we said no. Resigned, he climbed along with us. We passed adobes that could have been in Mexico or Persia, through a deep silence broken only by voices in the houses. The slanting muddy lane was strewn with garbage and goat droppings. Near the top, we paused, our lungs splitting. The man uttered just one word, which he knew I knew: *Coche*. "Car." I marveled at what a single word can convey. He was saying: "You fools – lungs bursting – I told you you could make it up here in your car but of course, you wouldn't listen. No, you knew better. And now, look at you. Serves you both right, etc., etc."

The ancient fabric stands there, stark and huge, on its neglected ground. It has a couple of towers surmounted by crosses, and there are carved lion faces over the arched entrance way. There are knot holes in the portal, and, for that key which the custodian refused us, a great iron keyhole (the Middle Ages were a time of enormous keys). Through these apertures we could look up to a narrow, vaulted ceiling, seemingly in perfect condition, and we made out a dark flight of stone steps leading up to the floor beneath it. And that was all.

The man in the beret said sadly that the Spaniards do not appreciate the things of Spain, like this castle. I told him it might be repaired, for the tourists. Too ruined, he said. He told us there is one fine old painting inside the great salon – not of *figuras* but *colores*. Otherwise nothing. He also informed us that the trees we saw blossoming were almonds. (How all this was communicated I do not know.) Afterward he would accept no money from us, only a candy, and that out of politeness.

These then were the experiences I shared with Pedro de Luna, elected Pope Benedict XIII by the Cardinals of Clement VII, Clement himself having been elected by the same Conclave who had, five months earlier, elected Pope Urban VI on condition, they said, that he would step down – only, Pope Urban refused.

And somehow, I felt I had found him – that never-yielding Benedict XIII, that man *de vida limpia, austera, generosa, sacrificada por una idea del deber.*

IV

The Diamond Bough

There were once two brothers named Chang and Eng, who were closer to each other than almost any two human beings have ever been. The two were even closer than Ruth and Naomi in the Bible; with them, it was truly a case of where you go I will go, for they were joined at the waist by a flexible ligament, five or so inches long.[1]

They were profitably put on public view (for a time by famed circus producer Phineas Taylor Barnum), and although mostly Chinese, were everywhere billed as the Siamese Twins.

In 1839 the brothers left show business, rich men for that time: they had over $10,000. Named Bunker by now, they settled down in North Carolina and became hard-working and prosperous farmers. Then the two of them (respectively, it seems) married two sisters, country belles, Adelaide (Chang), and Sarah (Eng) Yates, and the marriage produced twenty-one children.

Close as they were, as time wore on they (and the two sister wives, and some of the children) grew poles apart. For example Eng was only a moderate drinker, but Chang was a confirmed drunk. When violent he would smash things – his own, it is true – around the house. Once, under the influence, he even threw a feather bed on the fire.

The harassed four made an arrangement which helped a little: they would spend three days at Adelaide's house, and three at Sarah's.

When it got to be 1874, Chang fell ill, and died of something wrong with his lungs, and three hours later Eng too was a corpse.

But the thing that stays with me about these brothers is,

they seem to symbolize humanity in our present age, hopelessly bound together and at the same time worlds apart.

One day the two of them were working up on top of a roof, when yet another of their quarrels broke out. At that point a neighbor happened by, and according to him Chang grabbed a hammer and threatened to bash Eng with it and knock him off the roof.

I often wonder what it was that these brothers, who could never escape each other, needed and lacked. Certainly it must have been love, a too-much profaned term which explains little. What was absent from their lives was something like the Irishman's definition of salt: salt is what potatoes are no good without.

Salt is not far-fetched in this connection. Its credentials are age-old. It means both hospitality and loyalty in the Old Testament. It is used in baptism and exorcism by the Roman Catholic Church, because the Devil hates it. For the same reason, medieval witches banned it from their ceremonies. The disciples of Christ were the salt of the earth; and in Da Vinci's *Last Supper*, Judas is depicted as spilling the salt.

In his famed essay *On Love*, Stendhal also put love and salt together. He says that in the salt mines near Salzburg (Salt Town), the miners would throw a bare winter bough down into the old workings. Pulled out two or three months later, the bough, twigs and all, could be recognized no more: it was no longer a stripped, dried-out piece of wood, but a rainbow shimmer, a twinkling jewel, a "diamond bough," bits of which jewelry the miners would offer the tourists for souvenirs.

He goes on to describe the whole tour to Hallein, as it was in the early years of the nineteenth century, the visitors sliding rapidly down into the mine astride ancient tree trunks, the women with their voluminous skirts packed into huge trousers of gray serge. But what he uses for the development of his theme – love – what he dwells on, is that "crystalliza-tion," that transformation of stick to gem, "that process of the mind," he says, "which discovers fresh perfections in its beloved at every turn."[2]

Stendhal's four kinds of love have nothing to do with

'Abdu'l-Bahá's. The novelist speaks of passion-love, and mentions Héloïse and Abélard; of sympathy-love; of sensual love; and of vanity-love (this last by a man who shows off his mistress as he would a fine horse).

We are all familiar with aspects of love that effect a brief unity in the world: parental, romantic, patriotic, racial, political, team-love – we know about them; they are all limited, the Master says, and cannot bring peace. These kinds are among us anyhow, and, to paraphrase, there needs no Holy Ghost come from the next world to tell us so. These are not what Scripture means by love. As Jesus said, "For if ye love them which love you, what reward have ye? do not even the publicans [the hated tax-gatherers] the same?" (Matt. 5:46).

But what was it that the Apostle John meant when he was grown too old to walk, and had to be supported under his arms by a disciple to either side – too old to deliver his message any more, able only to condense it all into five words, no more: "Little children, love one another"?

He must have meant the same as what the Qur'án says: "Hadst thou spent all the riches of the earth, thou couldst not have united their hearts; but God hath united them . . ." (8:64). Or what 'Abdu'l-Bahá means on the same theme of the believers' unity through divine love when He says of our Faith that here "is neither rod nor blow, whip nor sword; but the power of the love of God has accomplished this."[3]

Bahá'í doctrine has it that a candle cannot light itself, that only God can rekindle love in the world. God, through His Manifestation. Human beings will not suddenly turn loving and lovable. Unless love comes from Somewhere outside, Something not ourselves, we will continue to hate and envy and punish and retaliate forever and ever.

Let alone national wars, urban guerilla warfare is daily on the increase worldwide; and current studies show that many American couples beat, maim and even kill each other and their offspring. The mindless murders that take place every day throughout the nation, now routine to the point where we hardly notice them any more in the news, do not derive from love in the heart.

People have forgotten, Shoghi Effendi writes, "those things of the spirit on which alone a sure and stable foundation can be laid for human society."[4]

Love must be taught, 'Abdu'l-Bahá says. All "must be taught to love their fellow-creatures . . ."[5] And He says again: "Let not a man glory in this, that he can kill his fellow-creatures . . . rather, let him glory in this, that he can love them."[6]

He says on love that love gets stronger if we practise it: "By the exercise of love," love is strengthened, and hostility wanes.[7] Again he tells us to treat people "as kindly as God treats them,"[8] and adds that there is no higher attainment for humanity than this. A New England artist, Daisy Pumpelly Smythe, when she asked Him how to live her life, was told: "Be kind to everyone."

Another of His well-known teachings on love is to look for the good qualities in those we meet. Such a procedure is bound to effect what Stendhal refers to as "crystallization," that magic change of a twig into a spray of diamonds. Obviously, this works both ways – people seem wittier when others think they have wit, more beautiful when others think them beautiful.

And subjectively, seeing only the unpleasant inevitably makes us like the fabled cow, wandering through the streets of beautiful Baghdád, looking through its gutters and saying: "Nothing here but orange peel and melon rind."

There are four kinds of love, 'Abdu'l-Bahá says: God's love for the transfiguration of His beauty in the mirror of creation – "Christ has said God is love." We could also remember here the Muslim ḥadíth, sacred tradition, on which the Master wrote a noted commentary,[9] when still an adolescent: "I was a Hidden Treasure, and I desired to be known, wherefore I created man, thereby to become known." ("Man" being the Perfect Man, emerging from time to time in history; God's Primal Mirror, through Whom alone we can see the Father.)

Second, there is God's love for humankind, His creatures.

Third, the love that flows from us to God.

And finally, the love that binds the hearts of the believers.

(These four are not necessarily listed in this order – He lists
them differently on different pages.[10])

As you look at it this way and that, Bahá'í history is
primarily a love story, illustrating these four kinds of love.
Think of the love between the Báb and Bahá'u'lláh,
Who never met. The Báb, Who established Bahá'u'lláh's
Covenant before His own; Who wrote to His Promised
One: "I have sacrificed myself wholly for Thee; I have
accepted curses for Thy sake, and have yearned for naught
but martyrdom in the path of Thy love. Sufficient witness
unto me is God, the Exalted, the Protector, the Ancient of
Days."[11]

And Bahá'u'lláh Who responded: "I stand, life in hand,
ready; that perchance, through God's loving-kindness and
grace, this revealed and manifest Letter may lay down his
life as a sacrifice in the path of the Primal Point, the Most
Exalted Word."[12]

Their chronicler tells how each tried to outdo the other in
proclaiming the new Faith. Both of Them, while of different backgrounds, young men from homes of comfort and
wealth, matched hardships in what to Them was the way of
God: They matched prison sentences, and hunger and pain,
matched ridicule and humiliation and scorn, matched the
bastinado (the ignominious throwing down of the victim on
his back, fastening his ankles tight to a horizontal pole, this
being held firm and continually twisted by a man at either
end, while a third man beats and beats on the soles of the
tortured feet). Then at the end the Báb was bound and
raised up on a spike in the wall at Tabríz, and
Bahá'u'lláh was chained and lowered into the Black Pit of
Ṭihrán.

"Such love no eye has ever beheld, nor has mortal heart
conceived such mutual devotion," writes Nabíl, and adds
in the terminology of the Persian poets: "If the branches of
every tree were turned into pens, and all the seas into ink,
and earth and heaven rolled into one parchment, the immensity of that love would still remain unexplored, and the
depths of that devotion unfathomed."[13]

What each saw in the other was undoubtedly the beauty

of the Unknowable, mirrored in the heart of His Manifestation. The mystery is perhaps fleetingly glimpsed in this strange colloquy between the Sender and the Sent One:

> O My Well-Beloved! Thou hast breathed Thy Breath into Me, and divorced Me from Mine own Self. Thou didst, subsequently, decree that no more than . . . a mere emblem of Thy Reality within Me be left among the perverse and envious. Behold how, deluded by this emblem, they have risen against Me, and heaped upon Me their denials! Uncover Thy Self, therefore, O My Best-Beloved, and deliver Me from My plight.
>
> Thereupon a Voice replied: "I love, I dearly cherish this emblem. How can I consent that Mine eyes, alone, gaze upon this emblem, and that no heart except Mine heart recognize it? By My Beauty, which is the same as Thy Beauty! My wish is to hide Thee from Mine own eyes: how much more from the eyes of men!"[14]

And again, in the Persian poets' language for an interrupted speech, He says:

> I was preparing to make reply, when lo, the Tablet was suddenly ended, leaving My theme unfinished, and the pearl of Mine utterance unstrung.[14]

Second and third of the four kinds is the love of God for the creature, and of the creature for God.

Among the Báb's followers one or two had been told that they themselves would see Him Whom God would manifest; they would see Ḥusayn, the Promised One.

This refuted the claim of the Azalís that the Heralded One of the Báb would not appear before the Day of Mustagháth, an Arabic word meaning "He Who is Invoked." To them, the Day of Mustagháth meant A.H. 2001; for each letter of the Arabic alphabet has a numerical value, so that words could add up to calendar dates; and the letters of this word add up to 2001. This 2001 was the date assigned by the Báb as the time beyond which the promised Advent could not take place.[15]

One of these especially prepared believers was Shaykh Ḥasan. The Báb told him: "You should proceed to Karbilá and should abide in that holy city, inasmuch as you are destined to behold, with your own eyes, the beauteous countenance of the promised Ḥusayn."[16]

And so Shaykh Ḥasan went to Karbilá, over by Baghdád, settled down there, and earned his living as a scribe, a profession underpaid, however necessary in that mostly illiterate society. Meanwhile, far away in Tabríz, the Báb was put to death. Meanwhile, too, Ḥasan was hounded by the Shaykhí sect in Karbilá – those followers of Shaykh Aḥmad who failed to recognize the Báb, just as in after-years the Azalís disclaimed Bahá'u'lláh. Ḥasan bore it all, to stay on at his post, never breathing to anyone the secret of why he was there.

Time passed and then one day – it was October 5, 1851 – when Shaykh Ḥasan was walking past the gate of the inner courtyard of Imám Ḥusayn's Shrine, he caught sight of Bahá'u'lláh, Whom he had never laid eyes on before. How he recognized Him, we do not know. We once asked Louis Gregory, first Bahá'í Hand of the black race: "How do we know Bahá'u'lláh was the Promised One of the Báb?" And Louis Gregory replied: "Bahá'u'lláh is His own proof, just as the sun is its own proof." We have often thought, since, how irrelevant it would be to pin a label on the sun; to introduce the sun.

Could he have perhaps heard the Stranger's name, Ḥusayn-'Alí? We do not know. This was three years after that watershed Conference at Badasht, where a woman had "sounded . . . the death-knell of the twelve hundred year old law of Islám,"[17] and where each of those present received a new name, the new name confirmed in every case by an individual tablet from the Báb later on.[18] It was at Badasht that Ḥusayn-'Alí had become Bahá.

Or did he perhaps have wind of that Shí'ih tradition, that in the Latter Days 'Alí would reappear twice, once before Muḥammad and once after Ḥusayn? Still, he could hardly have heard, so early, that the mysterious prophecy referred to 'Alí-Muḥammad (the Báb's name), and Ḥusayn-'Alí (Bahá'u'lláh's).

Shaykh Ḥasan was by now an old man, bowed over with the years. And he was so poor, with his ill-paid job, that he went hungry most of the time. So, a poor, shabby old man. Yet he was the individual singled out by this princely pilgrim who, judging by His dress, had come out of Persia, to visit the Shrine.

Ḥasan has left, at this point in his account, one of the few word-portraits of Bahá'u'lláh, then in the prime of life at thirty-four, His face still unmarked by the long anguish to come. He lingers on Bahá'u'lláh's great beauty, His probing glance, and the sweetness of His smile; tells how kindly His face was, how luxuriant His black flowing hair.

"How lovingly He advanced towards me!" says Shaykh Ḥasan. "He took me by the hand and . . . addressed me in these words: 'This very day I have purposed to make you known as a Bábí throughout Karbilá.' "[16]

Continuing to speak with him, never letting go of his hand, Bahá'u'lláh walked him the whole length of the market-street, the people who had come to buy, and the merchants in their raised niches to either side of the way, watching as they passed. Then at the end Bahá'u'lláh told him: "Praise be to God that you have remained in Karbilá, and have beheld with your own eyes the countenance of the promised Ḥusayn."

At these words Shaykh Ḥasan caught fire, and he wanted "with all my soul and power" to shout to the pressing crowds that the Promised Day had come. But Bahá'u'lláh's whisper was urgent in his ears: "Not yet . . . the appointed Hour . . . has not yet struck. Rest assured and be patient."

From that day on, Shaykh Ḥasan was never unhappy again. Never mind hunger, never mind his poverty and the constant persecution by the Shaykhís; what he had now outvalued all the treasures in the world, because what he had now was love.

Or, from the Báb's time, take that Mihdí who appeared above the ramparts at Ṭabarsí – the fort the early believers built when, on their march, they were betrayed by the guide and ambushed in a forest. Cut off by government troops, Mihdí and the others in the fort were living on grass and bones. Now he was called to by a Muslim, a former companion from his home city, and he stood up there on the wall, his head wrapped around with a white cloth, his sword girded on over his white robe.

"What is it you want? Be quick!" he cried, impatient to rejoin his starving friends.

The other looked up at Mihdí's non-seeing eyes, and could think of only one thing to say: "Your beloved Raḥmán . . . is alone and forsaken, and yearns to see you."

He knew that Mihdí so loved his son, whom he had named after God's name, the All-Merciful, that he had written a song for him and would sing it as he rocked the boy to sleep.

"Tell him from me," the father answered, "that the love of the true Raḥmán . . . has so filled my heart that it has left no place for any other love besides His."

Then the friend found himself weeping and said: "May God assist you in accomplishing your purpose."

And the starving man said: "He has indeed assisted me! How else could I have been delivered from the darkness of my prison-home in Kand? How could I have reached this exalted stronghold?"

And he sank behind the wall of the fort.[19]

We know, too, from Nabíl that in the Baghdád days the believers were as if drunk with bliss. He says the earth's kings never dreamt of festivals such as those impoverished lovers had; that a royal palace would have meant no more to them than a cobweb to be brushed away.

"Many a night," he writes, "no less than ten persons subsisted on no more than a pennyworth of dates. No one knew to whom actually belonged the shoes, the cloaks, or the robes that were to be found in their houses. Whoever went to the bazaar could claim that the shoes upon his feet were his own, and each one who entered the presence of Bahá'u'lláh could affirm that the cloak and robe he then wore belonged to him. Their own names they had forgotten, their hearts were emptied of aught else except adoration for their Beloved . . . O, for the joy of those days, and the gladness and wonder of those hours!"[20]

At a later time in our history, Juliet Thompson tells in her unpublished *Diary* of the kind of love continually expressed by 'Abdu'l-Bahá.

She was a young Victorian woman, very beautiful, and an artist, who in the early days would speak on the Bahá'í Faith (she well-chaperoned, but behind her mother's back) – down in the Bowery, in the slums of New York.

One bitter night she arrived at the Bowery Mission, to find it packed with hundreds of homeless men, forced in by the sleet and snow.

Among the crowd was enormous John Good, with his shock of white hair. He had been released from Sing Sing prison that day. They had tortured him, hung him up by the thumbs, and he had come out an atheist and full of hate.

Juliet, knowing nothing of John Good, told the men about 'Abdu'l-Bahá in His prison, and how He had come out, full of love. The minister in charge then rose and said that 'Abdu'l-Bahá was even then on His way to America, and would all those who wanted to hear Him please stand up, and the whole three hundred stood up.

Next the minister asked how many of them would like to study I Corinthians 13 with Juliet and himself. Thirty of them stood up. Among these thirty were John Good and a thin, redheaded, sodden individual named Hannegan.

"Then we will meet every Wednesday," the minister said, "and learn something about this love of which 'Abdu'l-Bahá is our great Example." This they did, Juliet, as ever, well-chaperoned and having wrested permission from her mother.

The night 'Abdu'l-Bahá spoke at the Bowery Mission was April 19, 1912. First He had sent Edward Getsinger and Juliet to the bank, each to secure a large quantity of quarters, which the bank gave them in two huge white bags, so heavy that Juliet had to drag hers.

They found the long hall packjammed with derelicts, the unwanted and rejected who would sleep on other people's doorsteps and on benches in the park. To her embarrassment, the minister asked Juliet to "introduce the Master."

'Abdu'l-Bahá rose and addressed them. He told them that they were His friends and His family. He said that in their poverty they were more like Christ than the rich, for the rich depend on their means, and the poor have nothing to depend on but God. He said that everyone must be a servant of the poor. He said that Jesus was a poor man; that one night, homeless, out in the fields under the rain, He raised up His eyes and said to the Father that although He had nothing, only the cold ground, the stars for lamps and grass for food, still He had a blessing the rich were deprived of: He had the poor. "Thou hast given Me the poor . . . They are Mine. Therefore am I the richest man on earth."²¹

Afterward, followed by Juliet and the others with Him, 'Abdu'l-Bahá walked down the aisle to the door. He had on His pongee 'abá, Juliet says, and was "shining in white and ivory." There at the door He waited, and He called on Juliet and Edward to stand one on each side of Him, each with a heavy bag from the bank.

Then, as Juliet describes it – she was an artist and visual-minded – came the long line of men down the aisle: the "sodden and grimy procession – three hundred men in single file. The 'breadline' – the failures. Broken forms. Blurred faces. How can I picture such a scene? That forlorn host out of the depths . . . ?" She asks if the Master greeted them like the erring, or like strays. "No, like His own beloved children."

And as He took each hand, He pressed into it "His little gift of silver – just a symbol and the price of a bed. Not a man was shelterless that night. And many, many, I could see, found a shelter in His heart. I could see it in the faces raised to His and in His Face bent to theirs."

He held out His hand to the first man, leaving His gift. Five or six quarters, maybe (and John Good told her afterward that the completely destitute got the most).

The first man looked up, surprised. "His eyes met the Master's look, which seemed to be plunging deep into his heart with fathomless understanding . . . The man must have known very little of even human love . . . and now, too suddenly, he stood face to face with Divine love. He looked startled, incredulous . . . Then his eyes *strained* toward the Master, something new burning in them – and the Master's eyes answered with a great flash, revealing a more mysterious,

profounder love . . . I saw this repeated scores of times."
She says some of them only "shuffled past, accepting the
gift ungraciously," but most were like the first. And she
adds, "Who can tell the effect of those immortal glances on
the lives and even, perhaps, at the death of each of these
men?"

Months afterward, John Good told her about Hannegan,
the Bowery derelict who by now had drunk himself into his
grave. Hannegan had been counting the days, John Good
told her, till it would be April 19 and he could go to
'Abdu'l-Bahá at the Mission – but he lost count and the
day came and went. Once he was conscious again, he realized there would be another chance – 'Abdu'l-Bahá was to
speak out in Flatbush the following Sunday. Flatbush was a
long way off and when the day came, Hannegan was penni-
less, and so he walked.

That midnight John Good went to Hannegan's room and
found him in his usual condition.

"Why did you do it this time, Hannegan – and you
straight from seeing the Master?"

"That's just it," said Hannegan. "I'm straight from seeing
Him. Why, John, He's perfection. The Light of the World, He
is, John. It's too much for a man. Too discouraging."

Afterward, recalling with 'Abdu'l-Bahá that scene at the
Bowery Mission, somebody asked Him if charity is advis-
able.

'Abdu'l-Bahá laughed and said: "Assuredly, give to the
poor. If you give them only words, when they put their
hands into their pockets after you have gone, they will find
themselves none the richer for you!"

Although a prisoner and exile Himself, He was known all
over the Holy Land for taking care of the poor. On His
travels He tipped generously. He also gave generously to
churches where He spoke, and gave in the poor quarters of
cities, which He sought out. He shared with the poor whatever funds came in, and although so poor Himself that His
daughter could not find an extra nightgown for Him during
His last hours, when He died, the destitute were orphaned.

What we in the world call love is not included in the

Master's four categories. Our kind is not true love, He says, because it changes. He calls it fascination. (The dictionary says fascination is a spell, sorcery, enchantment.)

As the wind blows, 'Abdu'l-Bahá says, the bough bends; if the wind blows from the east, the tree leans to the west, if the wind veers to the west, the tree leans to the east. Today you will see two souls ready to die for each other, tomorrow the same two not speaking. "This is not love; it is the yielding of the hearts to the accidents of life."[22]

What is it that people have found in the Cause of the Báb and Bahá'u'lláh, from its birth until this hour? Why have they offered themselves either to live or die for it?

What they see here is a restoring love, a beatific vision to blot out the world's augean hate. Here they have glimpsed once more, as in the ancient story, Joseph's face.

Joseph was a Prophet Who ruled in Egypt, and His beauty was beyond compare.

There came a time when His courtiers gathered around Him and said: "We shall go forth and search through every land, and each return to Thee bringing a gift, which shall be whatever thing he finds most beauteous in all the world."

The years passed by and one by one the courtiers came home, each bringing what to him was the fairest thing on earth. They came with white racing camels and comely slaves, weaves so fine they could be drawn through a ring, lacquers and rare animal skins and opalescent glass, jewels bright enough to light a room. Finally they had all come back but one.

Then at last he too was back, bowed with the years, wearied out with the roads and waves. Slowly he approached the throne and knelt, offering his gift.

It was only a mirror in a simple wooden frame, no more.

Joseph took it and held it up; and Joseph looked, and within it saw His face.

"I have travelled through every land," the old man said, "I have searched through all the world; and what in all the world is more beauteous than the face of Joseph?"

The Star Servant

Thinking over some of the great Bahá'ís that you remember is like going through a jewel case and selecting one jewel or another and holding it up to the light – watching it spatter lights around the walls. Martha Root was the "star-servant of the Cause of Bahá'u'lláh." She was the "foremost Hand which 'Abdu'l-Bahá's will . . . raised up in [the] first Bahá'í century."[1] The Guardian also writes that her "acts shed imperishable lustre [on the] American Bahá'í Community."[2]

She was a little woman with iron gray hair cut off – by herself more than likely – in a sort of Dutch bob. Her face was not remarkable in any way except for marvelous green eyes. Her voice was soft – we have a recording of it – and her accent over the years had become in a way international. She was a fluent Esperantist – one of the best.

I first met her in San Francisco, I believe it was, and spoke to her on the sidewalk after a meeting. My grandfather had just died back East. Young people don't know much about death – they think it's a great drama that happens to someone else. They don't know it is routine. Grandfather's death was the first breach in our American family wall and I blurted out to Martha, "My grandfather has just died." Martha looked at me with those marvelous eyes. All she said was, "He has gone into the Kingdom of Light." The words were not remarkable, but I've always remembered them.

As a speaker Martha seemed to us ordinary, but for some mysterious reason her impact was tremendous. Martha did not dress well. I remember one dead of winter in Vienna. Martha was due to arrive, and Herr Pöllinger and I were sort of her advance people to get platforms for her. We had one engagement for her at a very elegant American women's club. The American dollar meant a lot then, and the ladies had their wools and furs and high Russian boots. Martha had on a brown straw hat with a leather strap around it and a long, blue satin evening gown, this being in the afternoon. I understood it was the very gown she had first worn when she went to Romania's royal court and had her historic audience with Queen Marie. (This was long before the days when you did your own thing – and wore what you thought best or worst.)

I remember Martha walking ahead in the mud and snow, holding up her gown, and we following (often on such trips loaded with Bahá'í books for display at the meeting), on our way to board an already crowded street car. I thought, what if the friends could see us now. And I've often told myself since that this must have been the real glory – not those furs and boots and shiny limousines, but the mud and cold, fingers freezing in our gloves, the load to carry and those lurching street cars. On the occasion I'm thinking of we got to the club and suddenly Martha became nervous and she and I retired to a ladies' room. She said, "I get this way sometimes." It was a lesson to me, to find the great Martha Root, world traveler and converter of the first Bahá'í queen, nervous before a talk. I used to suffer anguish before getting up to speak, produce a wide range of symptoms and even lose my voice; it helped to know that other human beings, even great ones, felt the same.

Then she went to the platform in the midst of all those elegant ladies and gave her talk; not a very good one, it seemed to me. I was rather embarrassed, the way young people are often embarrassed for their elders. I thought that the talk was not right for such a sophisticated audience. But to my amazement, when she had finished the response was over-whelming. She had spoken to their hearts. In fact, my old diary indicates that Martha gave them a good talk: she told how Táhirih inspired Marianna Hainisch to free the women of Austria; and what various statesmen said of the Bahá'í Cause; and how she herself – Martha – was at one time ashamed to be seen carrying a Bahá'í book, so she left it in a drugstore and the druggist's wife became a Bahá'í. She also said that she – Martha – had studied by herself two years before looking up any Bahá'ís.

Actually, the only thing that matters where a speech is concerned is its effect on the audience – if not that audience, then on people who read the speech later on. You can give your talk in a Tibetan accent and swing from the chandelier, but if they take to it you've given a good speech. It was her great spiritual station that came through. I remember at a Vienna Bahá'í meeting (and some of those she addressed there lost their lives afterwards in the Hitler time) she quoted the words of the Greatest Holy Leaf. The Most Exalted Leaf had said that if, after death, she should be found worthy to meet her Father, Bahá'u'lláh, the first thing she would ask would be His help for the Bahá'ís. Martha also described the progress of the Faith that night; she told how Miss Knobloch had gone to teach in South Africa, and how she had wept there, and how the house where she wept became a Bahá'í home. How Miss Knobloch had formed a class by ringing doorbells up and down a street.

I realized later on that in those days Martha was actually doing follow-up teaching work for 'Abdu'l-Bahá. He had left the world, but it was He who had pioneered both in Vienna and Budapest and on many occasions Martha was looking up those still living who had seen and heard Him.

During the Vienna stay, Queen Marie of Romania and Archduchess Anton sent for Martha to have lunch with them and there were frantic telephonic and linguistic struggles before we somehow had her escorted to the lunch, this time in a taxi. She once told me, "I am sure of the Queen . . ."

In those days there were many Theosophists, and they would offer their platforms. Martha would tell them that we and they agreed on the principle of development, though not the place – in other words, Bahá'ís do not believe in reincarnation, though we do believe that we must go on progressing forever. Martha also told them that Annie Besant had said that 'Abdu'l-Bahá was the greatest man then living. And she said that two Theosophical Society presidents, in introducing Martha, had told their audiences that Theosophy was a philosophy, while the Bahá'í Faith was a universal religion. (My notes of the time often use the term Bahá'í Cause. The term "Movement" was used by earlier believers. At an early time a Bahá'í speaker had come to Stanford University, and a young reporter wrote in the college paper that she had heard of a lot of dances before, but had never heard of the Bahá'í Movement.)

I used to watch with amazement how ambassadors and scholars and editors would step around and do what Martha asked. She would say, "When a man says no, that's the time to begin . . ." She would go to a strange country, interview the leader, find a translator, and set him to work translating pamphlets and Esslemont. Then she would find platform after platform – schools, clubs, religious groups, Esperantists, old ladies at the Women's League for Peace and Freedom – all by herself, since she might be the only Bahá'í in the country. She would go to some poor hotel or hospice, set a little tripod in the wash basin and boil an egg over it; then she might give her lunch money to some poor person. My diary says: "It is remarkable how Martha endures cold, and insufficient food."

Third class on trains was – in those days – hard boards. Normally if you were in third you weren't rich enough to have much luggage – but Martha would have maybe a dozen suitcases (she was always counting) and they were loaded, not with worldly possessions but Bahá'í books. She was always giving little presents. If you gave her something you had to make her promise not to give it away and you weren't convinced she would keep the promise.

In Budapest we did not go to the Esperantists – they had split into two groups and weren't speaking. We did go to the Polytechnicum to see Professor Nadler's painting of the Master. I wonder where the original that we saw that day is now. A photograph of this portrait is in the Hungarian Esslemont. In Belgrade the Esperantists made much of Martha and even gave me a green star. A lady in Belgrade told us Christ wasn't a Jew because He was the Son of God. (Just the reverse of that old fundamentalist lady in the anecdote who studied Hebrew shortly before her death because she "wanted to greet her Creator in His native tongue.") Martha had tea with Prince Paul and Princess Olga; we also precipitated many theological discussions at the American Legation.

A note in my diary says, "It's some job keeping up with Martha – stamps fly, and wires are hot." One day I was in the lobby of a Belgrade hotel, having a lemon ice. I looked out the big window, and there was Martha, indomitably going about the Lord's business. I shall never forget the set of her jaw. By this time I was exhausted, and my husband Howard Carpenter was sick in bed. Howard and Martha were both very strong-willed, and one time they had an argument, over me. She wanted me to go and see the editor of some big paper, and he didn't. The debate raged, and since he was up on the third floor, sick, and she was downstairs somewhere, I had to keep running between the two of them bearing messages, relaying the argument. Martha always felt that her decisions were the will of God. "She says it's the will of God that I should go," I told him. "Well," he said, "you tell her I'm closer to God up here than she is down there, and it's His will that you shouldn't."

When Martha left Belgrade, the Esperantists were down at the station to see her off. They had brought their green flag on a cane, to wave. I knew that as she stood in the corridor of the train, waving good-bye, she was repeating over and over – as she always did when leaving a city – "Alláh-u-Abhá."

We stayed behind, as the Guardian had directed, first to visit Marion Jack in Sofia, and then to go to Tirana, before our pilgrimage en route to Persia. I never saw Martha again. She went her endless way, four times around the globe, till at the last, as the Guardian wrote, she would fall "in her tracks on an island in the midmost heart" of the Pacific Ocean.[3]

Martha was the star-servant, the first to arise when the Divine Plan Tablets were unveiled in the U.S., and who toiled virtually without ceasing for almost twenty years – "the nearest approach to the example set by 'Abdu'l-Bahá Himself."[4]

One thing happened in Vienna that stays in memory. One night, and it was midwinter, we had to get Martha through a mob so that she could give a public talk. There was a torchlight parade going on in downtown Vienna – striping with light and shadow thousands of people, and swerving horses of the mounted policemen, their riders trembling and the mob howling in the flickering night. Suddenly the torchlight flashed on a dark, foreign-looking man in that blond crowd. The thousands of people began snarling "Fooey" and "Jew" . . . Martha was very much frightened, but I was confident that Howard Carpenter would get us through . . . I can remember the mob hissing and hissing, like the "universal hiss" the devils made in Pandemonium when Satan came back to the infernal regions to report how he had seduced Eve (Milton, *Paradise Lost*, Book X). A scene like that, repeated over and over, against one race or another, one religion or nation or another, forever and ever – is enough reason for anyone to become a Bahá'í. Down the ages, mankind has been programmed for hate. Now the Bahá'í Faith comes to reverse the whole process and program mankind for love. No other religion is doing this, or attempting it. Look at Ireland. Look at the hate exhibited by the so-called Jesus groups when you disagree with them. Look at the warning of Bahá'u'lláh about the Shí'ih habit of cursing. Heaven knows, I often heard my Muslim relatives cursing leading Sunní Muslims, to say nothing of non-Muslims. We read in the Tablet of the World: "From the lips of the members of this sect foul imprecations fall unceasingly, while they invoke the word 'Mal'ún' (accursed) – uttered with a guttural sound of the letter 'ayn – as their daily relish."

Smoke and Din of Battle

Of many great Bahá'ís, one that I found especially easy to be with was Keith Ransom-Kehler. She had been a professor of English at Albion College. Our family thought of her – and indeed, of most American Bahá'ís – as new Bahá'ís. Anyway, I knew her best in Ṭihrán. Keith had been sent to Ṭihrán on a mission by our U.S. National Assembly to petition the Sháh and the Prime Minister to remove their ban on Bahá'í books coming into Persia. Keith was able to send back the following cable: "Mission successful." But the High Court minister who had responded favorably to the petition and told Keith she could have Bahá'í books mailed into the country without their being confiscated in the old way, disappeared virtually the next day. There was a massive walled building on a hill to the north of the city and many people were said to vanish there, and in any case were never seen again. One who had been escorted out of his newspaper office and taken to that place and held quite a time – and later freed – told me a doctor there would examine certain of the prisoners and inform them that they needed a supposedly remedial shot; their bodies would then be disposed of by night. Part of the unending story of man's inhumanity to man.

Anyway, the Keith I knew in Ṭihrán was ill, spending much of the time lying on her bed in the summer heat. She lived in the home of two devoted Bahá'ís, Raḥmat and Najmia 'Alá'í. Raḥmat's beautiful daughter Gloria later married Mr Faizi. Here in their house Keith wrote brilliant letters to the Sháh, to every cabinet minister, to the President of Parliament – still working away at her ruined mission, pointing out that other religionists in Persia freely circulated books that were hostile to Islám, while our books, which were pro-Islám, were banned. I heard the Guardian say later on that whenever Persia should lift the ban on our books, Keith would get the credit. I'm not sure whether the ban has ever been lifted. Keith was seriously ill, from the unfamiliar food and climate. She was in her late fifties. Her mission had apparently failed. Still, she was full of plans for the future. For one project, she expected soon to teach in India. In Haifa the Guardian had said to us, "Keith is very frank, very sensitive and very brave." He said she was the ablest of all to present the Cause adequately. He said he was very pleased with her article on Ṭabarsí. During her Haifa pilgrimage, she told me, he had sent over books on Islám for her to study – I gathered for many hours, at night, in preparation for the mission to Persia. To me the day he spoke of Keith he also spoke of our close bond with (Shí'ih) Islám. He said that the Imáms were divinely inspired, and that they were Guardians. He also told me to work on the Aqdas and to show Keith my material on the Aqdas. He always planned so many, many years ahead. One thing he said – speaking of planning far in advance – had to do with his letter to the U.S. National Assembly on the eventual non-participation of Bahá'ís in fighting wars. I seem to recall he had the letter with him at table that day, but he merely told us the subject of it. He said many books would be written about this letter of his – on what is now called a non-combatant status – in the future. He also, among many other statements, gave me instructions about how to act in Persia. He said: "Be very tactful." He also said the Persians are sensitive, devoted, lack initiative, can't decide, must be pushed. Also that I was to stress always that East and West are one. The reason we were heading for Persia was that the Guardian had written me (I lived in California at the time) to go.

Speaking of those national characteristics, I had to laugh in Austria, later on, when a European visitor to Persia came through. His advice was, "When you're dealing with a Persian and want action, don't speak English – don't speak French; speak German, and *bang on the table*." Americans are really mistaken to ignore the various attributes of a given people on the grounds that you shouldn't generalize. You should both generalize and particularize.

Now Keith was very frank, and frankness was no better appreciated in Persia than it is here. Keith said she had to win over the members of the American National Assembly. Well, if you've studied *Bahá'í Administration* you know that members of our elective institutions have no choice but to win the rest of us over. The Guardian writes that such members must "endeavor . . . to win, not only the confidence and the genuine support and respect of those whom they serve, but also their esteem and real affection."[1]

Although there were marvelous exceptions to the rule, we saw that Keith was not really properly valued at that time and place. The majority had no conception whatever of the myriad elements which must be brought together to produce a Keith. I'm told she is appreciated now in Persia, and that a number of girls have been named for her: not Keith, but Kehler. What they saw was a woman – not pink and plump and fourteen, which was the standard of beauty in those days – with a face round like the moon on her fourteenth night – but an older woman (old women have seldom enjoyed a good public image, least of all in Persia) and one whose vast erudition and gorgeous English could not reach them through a translation.

Keith, by the way, was always elegantly dressed. She told me that if she were invited to Buckingham Palace "tomorrow," she had the clothes. When she addressed the Women's Progress Committee she wore a pink dress with a long necklace of pink and lavender beads. (She used to play with her necklaces while speaking, liked to move about on the platform, or gaze skyward, or take off a little jacket.) Her hair was prettily waved. Later I asked her who did it for her and she said she did it herself. I told her it was lovely, and she said she was awfully glad I'd come to Ṭihrán.

Keith had a story she used to tell American audiences about the unknowability of God. She said a little girl drew some scratches and circles (Keith would make the child's gestures, agonizing over the drawing). The child proudly showed the bit of paper to her mother. "Look, Mother," she said, "this is a *skungg*. I think it's pretty good for a little girl. I didn't have anything to go by but the smell."

I might say here that my husband Howard Carpenter was having serious problems getting his permit to practise medicine. It was the more heartbreaking because he was highly trained at Stanford Medical and Vienna for what Persia needed most – he was an ophthalmologist. Instead of thanking God that he had come, since the Persians were in torment from their trachoma, the officials put every possible obstacle in his way; and eventually as a result of that journey, he died.

Keith told us she was praying the Remover of Difficulties for us. She said she was just as dramatic and emotional with God as she was with people and that when she prayed, "They know there's something doing in Heaven."

One day in Ṭihrán she said to me: "In future when I'm in my resting grave and people ask what I was like, it is your mission to tell them how I suffered in Persia, Bahá'u'lláh's country . . . There were battles every step of the way . . . My duty here is chiefly to awaken them to the nature and purpose of Bahá'í Administration." This last is something that Americans really have not understood: Persia is the cradle of the Faith – but America is the cradle of the Administrative Order. See *The Advent of Divine Justice*, pages 15 and 16. You will read there that these two countries were selected not because they were so wonderful, but because they were so awful – the first for decadence, the second for political corruption – and thus by the transforming power of the Bahá'í Faith they will serve as a demonstration to an unbelieving world of the power of Almighty God.

Keith also told me that she loved the Persians. Well, "Greater love hath no man than this, that a man lay down his life for his friends." (John 15:13) She left Ṭihrán and went on a teaching journey, going to Iṣfáhán. And there in Iṣfáhán she caught black smallpox. They say she caught it from kissing and holding a child that had had it. Nobody knows. Raḥmat and Najmia 'Alá'í disregarded their own safety and nursed her day and night. They told me her skin cleared up. And then, one day, they heard a kind of strangled cry from her bedroom – and ran in and Keith was gesturing helplessly at them. She could no longer speak. She tried for some hours to form words, and repeat the Greatest Name, and then she died.

The strange thing is that before she fell ill with smallpox, she visited her own grave. She went out to pray on the graves of the King of Martyrs and the Beloved of Martyrs, and took flowers there, and wept. Now she too is buried beside them. And I understand that in later years Robert Gulick, visiting there, was able to take steps which protected the area from a road that would have passed too close.

Keith left a diary and in it they found these lines, written not long before she was gone:

I have fallen, though I never faltered. Months of effort with nothing accomplished is the record that confronts me. If anyone in future should be interested in this thwarted adventure of mine, he alone can say whether near or far from the seemingly impregnable heights of complaisance and indifference, my tired old body fell. The smoke and din of battle are today too dense for me to ascertain whether I moved forward or was slain in my tracks.

Nothing in the world is meaningless, suffering least of all.

You remember that Keith was a professor of English. She had read Oscar Wilde's letter from prison, *De Profundis*, where he says, "Where there is sorrow there is holy ground"; a few pages on he says, "Now I find hidden somewhere away in my nature something that tells me that nothing in the whole world is meaningless, and suffering least of all." Keith goes on:

Sacrifice with its attendant agony is a germ, an organism. Man cannot blight its fruition as he can the seeds of earth. Once sown it blooms, I think forever, in the sweet fields of eternity. Mine will be a very modest flower, perhaps like the single, tiny forget-me-not, watered by the blood of Quddús that I plucked in the Sabzih-Maydán of Bárfurús̲h̲; should it ever catch the eye, may one who seems to be struggling in vain garner it in the name of Shoghi Effendi and cherish it for his dear remembrance.

To tell us who stayed behind that even if – as she thought – her own mission had failed, the fight was worth it, and the Cause of God would always win in the end, she chose these words from "Say not the struggle naught availeth":

While the tired waves, vainly breaking,
Seem here no painful inch to gain,
Far back, through creeks and inlets making,
Silent comes flooding in the main.

There are all kinds of Bahá'ís, and we cannot all be Martha or be Keith. As with your relatives, you don't get to choose your fellow believers. They're just there. A few years after Curtis Kelsey did the flood-lighting of the Báb's Shrine, I was up on the mountain, following the Guardian who was showing my mother the Shrine area. It was dark and the lights were on, and a wide band of golden light slanted down from the top of the Shrine across the gardens. This was long before the sheltering outer edifice was built, with the great gold dome. I noticed that the wide band of light was full of golden bugs. Every bug that floated into the band of light turned to gold. The moral is obvious. This Faith is the rightful possession of anyone who loves it; Bahá'u'lláh says, "I belong to him that loveth Me." Of course there's more to it: "that holdeth fast My commandments, and casteth away the things forbidden him in My Book."[2]

For John, With Love

September 4, 1946

Monday we went down from Cloverdale, driving a cautious thirty in the shiny blue De Soto – our first since the War. The low hills had that hard, baked feeling that seals you in, safe and dry from the wadded fogs of the Bay Region, down to the south, nonexistent and forgotten here in the bright heat.

We turned off the highway into the Geyserville School grounds, up the curving road the Maintenance Committee has enlarged, to the parking space they leveled off with the bulldozer, south of the Big Tree. We got out and walked, and ate a couple of the purple, stained-glass-window plums, with sky-blue dust on them, fallen in the dust of the orchard. Reluctantly, we crossed the wooden bridge over the gulley, going toward the ranch house. For nineteen years now, I had been coming to this place, and John had always been here, all that time, for me, and now he was not here.

Perhaps I was wrong. All around us, in the quiet heat and dust, I could feel him speaking.

"Núrání," he was saying, "Núrání"; luminous, luminous. It was the name 'Abdu'l-Bahá had given him, long ago. It was the white, radiant name. Now John was saying it to me, in the old way – with his voice, that had so much light in it (I can only think of light in connection with him; the tall, transparent figure, the shining white beard, thick, white silk hair, the light suit, the white felt hat. White candles, maybe; white sun on the hills; yards of white cloth for a turban. His hat, at least, I saw, a few moments later, hanging on its peg in the ranch house). His voice repeated the tones of 'Abdu'l-Bahá's voice as the Master Himself had spoken the name; vibrant and happy and as though everything in the universe was all right. Perhaps John was saying this to Harold and me now, because he knew how we felt with him not here. Or again, it was all in my mind; but what is the world of the mind; no one knows; no one can bound it.

We rang the doorbell and it seemed an incongruously natural, everyday thing to do. A handsome, brown Persian boy, Shídán, let us in. Louise is alone now, and Shídán is spending his vacation from college here at the School to be with her. Then Louise was at the door, bowed over, the gray hair cropped short, the blue-gray eyes smiling.

"We've come to take you for a drive."

"Oh, no, I cannot —"

"But we want to go and say a prayer at John's grave."

Shídán broke in, "Here's the car you needed, Louise."

"Well, get the shovels, then," Louise said, and started up the steep stairs, that she had gone up and down so constantly these years, serving John, who lay most of the time up there in the bedroom, withdrawing farther and farther from what we think is the real world but the dying and the dead know is only a reflection and shadow.

Louise moved rapidly over our heads, changing her dress, and Shídán told about the grave. Louise and John had bought their graves on a hilltop, in one of those dry, northern California cemeteries, all perpendicular dirt roads, dust and lizards and purple-trunked manzanitas, rocks and unexpected flowers, or sometimes a rare, elegant gravestone, decorously out of place in the lost hills. Since the War, there had been no caretaker, and there never had been any water here, except the winter rains. Louise, who hardly eats or sleeps, and works always, in the house and grounds, and at her correspondence that comes from all the friends of a long lifetime, was worried over this grave. She had been driven up there a few days before, and gathered the dry flowers left from the funeral to burn them; now she wanted the sandy gravel, piled up from when the grave was dug, leveled off or shoveled away.

"I can only take one shovel," the boy confided to us, "or Louise herself will take the other and set to work and no one can stop her."

We sat on the hilltop, gingerly, on the cement ledge of the

rectangular, parched lot. John's long body lay there beside us, under the gravel – as if he were lying in his bed, as we last saw him; the gravel folded lightly over him. I knew there was a coffin under the mound, but it was as if John were lying there, under the bedclothes. He seemed to share our problem about the grave.

A weaving of vineyards and blue mountains rolled away beneath us. The grapes climbed here almost to the cemetery line, clinging to the sandy hillside, close at hand, heavy blue bunches on the russet vines. I suddenly remembered John in his light clothing and white felt hat, with the vivid hills behind him, smiling, carrying a basket of these blue grapes to give us. "I am a fruitarian," he said.

The baked dust lay warmly around us. Louise wore a white and black print dress with a high collar, and over it a black coat. She sat on the ledge, her blue-gray eyes looking up at us. Then we had prayers, Harold's from *Prayers and Meditations*, page 77, and Shídán's low, mourning-dove Persian chant. Shídán, looking like a sunny, brown Italian, began with the casualness of youth to shovel off the top of the plot and smooth it. He, open-throated and strong, his brown hair gleaming in the sunshine, and Louise in terminal black, both against the far blue hilltops, talked back and forth through the spiced wind:

"This is the earth from the interior of the grave; this was removed for the hole to be made; now it should be put back on the plot again," said Louise.

"No, these are only rocks," said Shídán. "Look at the other plots – hard and smooth. Let me make this one like the rest."

Each of them smiled a little and winked confidentially to us, about the other. Youth and age, amused at each other, for being youth and for being age. Each one hopeless, the other thought; to be put up with and served, but to shake one's head over.

A line of pink flowers, amaryllis, like trumpet lilies only pink, several on a stem, pulpy and delicate, jutted on naked green stalks from a barren neighboring plot. A lizard rustled over the grave, a taffeta rustle, soft, like a thought that escapes you. We sat on the concrete ledge in the warm circle of heat, looking down over the sky and the world. It was during the prayer that I understood how completely selfless Louise is; I could feel the presence of Harold and <u>Sh</u>ídán there beside me but I could not feel Louise there at all, and had to open my eyes to make sure she was with us, holding on to my arm. The earthly Louise is already as ethereal as John.

"The void, the void he has left . . ." she began in the careful, almost whispering voice.

Whenever John said "Louise" he said it in a special way. You knew the word was important. He dwelt on it, italicized it; you knew he looked up to that word. Their marriage was a special marriage, as the Tablet revealed for them by 'Abdu'l-Bahá proves. It was a marriage for always. Even now there has been no separation, really. There we were, sitting on the grave-edge with Louise, and there beside us was John's long, light form; the long, light earth piled up, not away, but present and participating; after all, you can't bury sunlight.

"*Louise*," he would say, and the word was prolonged, solemn, humorous.

Once when I was trying to write his biography and wanted to know how tall he was, to put it down for posterity, he couldn't remember. "Let's measure you, John," I said. We were in his high-ceilinged office in the old ranch house, with the polished walls of redwood. Everything was in its place, and all immaculate. "Let's stand you up along the wall and put a pencil mark where your head comes. Louise won't see it."

"*Louise* sees everything," he said.

John was five feet ten and so registered with the Swiss Government at Neuchâtel in '74 when they wanted him to be a soldier.

Once, trying to unravel his history from the neat envelopes he had filed it in, and the sentences he had decided on, probably years before, and no longer altered (because often, when I'd ask him again about some episode in his life, he would reply in the same brief, economical words as before), I asked him, "Where did you meet Louise?"

"I didn't meet her," he answered. The meaning was clear. He couldn't imply a time when they were not together.

"I started to correspond with her through Lua Getsinger."

He had met Lua in San Francisco in 1912. She spent a week at Geyserville, staying in the long front room of what is now the Collison house. Lua said there was a young Suissesse at Briarcliff Manor,[1] serving as health officer, who was a Bahá'í. "So I dropped her a few lines." He thought a Swiss girl from Zurich who had a position like that would be just right for him. She had also worked four years in Eliot, Maine, with Sarah Farmer. "Did you propose to her before she came out West?" "Just as much as I could by mail."

"Was Lua very beautiful?"

"Most beautiful to me. She wore her regular costume. Looked more or less like a nurse, or like some of the Catholic sisters. Beautiful blue eyes. She was nearly as tall as Louise. Lua was a good speaker. Impressive. Spiritual."

"Who do you know now like that?"

"No comparison."

The day we had this conversation John told me that his letter to the Master dated September 18, 1919, was very important so far as the future Geyserville School was concerned.

Louise and John were married in San Francisco by a Swedenborgian minister at the Swedenborgian Church.

John had been married once before. It was in Los Angeles. She was a German singer, a lovely, blond soprano. When I asked why the marriage failed, John said: "She was a night woman, and I was a day man. My time was between six in the morning and six at night, but when I went with her she always wanted me to have late supper; it lasted till two or three o'clock." He was married to her about three years, and let her spend a year and a half of that period studying music in Europe. He saw it wouldn't work, and they were divorced in Los Angeles around '89.

"Didn't it break your heart?"

"Well, I don't know. It's all forgotten. We loved each other and at the same time it was a mistake."

Her name was Käthe. She became, John said, "only a small singer afterward."

John: "Oh, beautiful music. I love that. I just *melt* – don't you?"

Much of John's history cannot be assembled so early; the future must find it and set it down. He taught the Faith in Germany in the early 1920s. From 1927 on he was at various times active on the Geyserville School Committee and in meeting the thousands of people who came to the School. In 1935 he and Louise made a gift of the Geyserville property to the National Spiritual Assembly . . . All we want to say here is that he was John, and that simply by living he served the Faith.

Of the founding of the Summer School Louise writes: "The National Spiritual Assembly had the idea of the word 'Summer School' first. I will find their letter where they inform John that he was made one of a Committee of three to find a location in California on which a Western Green Acre could be established.[2] George Latimer and Leroy Ioas were the other two. So they took some trips together, two or three, when John said to them: 'Why don't you take mine?' In 1925 John had his 70th birthday and over 100 attended it (and I made 150 cups of the finest coffee). People from nearly every assembly of California came, also from Portland. The founding of a 'Bahá'í Village' then became the conversation for 2 or 3 years. In 1926 I made another 150 cups of coffee on same date of John's birthday, and in the evening of that day with 35 in number we started what later became the Summer School."

The journey to Tahiti came about through Louise. She had been reading 'Abdu'l-Bahá's *Tablets of the Divine Plan*: "I was reading that entire book from one end to the other and begging the Almighty to let me know when I had come to the place that was to be for me. When I reached the Polynesian Tablet I perceived a stir, so I stopped and read it thoroughly, many times. The next morning, or soon after, I awoke at the very earliest gray light of dawn, because something had wakened me. It was a voice that said, 'Loti. Loti.' I sat up and thought, 'Well, this is strange. What is this Loti?' So I went to John's small room next to mine to tell him about it but he was sound asleep." When John wakened they consulted an encyclopedia and found that Loti was an author. Louise left Geyserville for San Francisco that same day to get *Le Mariage de Loti* – since this particular book included his name in the title –at the Public Library, but the book was out. About this time Mrs Maxwell wrote her to come to Green Acre; it was hard for her to leave, as she was expecting guests:

"My husband had arranged a deer-hunting. He did not hunt himself."

"Why?"

"Well, because it wasn't in his life. He never even killed a chicken."

In any event, Louise packed and went to Green Acre, where she set out for Miss Farmer's house to find Mrs Maxwell. (Louise's friendship with the Maxwell family is very old; Mr and Mrs Maxwell took her on her first pilgrimage to 'Akká, in 1909). Mrs Maxwell asked her to wait a few moments in the big upstairs hall, while she got ready for luncheon. It was a warm day, but there was a draught through the hall from an open doorway. Louise started to shut the door, when she saw a little book on a small table just inside. Thinking from the size that it was the *Book of Íqán*, she picked it up, and sat down on the top stair in the hall to read. "I opened the book and instead of the beloved title, to my surprise it said *Le Mariage de Loti*. Imagine my feelings. That trip of three thousand miles I had to take to get it."[3]

And so John and Louise left for Tahiti. John said that on the boat he encountered a fellow-passenger carrying another work by Loti. "For heaven's sake," John told him, "don't let my wife see that book!" Its title: *Vers Ispahan* (Toward Iṣfáhán).

Louise has already described the essentials of their Tahitian journey, which lasted six months (cf. *The Bahá'í World*, III, p. 368). Prefacing the story, Louise writes that as a child she had learned from Robinson Crusoe that the Polynesians were cannibals and would "*eat* their enemies that they killed in warfare. So I made up my mind that if I ever grew up and travelled I would give Polynesia a wide sweep . . . But after having read 'Abdu'l-Bahá's words on Polynesia I was not afraid any more and after a most interesting happening . . . it came about all by itself and unsought for that both John and I went to that very part of the world . . ."

The first Tahitian Bahá'í was Ariane Drollet, a girl of nineteen.[4]

John remembered things for me, sharp details. When they arrived, their trunks were taken from the ship to the hotel by wheelbarrow. At the hotel, there were no rooms; then a Mrs Maui gave them her room. At a restaurant, the Tiaré, they met a young man named Martial Yorss; lunch times Louise would teach him the Faith there. His wife was in the hospital. In Papeete, not long before the Boschs came, 3,500 persons had died out of a population of 7,000, from the black plague. They piled the dead in the streets and burned them. The Yorss' four-year-old son had died, crying, *"Oh maman, ne me laisse pas mourir – ne me mets pas dans ce trou noir!"* ("Oh mother, do not let me die – do not put me in this black hole!") It was Martial Yorss who first translated Bahá'í writings into Tahitian: the "number nine" pamphlet, but owing to various difficulties this never got beyond the proof-reading stage.

The head minister, Pomeret, was against the Faith, but a Protestant minister named Paul Deane was for it. Pomeret warned Deane against the Boschs. Pomeret said, "You're too old to embrace the new Faith." Deane answered: "I may be old, but my tongue is young."

Deane studied *Some Answered Questions*, Dealy, Chase. He encouraged Ernest Marchal to study. He was seventy, Deane was.

When friends are about to leave, the Tahitians give them names; John's was: Teriitahi Papeete – "First king of the great family of Bahá'ís arrived among us."

"They were all beautiful to me," John said. "I like their dark skin. They are very generous; give away all their possessions."

John told me about the beautiful Madame Tepori, a leading personage, who lived on Moorea Island. They went to visit her in a small gasoline boat, perhaps thirty feet long. When they were five kilometers out in the open ocean, their engine gave out. John says there was wonderful sand, and wonderful fresh fish, at Moorea Island, and the ocean was warm. They would talk to her in French about 'Abdu'l-Bahá, and she would say, "Oh, Jehovah!" "She loved us very much. When we returned to Papeete, the first passenger on the little boat was an immense pig – the second was the minister – then some Chinese – then we followed." Madame Tepori stood on the pier, tears streaming, with outstretched arms – in white, against the dark, wooded mountains, two doves flying over her. "She had beautiful feet – always walked barefooted."

Louise brought the people of Tahiti into the Master's presence, on almost the last day of His earthly life. She placed before Him the photograph of a Tahitian lady; He asked who it was; she said, the wife of a chieftain whose descendants have listened to the Bahá'í Message. He answered, "She was a good tree, she has borne good fruit!"

They were always together, John and Louise, working, consulting. If Louise wrote a letter, she read it to John, and then she re-wrote it, incorporating his suggestions. In the middle of the night, if Louise happened to be staying at the old ranch house and John at the new, Louise would worry about John; she would cook him a rapid dish of scrambled eggs, and then, in heavy boots and poking the dark with her flashlight, would guide herself precariously through the night, under the trees, over the bridge, to wake John up and feed him.

Summers their home was overrun with people crowding to the School. A few would come later, during the empty weeks after School closed, when the autumn hangs like a weight on the hills, and leaves drift down the shallow river; the prunes, ready for picking, are blue then.

After a while it became an accepted thing that John was ill. It lasted anyhow two years, with the good days and bad ones. I saw him once during the long, last illness. He was propped up in the big bed; he was crisp and immaculate as usual, his beard rippling down silken white over light pongee pajamas. Louise had turned his bed away from the California light, because his eyes were sore. I wondered what he looked at in his mind. The hills of home, maybe: wooded hills, wooden houses, the big white church of Neu-St Johann; across the road from the church, and separated from it by other buildings, a commodious three-story white house, set in trees on a corner lot – the house where John was born. Criss-cross of roads on the hills, dotting white houses; the white clouds, the warm security of the long Swiss valley.

I talked, stupidly and artificially as you do to sick people; it is another language, not yours, a kind of sick-room pidgin, since a sickness is its own world and you are a foreigner in it. Some of the time he knew we were there; anyhow, he could feel our anxiety for him; and once there was a flash of his old humor:

"That's a handsome bed, John," I told him.

"It looks better from the outside," he said.

He died at one-thirty in the morning, July 22, 1946. He almost rounded out his ninety-first year. On the 24th, they gave him a memorable burial. Louise writes: "Leroy Ioas was the speaker and the Message of the Coming of Bahá'u'lláh that Leroy rendered so wonderfully was the glory of this funeral. The Message was all so delicately disclosed and so eloquently revealed by Leroy to a deeply silent and attentively-listening audience of townspeople, relatives and friends . . . [in] the Auditorium where in front of the stage the body was lying in state . . . Everything had been so perfectly arranged by the beloved friends that one could have thought it was a king who had died." The Master once told John that the Persians loved him; there were many Persians there, at his burial; two of them, 'Alí Yazdí and Shídán Fatḥ-A'ẓam, helped to carry his coffin. Tributes and flowers came in profusion, and about one hundred and fifty persons were there to say good-bye.

From Haifa, the Guardian cabled to the National Spiritual Assembly – in addition to his personal cable to Louise:[5] "Profoundly grieve passing dearly beloved, great-hearted, high-minded, distinguished servant [of] Bahá'u'lláh, John Bosch. His saintly life, pioneer services, historic contribution institution summer school entitle him rank among outstanding figures closing years heroic, opening years formative age Bahá'í Dispensation. Concourse on high extol his exalted services. Assure wife and valiant companion deepfelt sympathy. Advise hold special gathering Temple tribute his imperishable memory." Rúḥíyyih Khánum cabled Louise: "My father joins me deepest loving sympathy passing beloved

John." The Guardian wrote, through his secretary, to Mrs E. C. Newell who had helped take care of John during his last days and had written to the Guardian on behalf of Louise: "No doubt, when the Cause spreads more throughout Switzerland, this fatherland of his will grow to be proud of this heroic and noble soul it produced; even though the best days of his life were spent in America. The influence of such a pure spirit grows as time goes by and he wishes you to assure dear Mrs Bosch that the services she and her husband have rendered the Faith are very great and very deeply valued by him."

George Orr Latimer, who spoke at the Memorial in the Temple, said of him: "John, to those of us who remain behind, is like a comrade who rides ahead to link us with his eternity. He has found the trail out yonder and will be there to greet us when we are called to go . . ." Bijou Straun wrote: "His reputation in Sonoma County . . . was such that when a dispute arose between farmers both sides would choose John as a mediator and be willing to abide by his decision . . . He was essentially a country man, in no sense a city man. He loved his home at Geyserville."

September, 1947

The country had never been as it was the spring after John died. All green and dancing. Copious rains fell and the light was liquid and the colors all running together. Pink ostrich-feather trees came out; fruit blossoms trickled away, until evenings, the orchards were faint materializations in the dim moonlight. When it cleared, the strange brightness reasserted itself, Sonoma County light, a white glow with the colors suspended in it. That spring was all smoke and blue iris along the roads and bird calls.

I thought, he is really more present than before, up here in the valleys and on the hills. He spoke so little in life, and generally told you things that you could understand without words. He spoke with his love and his silence, and they are here.

NOTE

Except when otherwise specified, the historical material in this article consists of conversations with John (in 1939) written down by me as he spoke, and of written information supplied by Louise. Tablets, letters and cables were copied in the presence of John or Louise from documents supplied by them. This account varies in many respects from that in the *Geyserville Press* of July 26, 1946; certain of the statements there published were – through no fault of the paper and owing to the natural cares and confusion attendant on the funeral – erroneous.

A brief review of John's life, using data supplied to the writer by him, and after his passing, by Louise, will be of value to historians:

John David Bosch was born at Neu-St Johann, Canton St Gall, Switzerland, on August 1, 1855. His parents were Michael Johann Bosch and Maria Biegmann; he had three brothers and three sisters, and was his parents' fifth child. When he was nine, his mother died, and he was then brought up by his oldest sister, whom he loved all his life. After attending elementary and "repletitionary" school in Neu-St Johann, he left Switzerland with a sister and her husband (the Zuberbuhlers), arrived in America in 1879, and went to Amboy, Nebraska where on arrival the Zuberbuhlers purchased a farm. He practised his trade of cooper, "helped with the building of the railroad, and also farmed." He was in Los Angeles, California between 1884 and 1889, and became a citizen of the United States in Los Angeles County in 1887, the document also being registered in Sonoma County in 1892. He married Käthe Krieg in '85 or '86, the marriage ending in divorce around '89. It was about this period that he went to Germany, France and Spain to study wine-making. After holding various good positions in the Valley of the Moon, he purchased the thirty-five acres constituting the original extent of his Geyserville property on October 26, 1901 from Emily B. Smith of Geyserville. In 1905, John became a Bahá'í, his teachers being Mrs Beckwith, Mrs Goodall, Mrs Cooper and

Thornton Chase. John was delegate from California and Honolulu to the first Bahá'í Temple Unity Convention, Chicago, March 21, 1909. In April, 1912, when superintendent of the Northern Sonoma County Wineries, he went East to be with 'Abdu'l-Bahá, and on his return was instrumental in appealing to the Master to visit the West. He was Thornton Chase's literary executor. On January 19, 1914 he married Louise Sophie Stapfer of Zurich, Switzerland, in San Francisco. In 1920, with Louise, he left for Tahiti in March, pioneering there and leaving in September. In November, 1921, he and Louise were present in Haifa at the time of the Master's passing. Appointed by the National Spiritual Assembly with two others to locate a place for the establishment of a center "along the lines of Green Acre" John offered his property for this purpose, the institution beginning its functions in 1927. From this period on, he continued to serve in many ways until his long, final illness. He passed away July 22, 1946, and was buried in Olive Hill cemetery, Geyserville, following a befitting memorial service held July 24 in the Bahá'í Hall, Geyserville School. Under the auspices of the National Spiritual Assembly, a memorial service was also held for him in the Bahá'í House of Worship, November 24. His tomb is covered with a long plaque (the work of John Quinn) made of hammered bronze and bearing the Greatest Name. The underbrush has all been cleared away, exposing a whole new range of mountains, the western mountains that shut Geyserville off from the sea. When we saw the place recently, we knew we were watching one of the loveliest views in the world. It was a soft autumn day. "The mountains seem so near," Louise said dreamily. "That means rain." M.G.

The Days with Mark Tobey

Mark always travelled first class, even when low on funds. I would have met him sooner, otherwise. We were on the same boat crossing the Mediterranean to Haifa, but I was down in third. Disembarking at Haifa, Howard Carpenter and I, although we recognized no one, were greeted by an official at the Customs with, "So you belong to Shoghi Effendi!" We had been in a state of some agitation: this pilgrimage was especially critical, because Shoghi Effendi had written me (I lived in San Francisco) to go and settle in Persia; it was a watershed time in our lives. Now we felt welcomed and had no trouble getting through.

Effie Baker and Fujita received us with exquisite tea at what was then the Western Pilgrim House on Persian Street, across from the house of 'Abdu'l-Bahá. Effie was the frail-looking but wiry Australian who had, not long before, armed with the Guardian's long and detailed list, travelled six months across Persia, often by truck over haphazard roads, making photographs to illustrate *The Dawn-Breakers*. Fujita, the tiny Japanese, had served in the Holy Land from the days of 'Abdu'l-Bahá. He now sported a long beard because the Master, jokingly it seems, had suggested it, and for close companion he had an orange cat, two-thirds his size. The other pet I remember at the Pilgrim House was an ancient, rumpled parrot left from the days of the Master, a bird who could, on occasion, chant a line or so of prayer. It was evening then, and we knew we could not see Shoghi Effendi until the following day.

At this time the Guardian would lunch with his Western guests at their Pilgrim House, while his afternoon walks and many evenings were primarily given over to pilgrims from

195

the East. (Once or twice, as he walked over Mount Carmel, the Persians out of respect following behind, I would hear his voice echoing down the mountain, like the Báb's at Máh-Kú.) Now, at noon, we waited for the Guardian to cross the road from the Master's house, listened for his footsteps on the path outside. Besides ourselves, the other three were the international Bahá'í lawyer, Mountfort Mills, tall, slender, white-haired, one of the most distinguished men of his time. He was just back from a mission to Baghdád, connected with the question of the House of Bahá'u'lláh, a case he carried to the League of Nations. With him was the elegant Marjory Morten of New York, who had accompanied him on the mission (but had stayed, as directed, at a different hotel). And third was the tall, shy, brown-bearded young man, recently returned from a Zen Buddhist monastery, and with a name little known then, Mark Tobey.

This waiting, the anticipation of an advent, took me back to an earlier time at the Court in Ṭihrán, waiting with the Crown Princess of that day for the visit of her husband – he, although we did not know it then, doomed to be the final Sháh of the Qájár dynasty, that dynasty which had killed the Báb and done everything in its power to destroy the Faith of the Báb and Bahá'u'lláh. About to greet his wife and her guests, the Prince would walk alone across the great courtyard to the women's palace, his boots ringing on the stones.

I could still see the Qájár before me, that now-forgotten Regent, with his fair skin, long eyelashes, and eyes the Persians called *khumár* (languishing and seemingly half-drunk), traces of which features can be found across Persia even yet. For the Qájárs, one of whom was credited with 1,000 wives and 105 offspring (and this before computers), were fertile to the point where a proverb said: "Camels, fleas and princes exist everywhere." On an earlier pilgrimage, my parents had shown the Guardian this prince's photograph (the Guardian liked to see photographs; he was extremely interested in people), and Shoghi Effendi had pronounced the one word: "*Jilf*" – hard to translate but meaning in effect lightweight and frivolous.

Now we were about to meet one whose princedom was not

of this world, one who shaped the Bahá'í Faith for all future time, whereas the other, his royal contemporary, has been reduced to the footnotes long ago. Suddenly he was with us, and we following him into the dining room.

People speak of the Guardian as not being a tall man. In those days many individuals, especially, say, Persians and Frenchmen, were shorter than now. When we first met him in Paris, on his way to Oxford, he seemed to us of medium height. He "sat tall," he carried himself well, his walk was dignified (truly royal, in contrast to the swagger of Persia's Crown Prince), and even then he wore, at the Master's request, a tall, black Persian hat. "Learn not the ways of Europe," we understood the Master had told him, in saying good-bye. This hat set him off from the crowds and of course drew stares and comments. *"C'est le chah de Perse, non?"* I heard a woman cry. I wanted to tell her – even in those days – that he was the *chah* of a far wider realm than *Perse*. For even in the Paris time, to us, and to Father, who was certainly a man of the world and, also, had lived over a year in the Master's Household, Shoghi Effendi was someone apart. After he became Guardian, we were told by a Persian friend: "'Abdu'l-Bahá said, 'There is one among us who seems to be walking this earth, but actually he lives in the Kingdom.'"

It was his custom, at least when I saw him, to wear for an outer garment, a short coat like the trench coat he wore in Paris, or a sort of redingote or frock-coat to his knees; a white shirt and conservative tie: European trousers (rather narrow at the time); and highly polished black shoes. Outside the Shrines on Mount Carmel, where the pilgrims left their shoes any which way, you could recognize the Guardian's, because they were so well polished, and placed carefully side by side. His dress, although of fine quality and immaculate, was never luxurious. In fact, when Father wished to conduct him to the best shirtmaker in Paris – Charvet – he demurred, saying, "I might get to liking such things."

Now, although two tall men were in his presence, it was they who were overshadowed.

My American husband, a physician and hence of a scientific turn of mind, who had come here expecting to find an Eastern personality, commented later on how Western the Guardian was – like a young American executive, Howard said. Here was no robe, no turban, no prayer beads. The Guardian himself said in my hearing: "We are not Western nor Eastern. We are something new. We are Bahá'ís." It seemed to me that Shoghi Effendi was continually emphasizing that he was not in any way like 'Abdu'l-Bahá, that the Master, the "Mystery of God," was unique, that He was, "paradoxically . . . a perfect human being" and that one cannot *be* a perfect human being, to quote Shoghi Effendi again. Certainly the Guardian did not care for the adulation to which he was continually subjected. Howard told me how, at a men's meeting, an Easterner seized the glass Shoghi Effendi had used, and risking his displeasure, drank what was left. Personally, I sympathized with the drinker; but what the Guardian obviously wanted was service to the Faith, not displays of emotion.

Thinking of the relative stations of the four great Persons, the two Founders and two first Inheritors of our Faith, I recalled how, on an earlier pilgrimage, my father had said to me: "Shoghi Effendi stopped at a certain spot in the road (I understood it was the road along the mountain), and told me that as to his rank and being he was in no sense like the Master. It was the same spot in the road where 'Abdu'l-Bahá had stopped, long years before, and told me he was in no sense equal to or the same as Bahá'u'lláh."

Each new pilgrim was welcomed by the Guardian and would shake his hand – that perfect hand which you felt had taken thousands of years of high lineage to form, that hand which could be traced straight back through the Prophet Muḥammad, and through ancient Persian kings, all the way back to Father Abraham. He welcomed us, overlooking, with what I considered British reserve, my nervousness and embarrassment. His handshake was a gift he gave you, a brief electric contact that you could hoard through the rest of your life.

The Guardian placed Marjory at the head of the long refectory table and sat at the side of it, on her right, his back to the windows. And there before me, at the Guardian's right, sat Mark Tobey, brown-bearded, slender and timid, who made me think of a skittish deer that would pause to nibble a leaf from the Guardian's hand, before vanishing into the forest.

We could take notes at the table then, and all my attention was concentrated on the Guardian, so that I gave little thought to the pilgrims, all of whom I got to know better later on. Marjory told us afterward how the light would come over the Guardian's shoulder from the windows, and said she had never seen an eyeball so luminous. I, across from him, tried without staring to memorize his features. I noted the perfectly formed nose; the sculpted mouth, neither loose, nor full, nor tight-lipped, nor anything else undesirable that most adults' mouths become. When he smiled, there was a vertical dimple, cut into his right cheek. He had a way of brushing the palm of his hand straight down over his face, and when he did this, his skin seemed to glow. Sometimes he had a pensive, withdrawn look in his eyes, as if he were briefly away from us. He never stared, the way today's men do – he had what nuns call the custody of the eyes. The color of his eyes was, it seemed to me, hazel, changeable – and this was how my father described the Master's eyes too. One sunlit day, when the Mediterranean was blue and the Guardian was standing under the bougainvillea vine at the gate of the Master's house, I saw his eyes bright blue.

He was young then. He smiled often, and there was laughter at table too, increased by a certain tendency on the part of Mountfort and Marjory to pull Mark's leg. Mark was just back from a monastery at Kyoto (he became one of the first in the United States to spread the philosophy of Zen). He was also artist in residence at Dartington Hall, a kind of Utopia for creative people established by Mrs Elmhurst, an American benefactress, in Devonshire. Always a capable Bahá'í teacher, Mark gave us to understand that he had converted a number of residents to the Bahá'í Faith. "I would like to send you a group photograph of the Devonshire Bahá'ís," he told the Guardian. This was too good an opening for Mountfort. "Why don't you go downtown and have it taken here, Mark?" he said.

At one point the Guardian, who was very frank about the characteristics of different nationals and nations, which he knew well from innumerable contacts, said that Bahá'ís must always set an example, including, for instance, when they go through Customs. He spoke about the bribery and corruption which was, in Lord Curzon's words, "a cherished national institution in Persia," and asked if we had not read the introduction to *The Dawn-Breakers*, where he had quoted Curzon's definition of *madákhil* as "that balance of personal advantage . . . which can be squeezed out of any and every transaction." He indicated the delicacy we were having for dessert, a round pastry floating in honey, and told us it was called "the Judge's morsel" (*luqmatu'l-Qáḍí*). This was long years before bribery and corruption, which most Americans then thought "Oriental," would become common practice in the United States. Although he minced no words, the Guardian's attitude, far from that of a thundering reformer or denouncer, was one of amused observation, as if he were telling of childish games which a mature humanity would disavow. The only time I saw him angry was when, addressing Marjory, and sending a message through her to a Western believer, he stated categorically that Bahá'ís must not participate in political affairs.

This detached, observing attitude of Shoghi Effendi's was further illustrated for me on a later pilgrimage when he spoke of how the youth at Bahá'í summer schools must set an example. He said then that people, being weak, should always avoid temptation. Someone told him that at the German summer school the boys and girls shared the same dormitory. "Oh," said the Guardian with interest, "so they are even worse than the non–Bahá'ís!" "It's all right," the person added, "Mrs Braun is there." "Yes," said the Guardian, "but at the hour of temptation Mrs Braun might not always be there." We all laughed, including Fujita who was serving. "Fudge" loved to laugh, and nearly dropped a plate.

The Guardian would share some of his incoming or outgoing mail with us. He pointed to a letter he was addressing to the National Spiritual Assembly of the United States, regarding nonparticipation by Bahá'ís in military service. He said many books would be written about that letter in future. Sometimes he would ask our opinion. As the Báb's title, did we prefer First Point or Primal Point? We opted for the alliteration. (I heard from Emogene Hoagg, who worked closely with the Guardian when she typed the entire manuscript of *The Dawn-Breakers*, that on occasion she would tell him: "But we can't say it that way, Shoghi Effendi!" and sometimes he would change the expression, sometimes not. His consulting with us was remarkable in one whose English so far exceeded our own. In translation we should give the equivalent, he said. He praised the King James Bible, "not the revised." He spoke of translating the Bahá'í marriage verses, which differ only in being masculine for the groom, feminine for the bride. "It is more than 'We are all content with the Will of God,'" he said. "It is like, 'We will all *abide by* the Will of God.'" Then he turned to me, smiling, with, "Perhaps we should say, 'We are all resigned to . . .'" His English speech was a phenomenon, the distinguished accent unforgettable. It was far from that missionary American so widespread in the Middle East, nor was it that flutey, plummy British perhaps insufficiently appreciated on this side of the Atlantic. Years later, when as a standee in a New York theater I listened to Paul Robeson's Othello, I thought to myself, "Here is one other besides the Guardian who makes the English language sound right." Not that Robeson's English was similar, but it too was of high rank. As for his Arabic and Persian, no earthly sounds could equal the Guardian's chanting in the Holy Shrines – reverent, solemn, but unsentimental.

Shoghi Effendi told Mark that he could paint the Dawn-Breakers, the early heroes of our Faith, but not the Báb or Bahá'u'lláh. He also said to him: "Art must inspire. Personal satisfaction is not enough." Beyond these comments, the Guardian at one time wrote a letter stating that there will be no Bahá'í music as such – there will be a world music. This greatly pleased Mark. "He has freed the artist," Mark said: the creative person was not to be the instrument of an ideology.

After a little while the pilgrimage was ending, and we were

to be dropped back again into the unreadable, frightening world. I went with Mountfort to the travel bureau where he was booking passage home, or somewhere, and they said something about having a cabin available for three. "Mountfort," I said, "why don't you marry Marjory and adopt Mark?" "Barkis is willin'," Mountfort said.

Sonoma County

I went by Mark's bedroom door that morning, and there were his shoes where he had kicked them off, one pointing due north, the other due south. Geyserville Summer School was over, the dormitories empty, and Mark, Harold Gail, and I had been invited to stay on a bit, so I could write my articles on Sonoma County (they were published in the Santa Rosa *Press-Democrat* under my grandmother's name – she was Alice Ives Breed, and I wrote as V. Ives).

Mark was in his permanent condition of stress: should he go north to Seattle and paint, or south to San Francisco and visit? So long as there were points to the compass, Mark would always be pulled this way and that. Postponing decision, he came along with us that day, for the ride.

Nothing in that far off, not yet spoiled time, could have been better than Sonoma County, or lovelier, or emptier, at that season and hour. Looking through that pearly light, you could see for mile on mile over ripened vineyards to the hazy blue mountains – which were, Mark said, "like blue and violet tears."

We drove through parched, corn-colored hills, speckled here and there with oaks, and came to a small white school house that was up for sale. "Just the place for a studio," Mark said – but he always said that, made his decision to settle, and then started toting up the disadvantages. Hurrying by, we stopped at an ancient mill, its great wheel, three stories high, stilled forever now, and no water in sight. It had become a monument, preserved, a sign told us, by the "Native Sons of the Golden West." Mark wanted to set up an easel, start painting, buy the mill, turn it into a studio, and directly thereafter disappear to parts unknown.

By then he was already hungry, and led us, in Healdsburg,

to a magnificent apple pie, made fresh that morning. (Forget about truck drivers, I thought, if you want good food, ask an artist, or a poet, or a musician.) We sat there a long while, chiefly discussing how Mark's harem would have looked if he had been born a Muslim. It would have had mother-of-pearl walls for the moonlight to shine on, and woodwork the color of old red manzanita, and lapis lazuli floors entwined with gold grapevines. He got so interested in the decorations he forgot to tell us anything about the inmates, and when we asked, he said they were only background anyhow.

Having heard rumors of a mysterious "Lotus Pond," we drove on, and finally discovered it, lost in cattails and willows, with great, carved pink flowers floating on its quiet surface. These flowers close around noon, and Mark said why hadn't we come at early dawn. (One reason could have been that he never got up till eleven.) The seed pods of the lotus were like shower sprays, seemingly punched full of holes. "I never saw a flower that looked more like plumbing," said Mark. There were no signs in that deserted place, "and best of all, nothing to say 'Don't pick the flowers,' " Mark exulted. We did not, anyhow, except for one suede leaf, which Mark gave me to wear as a hat, and one cattail, which we picked because Harold said it looked like a frankfurter with fur.

Later we passed a solitary roadside fruit stand, and Mark felt called upon to get out and sample the honey. Poking with a straw, he tried the manzanita, the lilac, the wildflower – and finally, after long deliberation, bought the orange. We also spoke briefly to a frail, bearded tramp in a cowboy hat who was on his way along the road. The tramp held out a finger and showed us his ring, given him by his lady friend, he said. "An old, delicate Buffalo Bill," Mark commented.

After a while we went wading in the Russian River, where early autumn leaves were adrift on the brown and gold water. Mark's feet, well shaped and in proportion to his tall figure, were as beautiful as his long, tapering artist's hands. We talked, as we dried, about the Russian impact on northern California, still present in the place names: Fort Ross, Sebastopol, the Russian River, and also Mount Saint Helena, named for a lady who was niece to the Czarina, and looked upon as a saint.

It cost you fifty cents to get into the Petrified Forest, a respectable sum (children twenty cents; dogs could not get in at all). Once inside, the primeval stillness alone was worth it. "Like Japan," breathed Mark. We followed a sawdust trail under ancient oaks, and manzanitas, and came to a sign that read: "This forest was buried millions of years ago by volcanic action, turning the trees to stone." Each petrified exhibit was back of barbed wire in its own enclosure – the place was a kind of silent zoo. You almost expected another sign reading: "Do not feed or annoy the trees." The biggest, with a new oak tree sprouting from its trunk, buried a million years and titled "The Queen of the Forest," was a petrified monster thirty-six feet around. Tourists, unable to carve their names on the tree, had industriously identified themselves on scraps of paper and pushed these through the wire onto the great trunk. Appreciating the tourists' frustration, kindly authorities had provided a special building, three-walled and roofed over, where you could nail up your business card or scrap of paper to your heart's content. Another helpful provision, which had, that far, kept the tourists from driving off with the forest, was indicated by another sign: "Free specimens of petrifaction given away at the office." Noting from Mark's expression that he was planning to set up a studio in the Forest, we pulled him away and drove on. Soon we passed two red temples in a hillside field: huge stone bases, with upper stories and double towers of wood. "They're just kilns for drying hops," a young girl told us, "but no longer in use. We sit around and think, 'What can we do with all that beautiful stone work?' and then we just leave them there."

"A deep pomegranate color," said Mark, grabbing my fountain pen and writing paper and making off up the hill. We entered the higher kiln, and found that the sunset, coming through the cracks, was turning the woodwork blood red. Outside the kiln was an echo, and while Mark was at work, we shouted to that for a while, waking up some turkeys that had retired for the night in a nearby tree. Mark made several sketches with the colors all written in, and he planned to paint the kilns from memory, only what he really wanted was to establish two studios, one in each kiln.

I seem to remember at least two pictures that Mark created from what we saw that day; one had to do with the two kilns, and the other was called "Western Town." But who knows how many impressions of that time remained in his memory and were later scattered through his work.

Seattle

His Seattle house of those days was an ordinary-looking frame dwelling catercorner from a small market. The door had a little see-through mirror set in it – it was what is called in some areas a go-to-hell door – and every effort was made to keep the place looking deserted. Once you were accepted inside you found stacks of paintings leaning haphazardly against the walls. Most of these paintings were later very valuable. One we saw there and thought of buying hangs now in the Metropolitan; at that time we chose "Archaic Satire" instead. There was bareness, almost no furniture, nothing on the floors; yards of paper curing in some dubious liquid in the bathtub, a battered, rusty carrot grater and a magenta eucalyptus leaf nailed up somewhere for decoration, a priceless, splintery polychrome wood Christus propped up on the newel post in the downstairs hall. Mark usually camped out in his homes, doubtless feeling freer, more tentative that way, so that fate would not get his address. We would eat with him in the kitchen. He was an excellent cook, and wanted almonds on his veal and shrimp on his whitefish. After meals, in those days, he would linger at the table and play – do Japanese tricks with a paper bag, or sing fake Chinese and German songs. He could mimic anything. When he told us about the three dogs that met on the Champs-Élysées, his voice varied from a shrill piping for the French poodles to a subterranean bass for the English bulldog:

First poodle: "My name is Fifi: f-i, f-i."

Second poodle: "My name is Mimi: m-i, m-i. What's *your* name?"

Bulldog: "My name is Fido: f-i-d-e-a-u-x."

Anyone might appear there. I remember once when a young, gold-bearded artist, carrying a single pink rose, wafted in from the night, left his rose in a golden vase, and wafted out. Another time (I was not present) came Leopold Stokowski. "I paint too," said Stokowski, once inside the door. And Mark answered: "I compose." He did, too. We often heard him improvising on the piano, and still have a recording of his "Homage to Guillaume Apollinaire." Music was his *violon d'Ingres.*

He always had disciples around him, learning both the Bahá'í Faith and his art, and for ever after, to some extent, they all reflected Mark – even to the point of murmuring *"Strange, fantastic,"* in italics, and suddenly drawing in their breath with a slight rasp and shaking their heads if something was beautiful. He enhanced life. He communicated his own verve. Juliet Thompson, the artist who taught him the Bahá'í Faith in 1918, told me that in the early days he would have his pupils dance up to the canvas, apply a dot of paint to it, and dance back again. Another expert said that when Mark loaded paint on his brush he always knew the exact, right amount he wanted, ahead of time. And apparently, even from the time when, as a youth, he earned his living by wrapping up packages, he was an artist. To him, the artist was the eyes of the community, his function being to teach the others to see.

Everyone in Mark's ambience was expected to improve. The case of Swedish intellectual Pehr Hallsten is in point. Rumor was that during the (or a) Depression, Pehr was picking up trash in the park by day, using a nail on a stick for the purpose, and attending an art class by night, which happened to be taught by Mark. Under Mark's impact, and with his help, Pehr had to return to the University in his fifties, acquire a B.A., then an M.A. (with a thesis on Strindberg), and after all that become an artist. One time when Mark put on a meeting for me to address on the Bahá'í Faith in Seattle – large audience, elegant hall, Beethoven – Pehr was recruited for chairman.

One of Pehr's strongest holds on Mark was his diabetes – he was chronically sick, and Mark was partly a nurse; but above this he held Mark's close attention because let alone improbable, he was impossible. Mark had a great liking for people's quirks, and Pehr was an eccentric's eccentric. Once, in the early days of teaching him the Faith, Mark commented, "If this Cause is universal, it has room in it for Pehr." And indeed, he gradually became a devoted Bahá'í and translated the Hidden Words into Swedish. As the years passed, a number of Mark's friends, like the Gails, and Tom and Helen Sousa, became Pehr-sitters as a matter of course. For all his continental background, his five languages and erudition, he had the purity and translucence of a four year old, and after a while you grew to love him in spite of yourself. "It is the extreme variableness of human beings which makes everything so interestingly difficult," said Mark.

He often lamented the changes in Seattle, the freeways and how they were spoiling that city and many other places, including, way to the south, the Bahá'í School we loved at Geyserville. He felt that many people were being turned into machines. Once, observing Seattle's prosperous crowds, he said, "Mr and Mrs Automata. Miss Automata. Master Automata." As Bahá'u'lláh forewarned, if our civilization, "so often vaunted," were "allowed to overleap the bounds of moderation," it would "bring great evil upon men." He made a great effort to help save the Farmers' Market, where he would draw the old transients, seeing them as shabby birds, nestless and blown along the wind.

Of one ancient character, who habitually wore a pith helmet with a small unpainted duck on top, Mark said he had never been able to best him in conversation. "Will you pose for me?" he asked the old man. "You're an artist. Take an impression," was the answer. "See those buildings the Government is putting up?" the duck man asked Mark, another day. "You can't buy them. Is that democracy?" Once, home from a journey half way around the world, Mark came across him again. "Where've you been?" asked the ancient. "Oh," said Mark, casually, "Japan – the Holy Land – Great Britain . . ." "Well," said the man, "one has to be somewhere."

Mark was already being made the target of well meaning fans, and someone or other was forever pursuing him with kindly attentions. Of one anxious hostess he confided to me, "Wants me to go out in the garden and admire her *tuberous begonias.*" He hissed the italics as if referring to a loathsome disease.

Nice

Yesterday, refugeeing at the Scotch Tea House (we refugee
from shelter to shelter, out of the Mistral, out of the rains, out
of the crowds, out of the blare of Carnival music), Mark said,
"Arithmetic – I flunked it. I had to go through the seventh
grade twice. Then the next year we had algebra, and I cheated
over the shoulder of the girl in front: she held up the answers
for me. I passed, but then we had geometry and – flunk-dunk.
The only thing that saved me was that we moved to
Hammond, Indiana. Otherwise, I would have been one of
those inside-out people in the town; you know, no skin."
After two years of high school, Mark's formal education
stopped. We used to wonder how he could be so articulate, so
literary, especially when we would think over the titles of his
paintings: "The Return of Persephone" – "The Edge of
August" – "The Void Devouring the Gadget Era" –
"Threading Light."

Sara Kenny (wife of a former Attorney General of
California) and her mother, Mrs Duffield, were the first
Bahá'í pioneers to Nice. They asked Harold and me to stay
and help, and after a while down came Mark, and stayed five
weeks to help, too. I know exactly how long he was there
because of my diary reference to "his five-week hellish visit to
Nice last winter . . ." We learned then that geniuses are the
price we have to pay for art.

Like all chronically irritated people, Mark attracted noise.
First, although he had performed the miracle of finding a hotel
bedroom in Nice during the Carnival, that bedroom was next
to the hall toilet. From 7:00 A.M. on he lay exasperatedly
listening to a long procession of guests: "Some trip in, some
bang in, some glide in, some swish," he told us. "And if that
weren't enough, there's the elevator." Here he reproduced the
whine of an elevator interminably ascending. At last his
landlady, proprietor of the small hotel, moved him elsewhere.
In the new location, however, he was kept fumingly awake
"for hours" listening to "Il Trovatore" from the next room.
Finally he summoned the porter, who pushed in and
discovered a radio at full blast and a teenage opera buff
peacefully asleep. No wonder each new environment was

208

THE DAYS WITH MARK TOBEY
THE DAYS WITH MARK TOBEY

approached by Mark stiff legged and with the hair on his neck
bristling; he was asking himself what unguessed, intolerable
annoyance would be next on the list.
Sometimes I would jot down his comments at random.
Mark: "To be mature really means to know what you've
missed in life." On marriage: "There are two hells: marriage
and celibacy. Take your choice." On the English: "Every
Englishman has two wishes: that the sun will shine; that he can
get to the Continent for a meal." On life: "Sometimes I think
life is exactly what those American traveling salesmen think it
is." Again, on life: "We have to be *moved* by something." And
once he said: "People don't understand the truth, but they'll
accept an untruth." Once, along the rue de Verdun, we met a
tall man and woman striding, with white, tufty hair streaming
from each head, the man's white tufts like horns, his face a pale
oblong, his body a black oblong in its straight wool cloak.
"That face," said Mark, ecstatic. "That man is *somebody*." "He
knows it, too," said I uncharitably; "I guess a man always
knows who he is." "There are always plenty of women
around to tell him," replied Mark. In the crowded and
fashionable Place Masséna, a nurse held a little girl bottom
out over the gutter. I made some noise or gesture. Mark
laughed. "After all," he said, "that is the essence of art:
revealing the concealed."
    In line with this were his sober, technical artist conversa-
tions with Leon (Leon Applebaum, an artist then awaiting his
American bride in Nice), as he showed him walls – stained
walls, mottled, crumbling walls, walls with old dripped paint
from former signs fading down them. "I especially wanted
you to see *these*," he would say confidentially, rounding some
favorite corner.
    When Harold, Mark, and I arrived in Marseilles to conduct
a Bahá'í meeting, the cab driver took one look at Mark's
substantial form and groaned: with their tiny cars, they judged
all passengers by bulk. He ended up with Mark beside him and
one of the local believers on Mark's lap – so that the man was
almost squeezed outside and the car driving itself. At the
public hall (freezing) Mark spoke very eloquently in English,
and they called him "cher Maître." I then came on in French,

and between us something must have been accomplished, since the local friend told me afterward: "Bombe atomique!" and said that a newcomer, a Frenchman in the audience, had accepted our Faith.

Inevitably, back at the hotel, it was Mark who got the room with the cockroaches.

The next day, as we sat in one of those restaurants with the glassed-in fronts, Mark was enchanted, surveying the incredible variety of faces passing in the crowds. We walked, so that he could look at walls. Coming to a ruined wall along the waterfront he pointed out the patterns he saw, the interrelationships and contrasts. "I want to paint what nobody else sees," he told us. "The ignored and forgotten things. The unregarded."

On the train returning to Nice, conversation went on in the usual way, if not to each other, at least past and around each other. I happened to speak admiringly of Mabel Dodge Luhan, who brought D. H. Lawrence to America. "She attracted a lot of celebrities," I said. "Oh," said Mark, "she had a lot of money, and she offered those poor apes a place to sit down." The train did not escape its share of blame in the new and of course hostile environment: "French trains never know where they want to go," he said, "unless they're actually going there. They back and fill, back and fill." Rocky hill towns slipped by. Mark commented, "A rock is a long time ago." I mentioned some land we owned in California, and said, "A deed is a friend indeed." This led him to the opposite coast: "Long Island," he said, "that gentle, used-up landscape that doesn't mean anything to me. That's why I like the Northwest – except Portland, which is an old dried pea in a pod. I always feel so *little* in Portland." "This is more beautiful than America," I said. "There is more total beauty here," Mark answered. "The trouble is, America is a part of you – and this you look at." I recalled him speaking then, back in Seattle, of "the voltage of beauty." Once, when we were almost home, he sang out, "O, Half Moon of my delight . . ."

On February 10, 1955, four of us – Sara and Mark, Harold and I – made a long-awaited expedition to the Matisse chapel at Vence. We three laymen wanted to see the chapel, not as simple tourists, but through an artist's eyes.

We met with ceremony at the Scotch Tea House at high noon. Mark had consumed one meal while waiting, and as we had our own bacon and eggs, buttered toast and scones, he consumed two more. Afterward there was quite a delay while Mark figured out his bill; the system there was, instead of being billed, you went to the proprietor at the cash register and recited the list of whatever you'd eaten, but no one could remember exactly what Mark had had.

On our way to the bus terminal, Mark admired the huge illuminated Carnival cutouts decorating the sky over the Place Masséna – only he pointed out the empty backs, whereas it was the decorated fronts that you were expected to admire. We caught the 1:30 bus, and wound up and up, mile after mile, through the spring-maddened hills, saw the wind in the white fruit trees, the air blue, the earth softening, only glimpses here and there from the bus, no way to be alone with it. Up and up the bus labored into the hills, going the long way round because the Nazis had dynamited the great bridge, leaving huge, dizzy ruined shards in the chasm. We finally reached Vence and looked for a conveyance to the chapel, about a mile out from the center of the town. We fitted ourselves into a taxi, or *the* taxi, and at last arrived at our world-famous, and long anticipated, goal.

We found a little white building with black line drawings on it, jammed between two other structures. Pushing inside with the crowd, we came to a nun with a plate for money, and then we were in the little chapel itself. I had an impression of blond woodwork and white walls, black line drawings scrawled, and sunlight throwing bright green shadows on the floor. Mark stood and looked. The three of us stood and looked at Mark. Then suddenly he was not there any more, and we pressed out through the crowds and caught up with him. With an air of finality, he was purchasing postcards from another nun. We three lined up behind him, and followed him back to the still-warm taxi. Total time elapsed: four minutes.

Mark's explosion took place in the cab: "It ain't worth the trip. The whole feeling is awful. Such bad, weak drawings on the wall. It's a pain in the neck. I always thought it would be. I knew he couldn't do it – a man with that past couldn't paint naked women and flowers all his life and then at the very end, draw a religious thing. I knew it, but I had to see for myself." Between snorts, wails, and roars, as the taxi rocked, he continued, "It makes me all sick. And those money bags in there – I hate any money mixed up in it. Such bad drawing! The only thing I like is when the color comes in there on the floor – it's the only thing that inspires me . . . I didn't come to see the chapel anyhow," he now decided, "I really came to get out in the sun."

We sat quiet, out of the battle. After all, we simple laymen had gotten what *we* came for – an artist's appreciation of an artist.

Eventually we managed to board a bus for the long, long ride, via Grasse, back to Nice. The trip was marred only by our not being able to get seats, and having to jerk and sway a couple of hours in the crowded aisle, holding on to whatever offered. Mark broke his silence only once: he was jostled, going over a bump, by a fellow hanger-on, a respectable, gray-haired matron, wearing a gray-and-white dress – at which time he informed us and the other passengers, with perfect clarity, that she was a *blanquette de veau*.

Our Villa Christiane, just off the Grande Corniche, was probably not the last word in comfort. The high-ceilinged, minuscule living room had a Renaissance tiled floor (cold) and a minute fireplace that smoked. It also boasted a small electric heater that offered no warmth but scorched you on contact, its plugs and fittings given to spitting and throwing sparks. The bathroom contained a theoretical water heater, called a *Vésugaz*, that exploded when you turned on the hot water, hence its name. With luck, if the room got warm, drops condensed on the ceiling and spotted you with yellow paint. In the kitchen, electric wires were looped here and there like entrails at a bullfight. As for the two-burner gas stove, it was hard for an onlooker to tell whether you were making a suicide attempt or just cooking dinner. "Do you ever smell escaping gas?" the gas man had inquired. "Invariably," I replied. "Then we must look into it," he advised (we never saw him again); "gas attacks the liver and the bile, you get a dry cough and you vomit, you wonder what you have, only the doctor benefits. Then one day you set a match to your stove, and it explodes in your face."

Hoping this would not be the day, we asked Mark up to visit, because there was one thing about the Villa Christiane that no one could disapprove of: its "*vue*," even as the ad had promised, was "*imprenable*." Down over orange roofs it looked, and way, way out over the Baie des Anges. When the season was right, lemon trees bloomed in the sun under the high windows.

"I knew you two would be on a hill," he grumbled, as we toiled up the Grande Corniche. He sat at the table, saying as a preface to the food (neither Harold nor I can really cook, as he was well aware): "Gather ye tastebuds while ye may." To which I, shivering in the kitchen, could only reply: "Cold hands I loved beside the Vésubie . . ."

London, Frankfurt, Salzburg
Mark deviates unerringly to some secret goal, which usually turns out to be Seattle. Once he has made his decision to return there, he loudly condemns both the trip and that city: he dreads the ocean, but is afraid to fly; his Seattle agent is "gloomy"; two of his best friends have died; he hates the way they page people in the Coffee Shop at the Hotel Meany; the freeway is ruining all; he cannot bear to think of the atomic bomb. (We ourselves had come from Portland, Oregon, with its weekly bomb warnings, to Nice, a city apparently bomb free; Europe never thought of the bomb; such a relief.) He has temporarily forgotten the all-time worst, and we dare not remind him: the Seattle woman, a disturbed artist, who used to haunt his porch, slip up his stairs, stick notes in his mirror. From half across the planet, she would mail him bulging letters and packets with hearts pasted on them, sprawlingly addressed via places and people like New York's Museum of Modern Art or even c/o Picasso in Paris. (I saw a number of them, returned for more postage.) She did not fail to approach the media with news of the phantom relationship, and even produced two imaginary children by Mark – Markinita and

Markolino – before he was at last rescued by the authorities. Once he sat down and wrote her a very long letter citing all the sober and logical reasons why she must stop, and go out into the world and lead her life, how he did not love her, never had, never could, how she had created something out of nothing. On receiving it she sat down and scribbled her thousandth letter to him. It said, "Write me again."

On one visit, in the days before he was rich, I asked him, "Why don't you get married, Mark?" "Why should I?" he replied indignantly. "I've supported myself all winter."

We understood, from a source we trusted, that Mark actually had been married at one time, that the lady was of a well-known New York family, and things had gone so badly between them that he had to sneak back for his clothes. We could not find out much about this, being afraid to ask. He had an equally difficult experience, trying to learn to drive a car.

In London – Mark virtually the only man in that city to be wearing a beret – in those years, the mid-1950s, correct London men all looked to us like Howard Chandler Christy illustrations for 1910: tall and tight suited, gloved hands clasped on a furled umbrella, bowler hat, moustache, stiff collar – he took us to his show at the Institute of Contemporary Arts. Here we noted Mark's reactions to compliments from his fans: A red-headed man in a French woolen coat with cowl said to him, "It's been a long time since I've seen anything like this." "And when," asked Mark, "have you seen anything like this before?" A handsome woman said, "This is exciting. I hadn't seen any of your work – hardly any." Mark brushed her off by turning to us and saying, "Well, we must be going now."

After thinking it all over I decided that the endless compliments from laymen made him suffer because what they took for pictures on the wall were pieces of Mark himself. And somehow it called to mind an old verse from a Persian poet: "Do not mock the wine. It is bitter only because it is my life."

He came to the big Bahá'í Intercontinental Conference that was held in Frankfurt in 1958, and here, too, we seemed to be gathered with him around a table, this time out at a restaurant in their beautiful zoological gardens. Because of their constant altercations at table over Pehr's slipping off his diabetic diet, the meal as usual was a special event. (Of another occasion when Pehr was absent, I complained in my diary: "The atmosphere was almost normal.")

"What's it like to be famous, Mark?" I asked him. "I only know it when I go somewhere, and all the doors open," he said. "It's a pain in the neck. Fame is for your friends." An eminent European had told him that his work didn't look happy. This infuriated Mark. He returned again and again to that comment: "Are you 'oppy?" Hearing of a statement made by the Guardian that it was the presence of Mr Banání in Africa that was responsible for the great advances there, Mark said, "I can readily accept that. I believe in *sieves*." I knew he meant that some, like sieves, let the divine light through.

This was the day when Mark announced that he was not an Abstract Expressionist. "What are you, Mark?" I asked him. He sat up straighter and answered testily, "I *hope* I am an artist."

I remember that Mark stopped by to see us in Salzburg, where we lived six years as Bahá'í pioneers. Salzburg, he said, was not for artists; it was a music town. We pondered this, knowing that artists crowd to that city from the ends of the earth. We decided, finally, that Salzburg already was a work of art (was before highrises, anyway), and Mark felt it left him with nothing to do.

He was fresh from winning first prize at the Venice Biennale – the first American to win it since Whistler. It took me back to a dream he told me about once, a dream he had after becoming a Bahá'í. He was in the presence of 'Abdu'l-Bahá, and the Master showed him some kind of tablet or scroll bearing a long list of names. "Here you are, way down here," said 'Abdu'l-Bahá, pointing to the bottom of the list. "But look," the Master went on, showing another scroll of names, "here you are, in the future –" and Mark saw his name, heading the list. His fame was late in coming, but did not surprise him. "I painted just as well thirty years ago," he said.

As usual, Mark was looking for a center, a place to be and stay. "During the four days I was with him in Venice," Otto Seligman confided, "I nearly went crazy. He's looking all over Europe for a house. He's even got it planned – Swiss or Austrian; cement downstairs, for car and storage, living upstairs. However," his agent went on gloomily, "I know it will all end in Seattle again."

As usual, Mark surveyed our Tobey collection, especially "The Void Devouring the Gadget Era," which we owned for many years and finally sold back to him. "My wife's sewing basket," "The town dump," "The product of a deranged mind" had been typical evaluations of "The Void" by our nonartistic friends – but it was one of the sanest commentaries that has ever been made on our times: that great, advancing, eating Dark – and its hot breath blowing our "civilization" to rubbish. "That's a top Tobey," Mark said of "The Void." He told us the two central drips had simply happened, but he liked them and let them stay. He also showed us the symbolic mouth, vomiting. Mark never, in our opinion, sold a painting – he warehoused them here and there, with nominal owners, but so far as he was concerned, they always remained his.

For some reason, he liked to pose for me, so we repaired to the terrace of our apartment, outside the bedroom window, and I snapped him in shirtsleeves – getting a portrait which has been reproduced several times: it appears as a full page in *Arts* (September 1959), and again in the April 1976 *Atlantic*. Another photograph, which I took of him in the gardens at Èze, and think of as "Plato's Cave," was also a favorite of Mark's. Since he had even rejected *Life* magazine's first portraits of him, and made them photograph him all over again for their September 28, 1953, issue, I was proud of my achievement, however accidental.

Basel
"I judge all art critics by whether or not they like Pehr's painting," said Mark. "If they don't like Pehr's painting, they don't know anything about art."

Pehr in old age, the way we found him the last time, in Basel, 1964. He had grown outwardly calm, his face round, white and soft, like the faces in a Klee. His function seemed to be to lie on a chaise longue under a fluffy orange blanket, read three Swedish newspapers a day, and bait Mark. Across the round table, sideways from Pehr, sat Mark in a high-backed, dark upholstered chair with stool to match. The two would pass books and cups of tea across the table. Sample conversation:

"An American came here. Visited. I would have taught him to be an artist. I sent him to Spain, to the Louvre. Did everything. A European would have given his eyeteeth for it – and then he left. Spoiled." "He left because he said you were so unreasonable, Mark," said Pehr calmly from his chaise longue; then continued with deadly aim, "Unreasonable *to me*." "When I'm painting, Pehr," said Mark in a fury, but dangling an obvious red herring, "I can't be being considerate to a guest. Consider, consider, consider –" I remembered complimenting Mark one time on how kindly and thoughtful he had become, in view of all he had to go through. "It's all made ground," he told me.

"Why," asks Pehr, screwing up his face as if biting into a lemon, "would anyone buy this house in a place where he doesn't live?" The house was perfect for Mark, the kind of jewel most of us can only dream of, built in early Renaissance days as the administration building of a monastery. You let yourself into a red carpeted hall, filled with high, neat stacks of fragrant firewood. A polished wood staircase wound into a great, bare chamber, shadowy, with a large fireplace – and one corner an oasis serving as the main sitting room, its decoration an orange-patterned rug from Morocco. There was no modern city outside these walls, no twentieth century; you looked out on wide gardens, trees, steps, you heard only a bird note or the licking of a fountain. Basel was the town favored by Erasmus, Luther's friend, and where he died. This house probably went up before he was born (1466?); he himself was raised in a monastery and hated them.

Of many who drifted here to see Mark, staying for various lengths of time, Mark mentioned a special one, and added, "But he has *visitors*." Alerted by the italics, I asked, "You mean, imaginary?" "Yes," said Mark. "They crawl up his arms." "What are they exactly, Mark?" "He doesn't know for sure. They're little animals. He fights them all night, and dozes all day. It's no pleasure for me, just when I'm telling him something, to have him doze off." (Mark, the insomniac, was always looking for someone to stay awake with him.) "Sometimes he thinks they're mice. Once we put out a plate of nuts for them. Didn't help. Nothing was taken, as he could see." Somehow in that tall, ancient house, the guest with his furred, pullulating entities was not too ill matched with those drifting ghosts of monks and abbots past.

Mark took us all over the house: the dull red dining room, furnished with an encroaching rubber plant, Otto's gift, and a kind of armoire, black, with a piece of Staffordshire on top: a lover in long white socks, and a billow-skirted lovee, the two in a china arbor. The prize bit of decor, however, was a tall cardboard box, half of it daubed with blue paint, serving as a pedestal for a Victorian fruit bowl which Mark had bought for two Swiss francs. Then there were long rooms where he painted; and the upstairs, where many rooms were almost empty, each with an island of bed, beautiful blanket, and rug. One, obviously unused, had no furniture at all, except that right in the center, and sporting a wooden cover, was an antique bidet. There was also a studio for Mark, with a north light, but of course he never painted there.

"What made him take this house?" complained Pehr to anyone who would listen. "The house took him," I said. What Pehr himself would approve of, we did not know, since he volunteered no information. But certainly if you asked him a direct question, you got a wonderfully surprising answer. "Pehr," I said, "do you paint from the inside or the outside?" "From the inside," he said like lightning.

My mind went back to Salzburg, when Pehr visited, alone and trying as usual to catch up with Mark. Mark invented "white writing" but plain writing was beyond him, and I seemed to be the only one who could read his letter of instructions to Pehr. It was postmarked Biarritz and included many remember-the-time-when touches: "That snapshot of us two in Venice is before me as I write. The one feeding the pigeons in front of St Mark's." (Who has been able to miss this photograph – millions of tourists have been taken in front of the same St Mark's, feeding the same pigeons.) "Why does he talk about the pigeons," Pehr snarled. "Everybody knows about pigeons! I want to hear about *plans*: Come here on such a date, go there. Mark is always writing comments about people he meets, and ideas. Who cares about that!" What he wanted was a timetable of Mark's comings and goings, and such a timetable existed nowhere on earth. Mark could not make plans. His preferred trick, which he actually carried out at least once, was to book passage on an ocean liner, say his farewells, go down the day of the sailing, stare morosely at the ship, turn around, and go back to his last base. (Later he was chagrined when the ship didn't founder.)

It was clear from what I could decipher of the letter, shared by Pehr with all comers, that Mark – no matter what his current geography – with the punctuality of the swallows returning to Capistrano, was on his way back to Seattle. Time after time he had left that city, only to home back again. "He hates it there," Pehr explained.

"Joseph will go back to New York and work the elevator," the letter went on, "and you and I can return to Seattle and paint." Joseph, a Spanish elevator man who savored Rúmí, was on a visit to his family in Spain. Mark was always looking for an attendant who could be of some use; most of them offered all aid short of help. In Joseph he thought for a time that he had found the answer: "He can not only drive a car, but he has a license," Mark had told us, with admiration.

" 'I have landed in Biarritz!' " quoted Pehr. "Landed from where? He must have left Paris for London, gone to St Ives and then gone to Biarritz." "Write me at once," Mark continued, giving no address. "I will go to Spain, if I do, on Thursday, or Friday; if we don't go, Joseph will ask them to forward it to where I am. So write me there." "I don't quite understand that in any language," I told Pehr. "You're like being tied to the tail of a kite."

In the end we had sent Pehr off to the long-suffering American Express. He left for Spain, and we tried unsuccessfully to intercept him at Geneva with an urgent letter, bearing a Paris address, which reached him in Salzburg, from Mark.

("We've opened a blasted branch Post Office," Harold groaned.) Besides his gifts of being chronically ill, and also impossible, Pehr remained important to Mark all through the long years. He afforded Mark a witnessed past, and continuity. To Mark, he was a kind of human Seattle.

We tried, on our trip with the two of them to Winterthur, to keep everything peaceful between them. We lay low, made them do all the choosing, where and when to go, what to eat, so that nothing that went wrong could be pinned on us. Our restaurant lunch went like this: "Pehr, make up your mind, will you, for God's sake! No! That drink is *too sweet*! You take iced coffee – don't be silly – take ginger ale! Why don't you ever relax? You know, a cow's tail relaxes more than you do! *Pehr, don't lay down the law!*" Pehr to Mark, re dessert: "Give me some of yours." Mark: "I'm sorry – you can't have the sweet stuff!" Mark's comment on Swiss food: "I don't like it. It's all edible, and there's something the matter with it."

"When do you work best?" I asked him. "Is it better when you're full of food and happy, or when you're miserable?"

"When I'm stimulated," he said.

His real goal that day was to visit the Museum at Winterthur, to see just how they had hung his two pictures. The museum was closed, but once the visitor made himself known, the doors opened, and the Director, busy hanging a show, came down and escorted us around for an hour. Mark said both his pictures – a large Sumi and a little one of white lines with brown margins – were untitled, but the Director told him no, the little one was called "Channels." We followed Mark around, listening for crumbs from the Master's table. He admired the Museum's three Vuillards. Said their Pissaro was the best he'd ever seen – "*So free.*" He apparently meant not so defined.

"How much of criticism is subjective, Mark?" I asked him.

"*All* of it," he answered.

Of a representative turn-of-the-century landscape he said they were out of fashion, but he liked this one. He would not even glance at the two small Renoir bronzes, or the Renoir painting. I told the Director, introducing Pehr, that Pehr was a fine painter, and Mark said, "One of the best of the naïfs," so we learned Pehr's category. Afterward, I asked Pehr which was his favorite of all we had seen. "The Renoir," he said.

Somewhere along the line, when I was alone with Mark, he said, "Pehr's changed. He's so negative. So irritable. You can't contradict him. He won't budge. He has hardening of the arteries of the brain."

A bit later, when I was alone with Pehr, he said, "Mark's changed. Doesn't like anything. So irritable. You can't oppose him in any way. I've learned that in this life, you've got to be *flexible*."

There were none of what the books call untoward incidents during the long drive back from Winterthur. We tried hard to keep everything smoothed over. All gushers stayed capped. As Mark got out of the car, he laid a tentative hand on Pehr's sleeve and said gently, "Pehr and I are getting old, aren't we, Pehr?"

Back at the house in Basel I asked him about another famous modern. "He's an alley man," said Mark. "He goes down the alley picking things up, and then he makes a collage. A baby art for baby adults." Of another celebrity he told me: "A collector came into a Basel gallery, saw one of his paintings and said: 'Moon Over Cow Dung.' " Mark did not say dung. I asked about Henry Moore. Of Henry and his kind, Mark had this: "They make me sick to my stomach. They leave enough to make the body recognizable, but they don't love the body. He's a surgeon. He makes some kind of a gosh damned operation. Those figures – they will all die because they don't breathe. Older I grow, the more I like Rodin."

Again, he said: "The artist has to exaggerate. He has to de-form in order to make form move."

Me: "Aren't we going away from abstract to representative?"

Mark: "Yes. We need intimacy in art. We can't get so far away – it's no use." Then he carried on against what he called "impersonalism," his arch foe.

Me (I admit it was stupid): "Are you planning to do something *new*?" I remembered those things he painted in Seattle: one perfect dripping drop, for example. Or those old men, the tattered birds with ruined nests.

Mark: "Gosh. I'd certainly like to." He said we were lucky to own paintings of his done in the 1940s. Of our "Archaic Satire," all bang-bang, black calligraphy and verve, he smiled indulgently, and said it was "naughty." One of his and our favorites we owned was "The Night of the Prince," a flat Persian house, in its segments a Prince, his executioner with sword, and Bahá'í martyrs proudly going forth, their straight backs to the world, walking to meet their death for the oneness of mankind. Over all the darkened scene, a black raven brooding, a concentrate of the evil being done.

Now he was at work on a gorgeous mural for the Seattle Opera, a painting which was to have a back on it and be transported rolled up. It looked like music, and included some great egg or football forms that seemed to float out of the picture. I wondered if these were Pehr. Mark took Harold into the painting room and consulted him about the work in progress. The mural had great black bar-like lines toward the bottom. I wanted these to reach up higher and not all sink to the bottom, and was surprised to find he had already planned to make the change. There was much collage in the painting, bits of amusing newspaper, and whenever he wanted color, pieces done by Pehr.

He spoke of his Bahá'í work, and said he had his usual problem: how much time to allot to the Faith, how much to his art. He preferred, he said, to teach in other Swiss cities, and work here.

I decided he had chosen to live in Basel because it reminded him some of Seattle. "That strange virgin promise," he said of Seattle. "This thing (Europe) has been breathed into too long."

A day or two – Mark put us up overnight in a nearby hotel – and we had to leave them, and the old monastery office, and Basel. We had no way of knowing that we would never see him, not in this world, ever again. "There are no ends," Mark had said, meaning terminations. We left, continuing our long drive down to Peñiscola, and Mark got ready to receive his next visitor, Lord Snowdon.

Mark hated death. He hated funerals. He did not so much die as slowly withdraw from this world's life. A year or so ago

I had a letter from the famous potter, Bernard Leach, whose book, *Drawings Verse and Belief* is dedicated "to my friend Mark Tobey . . . who introduced me to the Bahá'í Faith." "I visited him," Bernard Leach wrote me, "and he was doing some of his best paintings, although not always certain which continent he was living on. His painting . . . had in it I think a world message redolent of his faith . . ."

When Mark was still young enough to talk about it, I happened to ask him about his future dying. His answer was: "I'm going to throw myself on the mercy of God."

V

Juliet Remembers Gibran

On Saturday, December 8, 1956, the Paris Herald reported that "Miss Julia [*sic*] H. Thompson, a portrait painter for nearly half a century who painted such notables as President Woodrow Wilson and Mrs Calvin Coolidge, died Tuesday." Some of us, then living as Bahá'í pioneers in Salzburg, Austria, learned in this way of Juliet's passing, at home in New York.

Juliet, a Virginian by birth, was related to Edward Fitzgerald, translator of *The Rubáiyát*. Her father, Ambrose White Thompson, was a close friend of Lincoln. Both a serious artist and a great beauty, Juliet was well known in Washington society and was listed in the Social Register, although, as she pointed out, as a junior.

For many years Juliet and Daisy Pumpelly Smythe, also an artist, shared a house in Greenwich Village, at 48 West 10th Street. They made their home a famous gathering place for people of many races and religions; and visits there, and fireside meetings, were almost continual. They especially welcomed members of the black race, often quoting 'Abdu'l-Bahá's words that unless America healed black-white tensions her streets would run with blood. Juliet's friend and companion, Helen James, a black woman, also shared the house. So close did Juliet feel to the black race that, shortly before her death, she asked that her funeral cortège be led through Harlem, and this was done.

Many guests stayed there at "48," some for days or weeks. At one time Dimitri Marianoff, the former son-in-law of Albert Einstein, was writing a Bahá'í book on the third floor, Juliet herself was revising her *I, Mary Magdalen* (a story inspired by 'Abdu'l-Bahá, Whom she visited, as told in her Diary, in the Holy Land, Switzerland, and New York City) on the floor below, while I was in the basement sitting room, finishing *Persia and the Victorians*.

Every room of the old house had been blessed by 'Abdu'l-Bahá, and Juliet said that He particularly approved of her studio-room. He said it was eclectic – part Eastern, part Western, and that He would like to build a similar one. In a corner of the downstairs living room, with a cord across it, stood the fragile antique arm chair in which He used to sit.

It was on April 6, 1943, in her studio-room, upstairs at the front of the house, that Juliet shared with me and a few other guests, these memories of Kahlil Gibran.

"He lived across the street from here," said Juliet Thompson, "at 51 West 10th. He was neither poor nor rich – in between. Worked on an Arab newspaper; free to paint and write. His health was all right in the early years. He was terribly sad in the later years, because of cancer. He died at forty-nine. He knew his life was ending too soon.

"His drawings were more beautiful than his paintings. These were very misty, lost things – mysterious and lost. Very poetic.

"A Syrian brought him to see me – can't even remember his name. Kahlil always said I was his first friend in New York. We became very, very great friends, and all of his books – *The Madman*, *The Forerunner*, *The Son of Man*, *The Prophet* – I heard in manuscript. He always gave me his books. I liked *The Prophet* best. I don't believe that there was any connection between 'Abdu'l-Bahá and *The Prophet*. But he told me that when he wrote *The Son of Man* he thought of 'Abdu'l-Bahá all through. He said that he was going to write another book with 'Abdu'l-Bahá as the center and all the contemporaries of 'Abdu'l-Bahá speaking. He died before he wrote it. He told me definitely that *The Son of Man* was influenced by 'Abdu'l-Bahá.

"He wrote his books in the studio across the street. Then he would call me up and say come over and hear a chapter.

"He was from an old Syrian family. His grandfather was

228

one of the Bishops. I think he always remained a Greek Christian.

"I've seen Armenians and Syrians kiss his hand and call him Master. It was very bad for Kahlil. He had hundreds of followers. He kept that place closed to all except his intimate friends and his work.

"He was in love with a friend of mine – but he just loved me, and I loved him – but it wasn't that kind of love. He just wasn't a lover. He wasn't that kind of a man.

"He had a high, delicate voice and an almost shyly modest manner, until he came out with something thundering. I don't know how to describe him except to say he was the spitting image of Charlie Chaplin. I used to tell him so. It made him frightfully mad.

"How Gibran got in touch with the Bahá'í Cause: I'll just frankly tell you the story, just as it was. I hastened to tell him; he listened. He got hold of some of the Arabic of Bahá'u'lláh. He said it was the most stupendous literature that ever was written, and that He even coined words. That there was no Arabic that even touched the Arabic of Bahá'u'lláh.

"And then Kahlil, 'The Master,' got a following. He told me that he belonged to the Illuminati in Persia. He would rise up and say, What do we need a Manifestation of God for? Each one of us can come into direct contact with God. I am in direct contact with God.★

"I wouldn't say anything. I'd just let him talk.

"He wore American business clothes. Had lots of black hair, wavy.

"Time passed. I told him the Master was coming. He asked me if I would request the Master to sit for him. The Master gave him one hour at 6:30 one morning. He made an outstanding head. It doesn't look like the Master – very faint likeness. Great power through the shoulders. A great radiance in the face. It's not a portrait of the Master, but it's the work of a great artist. I do consider him a great artist.[1]

"He was very modest and retiring in his personal life. He'd never met the Master before, and that began his friendship. He

★ The Bahá'í Faith teaches that the individual reaches God through acceptance of the Divine Intermediary.

simply adored the Master. He was with Him whenever he could be. He would come over here to this house (48 West 10th) to see the Master. In Boston, he was often with the Master. All that's sort of blurred because it's so long ago. He told me two stories that I thought priceless: One day when he was driving with the Master in Boston, 'Abdu'l-Bahá said: 'Why do they build their houses with flat roofs?' Kahlil didn't answer for a moment, and then the Master answered Himself: 'Because they themselves are domeless.' Another time he was with the Master when two women came in. They were women of fashion, and they asked trifling questions. One of them wanted to know whether she was going to be married again. The Master was pacing the floor. Drawing in His breath, expelling it, His eyes turning from side to side. When they left, 'Gilded dirt!' He said.

"The Master went away and Kahlil settled down into writing his books. But he often talked of Him, most sympathetically and most lovingly. But the only thing was, He couldn't accept an intermediary for himself. He wanted his direct contact.[2]

"Then one night, years afterward, the Master's motion picture was going to be shown at the Bahá'í Center . . . He sat beside me in the front row and he saw the Master come to life again for him in that picture. And he began to sob. We had asked him to speak a few words that night. When the time came for him to speak, he controlled himself and jumped up on the platform and then, my dear, still weeping before us all he said: 'I declare that 'Abdu'l-Bahá is the Manifestation of God for this day!' Of course he got it wrong – but . . .[3] He was weeping and he didn't say anything more. He got down and he sat beside me, and he kept on sobbing and sobbing and sobbing. Seeing the picture – it brought it all back. He took my two hands and said, 'You have opened for me a door tonight.' Then he fled the hall.

"I never heard anything about it again. He never referred to it again.

"Poor Kahlil! The end isn't so good. I was away. When I came back he was very sick. He asked me if I wouldn't come every day to see him. He was in bed. These were his last days.

'I want to give you all I can while I can.' He would pour out the story of his life. So much of it has evaporated.

"He told me: 'When snow begins to fall it always wakes me up. One time at three in the morning I decided I'd like to go out and walk in the snow and get my thoughts together. So I went up to Central Park. I was walking with a little notebook in my hand. I was finishing *The Earth Gods* (an early book but his last). I was writing in my notebook in the snow. A big policeman came along.'

" 'Whatcha doin'?'

" 'Writing.'

" 'Writing? Are you an Englishman?'

" 'No.'

" 'Are you a Frenchman?'

" 'No.'

" 'What are you?'

" 'A Syrian.'

" 'Oh. Know anything about that Syrian – think his name is Kayleel Guibran – fellow who writes books?'

" 'I think so.'

" 'Well, since he came into the life of our home there's never been any peace in it. I used to have a good wife. Now she don't do nuthin all day long but read that Kayleel Guibran . . .'

"Those last days he just wept and wept and wept. His head on my shoulder. He never said he was dying. He never said a word. Except that one thing: 'I want to give you all I can while I can. So come every day.' His followers stayed with him. He's quite a cult. Buried in Boston.

"Large, tragic brown eyes. The eye was very important in his face. His forehead was broad – very high – very broad, and he had almost a shock of black hair. Short, slender, five foot two or three. Very sensitive mouth – drooped a little at the corners. Very sad man who had a reason for it. Little black moustache, like Charlie Chaplin."

"Love – Whatever That Is . . ."

The queer thing is that anybody who ever met D. H. Lawrence or even heard about him wants to write it all down. People who so much as shook hands with him seem to have left a memoir. We ourselves, who never even saw him, went to Taos on his account; he was long gone, we had no thought of meeting anyone there who knew him, we simply wanted to be where he had been.

Whatever you may think of "Lady Loverley's Chatter" – and the truth is we doubt if Lawrence's novels are much read any more; surely he will live for his letters and stories, for books like *Mornings in Mexico* and that poem to his dead mother – he touched off such an explosion of biographies and personal accounts, of tributes, analyses, criticisms, complaints, law suits, viewings with alarm, jottings, footnotes, and, no doubt, initials on trees and also tattoos, that after a while he becomes a sort of relative and as you go through life, busy with your own problems, you find yourself thinking: "I wonder why Lawrence . . . ?" What would Lawrence . . . ?" "Did Lawrence and Frieda . . . ?" And you recall with a sense of accomplishment an ever-lengthening, sort of Madame Tussaud's gallery of people that are on record as having had some connection with the Lawrence story: Baronin von Richthofen. Lawrence *père*, coal miner. Katherine Mansfield. Mabel Dodge Luhan (in turquoise blue, her Indian husband Tony beside her, and behind, Taos Pueblo). The Honorable Dorothy Brett. Susan. Witter Bynner. The Spoodle. Two Danes. John Middleton Murry. Catherine Carswell. Lady Cynthia Asquith. Richard Aldington. And to top all, those majestic Edwardian syllables: Garsington, Lady Ottoline Morrell.

Crazy or not, that is why we found ourselves one cold day in May, bowling along the far reaches of Cornwall on the bus from St Ives. British bus schedules being as easy for laymen to decipher as the Dead Sea Scrolls, we sat there in triumph to have caught the vehicle at all. The day was gray and misty, and we looked out on outcroppings of bare rock, and wide fields of bluebells; also ferns, stone walls, and butterflies. The bus was bound for Zennor, but when we reached the place which we thought would be nearest to Higher Tregerthen, we tried to get off. The conductor warned us against this, however.

"He's one of the ones who won't stop," he confided, of the rigid back up ahead, behind glass at the right side of the bus. "You can ring if you like – won't do you any good. He's regimental, he is."

So we did not ring, and sat on till the proper stop at the Tinner's Arms in Zennor, which is a small cluster around a church. Then we walked back over the moor-like fields to the scattered stone houses where the Lawrences once lived. The fog curtain was lifting off the sea, and a pale sun shone. It was on these very paths, we reminisced, that Frieda used to walk with Katherine Mansfield. It was here that Katherine, hating the Cornish wind, would stamp her foot at it.

Of all the people of that day, only Stanley Hocking, the younger of the two farmer brothers, was left.

"I'd then become eighteen," Stanley told us. He had received us in the neat, dark kitchen of Tregerthen Farm, with a fresh loaf of white bread on the table and the only functioning Cornish range we ever saw. It was warm in there. A haven. He looked for a letter or card from Lawrence to show us.

"I lost one or two of these letters," he said, half to himself. "I don't know if . . ."

We gathered that some visitor had made off with a memento.

"Quite a nice little inoffensive man Lawrence was," Stanley went on.

From out of his papers, he showed us a post card in Lawrence's beautiful hand. It said something about "Italy spoilt by war." It was formally polite and referred to Frieda as "Mrs Lawrence."

He then found and read us a letter, as friendly and polite as the card, from Lawrence soon after leaving Cornwall. It was carefully dated from Berkshire. Lawrence was very well, Frieda had pleurisy, the Army had listed him as number three, Berkshire was not so bare as Cornwall.

"He'd come in here. Had a red beard. Kind of tall and thin. You couldn't say he was suffering from TB – he was delicate."

"Did he look like a fox?"

"I dunno. We got so used to him we never noticed. I'd become eighteen, and Lawrence was learning me French. He'd knock and say (Stanley's voice took on a rising tone), 'I'm coming in.' If, maybe, we were frying potatoes, he'd take some.

"They, he and Frieda, they got suspected of being spies, signalling and that. You look at our big expanse of sea. In '17, there were three ships out there, all sinking at once. The whole hills were shaking some days. Bombs dropping. We saw more activity in the 1917 war than we did in this war."

Stanley Hocking was a large man with a red face and big boots. He spoke in a high, pleasant voice. We were outdoors sitting on a stone by then. "It must be his stone for telling tourists about D. H. Lawrence," I thought, because his side had a bit of carpet on it. We knew he'd had quite a spate of visitors recently because of the Lawrence commemorative exhibition at the University of Nottingham.

Lawrence and his German Frieda had, in the end, been ousted from the county, and as Frieda recorded later on, "When we were turned out of Cornwall, something changed in Lawrence forever."

"Farmers rent in England," Stanley went on. "The Hocking family have rented here for three hundred years. We've paid for it!" His face was purple-veined and stubbled. He had round, occasionally gleeful brown eyes. He would look away as he talked, his head swivelling, then he would swing round at you, and steadying his gaze he would home in at you like a gun. He had, he told us, been on the BBC with his Lawrence account, and of course he must have read the various Cornwall memoirs, the same as we.

"The police came, and army officers. Lawrence had to go for inspection. He was shoved down into grade three; he

234

turned parson," Stanley added with glee. ("It is the annulling of all one stands for, this militarism," Lawrence had written from Higher Tregerthen; "the nipping of the very germ of one's being.") "I went up in October, 1918. I've got a gammy leg."

Their cottage – Tregerthen* Cottage, accent on the *garth* – a short walk from Stanley's, had cost the Lawrences five pounds a year. "As usual," wrote Frieda, "we made it out of a granite hole into a livable place." The tenants let us see into it later that day. It was the customary thick-walled fisherman's little house, dark, with a crude fireplace, and with the Lawrences' decor and color-scheme gone we found, in a hasty and polite glance, little there to remember him by. In St Ives they had picked up furniture, good old pieces the fishermen were selling for nothing, to exchange for hideous modern. He got a bedstead for a shilling.

"You see, we must live somewhere," Lawrence had explained of this refuge, "and it is so free and beautiful, and it will cost so very little."

"He was in North Cornwall," Stanley went on, "when he heard about Zennor from friends. He and Frieda walked over here from Zennor. They stayed at the Tinner's Arms.

"We liked him as a person. Nothing to dislike about him. Always ready to help you. But he was terrible poor. They could scarcely pay for a pint of milk, tell you the truth – but we didn't bother."

We hoped Stanley would tell us about the time Lawrence broke the plate over Frieda's head but he said, "That's a little too personal."

He told us a woman who had been in love with Lawrence took their cottage here in after-years. "There had been talk about them in Nottingham," he said.

"What was she like?" I asked fearfully.

"Big, buxom lady. She said Frieda's book is all lies. She said her Bert (the D.H. stands for David Herbert) was always with her."

Stanley had on blue jeans and a dark green felt hat. He

---

* Spelled *gerth*, pronounced *garth*.

smoked a cigarette, shielding its burning end in his palm. His grayish work jacket had once been blue. With it he wore a blue serge vest, and a gold watch-chain anchored on a button and crossing to his vest pocket. Also a thick cotton shirt, brown-striped and frayed. His hat, full of character, was much dented, and its rolled-up, battered brim was matted in front with short hairs, apparently from leaning his head against the cows' flanks when he milked.

"My elder brother – he's dead now – was in more contact with him," Stanley said. "Lawrence was one of us. Worked in the fields with my brother. He'd come to help with the hay-fields and the harvest. Seemed delighted to. He showed us the Midland method of tying a sheaf of corn. I prefer the Cornish method.

"I am Arthur," Stanley added, "the boy in *Kangaroo*. My brother was William Henry. There was an old song then. It went:

> William Henry Hawkins,
> Are you coming back to me?
> Ever since last Tuesday
> You've been out upon the spree.

Frieda, she used to sing that to my brother. Frieda didn't pronounce her r's right. She would sing,

> Woe, woe, woe your boat
> Gently down the stream . . .

She was a lovely looking woman. Very good looking.

"They had lots of company. Thomas Hardy. Aldous Huxley. Lawrence would tell us afterward." A swallow flicked past us.

"And Mrs Murry (Katherine Mansfield) had consumption of the lungs and couldn't go out of the house. I remember one time Lawrence told us, 'Murry is flourishing, which isn't so – something – considering the condition of his wife.' Lawrence was sore because Murry was not suffering. Lawrence spoke about Clemenceau and Lloyd George and something about the Slough of Despond in there but I can't remember what.

"There were German submarines active off that coast," Stanley continued.

We looked across the fields at the peaceful water.

"One of them had been hunted by destroyers and seaplanes. They exploded depth charges. Frieda said: 'What an awful thing war is. In that submarine may be some of the boys I went to school with.' Anyway, the sub was destroyed. Patches of oil on the sea for days."

We had imposed on Stanley's hospitality too long. He had been good to us – total strangers, tourists – because we shared a common bond. He, the only one left. Only a boy in that long ago, having his own problems and not knowing that those everyday comings and goings, that haying and harvesting, would ever be of moment or have to be recalled again. It was time to leave now, and go along the paths to the Tinner's Arms.

"They were given three days to get out," Stanley concluded. "Here about a year and a half." And then he added wistfully: "Always said he'd come back."

Leaving the sea for the foothills of the Maritime Alps, we took the bus from Nice to Vence. The driver stopped and let us get off where we wanted, in the cold medieval streets. Those age-old mountain towns seem to have been built with one basic idea in mind: protection. Their narrow lanes are dank, except briefly at noon. The sun must have been repugnant to people then. Here they still lived trapped in darkness and cold, in all the surrounding golden light.

We pushed through the bead curtain of a small bakery and bought the regional delicacy, a soft, perforated flat loaf of bread called *fougassette*. In France, we did not find it helpful to ask questions without buying something in return.

The woman at the bakery told us the cemetery was two alleys below. We walked down, getting out in the open, and came to the cemetery gate. Living in a tiny house just inside the gate was the concierge.

"Where is the grave of the English writer, Lawrence?" I asked.

"He isn't here any more," she said. "There is nothing of him here."

"Where have they taken him?"

"To the United States."

"Where in the United States?"

That stopped her. She had thought of the United States as all in one piece, a single point, like Vence.

"Well, show us where he was," I said.

She led us quite a way through the cemetery, to the right and down steps and to the right again. She was a wide, square, self-assured woman with a gray knitted cap, gray hair, a gray knitted sweater, a blue-and-white checked apron covering her gray skirt, also gray knitted stockings and dark blue shoes with crepe soles. Her walk showed she had taken on some of the importance of the dead man who was no longer here.

A wall blocked us. Ahead and above us were the bare mountains. I looked around and saw the tall black cypresses climbing downhill in the sun. In the silence and the pebble-scrunching of our feet I could hear roosters crowing. Miles off to our left, away down at the edge of the plain, was the plumy blue sea.

"It was here," she said. "There is nothing now."

And there was nothing, only a depression at the foot of the wall, the flat earth faintly indented where the hole had been, and sparse, irregular grass springing up. Some gray boards clumsily nailed into the shape of a cross stood against the wall.

"Was that here then?" I asked.

"No. We just set it on the empty place so they won't throw rubbish here. They took him and his phoenix and everything." She meant the phoenix that a peasant who became his friend had carved for him on a stone.

"When was it?" I asked.

"Before I came. In '36 it was," she hazarded. ('35, we found out later.)

The shadows of bars fell across the plot. Next to it, on the west, was a rusty, weed-covered enclosure, barred in. Two white hearts, something like policemen's shields, identified the grave: "Ici repose Ramy Ludovic né en 1865 décédé le 6 oct. 1922. Priez pour lui." Metal bands at the foot of a small metal crucifix, all awry and unpleasant, read: "À mon époux et père." They had buried Lawrence beside another foreigner, for company, and out of the universal human wish to match things up. They had brought him up to this town that is flattened against the sealed mountains – this curiously terminal place, away from the escape offered by the sea, and buried him with his back to the wall.

They had been in Bandol and Frieda had thought: "Now I can do no more for Lawrence, only the sun and the sea and the stars and the moon at night, that's his portion now . . ." Then a doctor sent them up here to the foothills, first to a nursing home, the Villa Ad Astra, where there was too much coughing; then they rented another villa, so far as he was concerned just overnight. For those who collect coincidences, this name Ad Astra is as odd in the Lawrence context as the name of the ship that put in at St Helena while Napoleon was dying: she was the *Waterloo*.

From there he had written a postscript to one of his last letters: "This place no good."

"I didn't know they had moved him," I said.

"They tell me it is on the books," she answered, leaving me at a disadvantage. Hoping to score I said, "His wife has remarried."

"I know it," she said. "They have told me. Many come to see this place."

There were thousands of flowers elsewhere in the cemetery, fading over from All Saints' Day. In fact the cemetery looked in the main like a ghostly flower market or china bazaar. On all the better slabs were rotting flowers: mauve chrysanthemums with stringy petals, pink carnations turned yellow, brown roses, dried up daisies. On a spring day in 1912, Lawrence was picking daisies and floating them on a brook to amuse her little daughters, when Frieda suddenly loved him: enough to leave her professor husband, home and three children for him, and go away.

The flowers were stuck in flowered vases, in pots, in pitchers. Photographs peered from tall headstones. Here and there a sculpted nude reclined in mourning posture. We saw rude, gray metal crucifixes and glass-bead coronals, and

239

ceramic, unconvincing pink roses sitting on slabs. A ceramic wreath of pink roses and black leaves bore the word "Regrets." The French, whose taste – sense of balance, moderation – is often impeccable elsewhere, go unhinged in a cemetery. Just as they are in love with love, they are in love with death and their passion turns them humorless and carries them beyond the bounds. Come to think of it, they overdo things in the bathroom too. Result, those two perennials of French society, the bidet and the ceramic rose.

"Do they bring him flowers?" I asked stupidly.

"They *can't* bring him flowers," the concierge told me. "He isn't here any more."

We gave her some money and asked if it was all right to sit a while. She at once offered us the hospitality of the whole graveyard. After she had scrunched squarely away we sat on a tomb in the cypress shadows and ate our *fougassette*. The bread was pleasant and sweet. H thought it tasted like grapes, I said like orange water.

I thought of Frieda coming down the steps here that March day ("Then we buried him, very simply, like a bird we put him away . . ."), coming down here with her husband like all widows, then going back without him.

"If I die," he told her once, "nothing has mattered but you, nothing at all."

I thought of Lawrence being driven up to Vence all the winding way from the sea; passing details of the road which we, on the bus, would review in a few minutes, but which he, when he journeyed up, was not to pass again. For him it was a one-way road, here to Vence.

I asked myself what the man had that made people come all this way to see an empty hole that his corpse had once been in. Perhaps the best explanation is that noted down by one of the women who loved him: she said he enhanced everything.

And Frieda, to give her the last word, has written: "I only know that I felt the wonder of him always."

VI

Poggio at the Baths

When a flock of chaffinches flew over the city of Constance, making a cloud one mile long and half a mile wide, the citizens said it was a happy omen. They told each other, as they took cover, that a multitude of visitors would soon, undoubtedly, be coming to their peaceful German town, leaving plenty of *gulden* behind.

Sure enough, the very next autumn, 1414, crowds did assemble here from all over Europe and even beyond. Attending the sixteenth Ecumenical Council of the Catholic Church, clerics and laymen came together to heal the Great Schism of the West. Their gathering was one of the most brilliant ever held in the western world. Even the Holy Roman Emperor, Sigismund, was here, with Empress Barbara, his wife. Princes of the Church and of the laity were present, archbishops and leaders of Catholic orders by the dozens, bishops by the hundreds, doctors of theology by the thousand. The main business of the Council was to remove the tiara from three rival heads and place it on a single fourth. Another vital objective was to stamp out heresy; and this in particular quickened pulses because it was obvious that somebody at this Council would have to be publicly burned to death.

One of the remembered men of Constance was the "Florentine Voltaire," Giovanni Francesco Poggio Bracciolini. He was born in 1380, five years after Boccaccio died. For fifty years he held the post of Apostolic Secretary. He wrote many things that were "long, laborious and useful," but the world being what it is, he is generally thought of in connection with his Joke Book or *Facetiae*.

Papal secretaries were officers of the Pontiff's court who

composed, in Latin, all the correspondence, pastoral letters and other documents issued by the Pope. Higher than these men was the Pope's private secretary, an office which Poggio first held under John XXIII – that is, John XXIII the First. Neither job was well-paid and Poggio often resorted to the medieval equivalent of moonlighting. Italy was in its usual ferment then; there were internecine wars, armed bandits roaming and ravaging the country, the Bubonic Plague, the Great Schism, but Poggio lived, though not rich, still happy and secure above it all, while eight Popes willed him, one to another.

He studied Greek with Emmanuel Chrysoloras in Florence, for the Italian Renaissance was getting under way. Emmanuel had come from Constantinople and finally settled in Florence in 1397, and here for an annual stipend of 150 florins he taught Greek to anyone, free. Poggio studied Hebrew as well. At twenty-two he went to Rome to seek his fortune, and Boniface IX, the Roman Pontiff, was his first Pope. Later he transferred to Alexander V, who was elected Pope at Pisa. After that he went to work for Alexander's successor, John XXIII. When John XXIII, forced by Sigismund, convoked the Council of Constance and arrived at that city on October 28, 1414, Poggio was one of his suite. And when John XXIII was removed by the Council, Poggio stayed on.

There was always something doing at this Ecumenical Council. Poggio's Greek teacher, Chrysoloras, died here, and it was Poggio who pronounced his funeral oration. With his own eyes, Poggio saw Huss – and later, Huss's disciple, Jerome of Prague – burned alive. Poggio himself, though a cleric, was not interested in religion, but his letter to a friend, Leonardo Aretino, on Jerome's way of dying is history.

Parts of the letter, in summary here, cited words of protest from the victimized Jerome: "What an injustice is this, that after being kept in the strictest confinement for three hundred and forty days, in dirt, squalor, and filth, in fetters, with the lack of everything, while you were listening to my calumniators, you will not hear me for a single hour . . . You have made up your minds to sentence me . . . The lights of the world, the most learned men of the earth, are said to be here, but . . . I am the creature whose life is at stake . . . "

After the charges were read, Poggio continued, Jerome rose, spread out his hands, and with a piteous voice called out: "Where shall I turn me now, conscript Fathers? Whose help shall I implore?"

Examined by the inquisitors as to his views on the Eucharist, he even jested, wrote Poggio. "Being asked what he held as to the Sacrament, he answered that before consecration there was bread, but that after consecration there remained only the true body of Christ, and no one but a baker would think there was bread."

Jerome even dared to praise his mentor, the Bohemian reformer Huss, then (by the Council), freshly burned. He shouted his interrupters down, he talked himself into the fire. At the stake, when they tried to build up the wood behind him, where he could not see, Jerome cried out, "Come, light the fire in front. Had I feared it, I would not be here now." And the crowd laughed and applauded as he went up in flames.

Jerome, said Poggio – and it was his highest accolade – was comparable to the ancients of Greece and Rome.

As for Leonardo, he wrote back, terrified, warning Poggio against such sentiments, for there was guilt by association, and they were a danger to all. Leonardo was right: Constance was hardly a mild Council, and it had tasted blood.

After a while, as the Council wore on, Poggio decided to rummage through the libraries of neighboring monasteries, to look for books. He set out when spring came, despite bad roads and weather. He discovered a large number of classical manuscripts, long sought after. The famous Abbey of St Gall provided an especially rich yield, and here, in addition to those in the library, quantities of books were found stored in a tower, among them works by Valerius Flaccus the Paduan, Asconius Pedianus the Roman grammarian, and Lactantius, the "Christian Cicero." Indignantly, Poggio reported that the manuscripts were buried "in dark, damp hideaways in the depths of a tower where you would not even . . . have wished to throw criminals sentenced to death." Completely indifferent, the Abbott of St Gall allowed Poggio and his friends to carry off all the manuscripts they wanted. They wanted two full carriages worth. The monks of Cluny, at Langres, let Poggio have a discourse of Cicero for Coecina. From that time on, throughout his life, Poggio indulged himself in the pleasures of book hunting at whatever cost to his health and funds, contributing much to the revival of learning.

Poggio never did care for monks. He doubtless would have liked them had it not been for what he considered their ignorance, coarseness, lack of appreciation for antiquity, avariciousness and immorality. The monks on the other hand were not particularly attracted to Poggio, because of his paganism and, too, his loose morals. It was a day when most people censured one another for turpitude.

In the summer of 1415, like others among the great who attended the Council, Poggio betook himself a short distance out of Constance to the baths at Baden. Fortunately for posterity, he wrote his friend Niccolo a graphic account of the thermal goings-on. His letter tells how the town, encircled by mountains, had its watering place, its inns and tourists. How each house was equipped with its own baths, while there were also two public establishments for commoners. The people bathed virtually naked, says Poggio, the men separated from the women and children "by a light and inoffensive partition." It all reminded him of the Floral Games.

In the more elegant private establishments the partitions had numerous openings at which men and women could and did drink together and exchange caresses. Most of the men wore short drawers, while the women wore a linen chemise open on each side down to the legs and covering neither neck nor breast, arms nor shoulders. For the convenience of picknickers, there were floating tables in the pool.

As he watched from a walk above, Poggio noticed that nobody's husband seemed to object to the proceedings. Three or four times a day the people used the baths, drank, and danced in a band, getting in and out of the water. There were also symphonies of horns and citharas. The women solicited rewards from the male spectators above, and the men threw down coins to the prettiest ones, who held up their hands to catch them, or coyly, the edge of their chemise. They fought for the coins in the water, displaying, as the battle raged, their various charms. The men also threw down crowns of flowers which the women put on in the water.

The only thing that kept Poggio at his observation post instead of down in the pool was, oddly enough, the language barrier. As is often the case with men, he could not adjust to an unknown tongue: "Indeed, it seemed ridiculous to me for an Italian, not speaking their language, to remain in the water in the midst of the ladies, dumb and as if he had lost his tongue, spending his time solely in consuming drinks and sherbets." More enterprising, two of Poggio's friends plunged in with an interpreter, ate, drank and caressed the ladies "through the interpreter, meanwhile frequently fanning themselves with their fans."

Out of town along the river, Poggio reported that there was a vast meadow under the shade trees where people would sing, dance and play tennis. They also played a kind of tag: men and women would alternately toss back and forth to each other a ball full of bells; whoever caught the ball was It, whereupon everyone ran after him and he, after preliminary feints, would throw it on to someone else.

Poggio, a capable judge, maintained that the waters of Baden were excellent for sterility. He also deplored the fact that many who visited the Baths had nothing wrong with them – they had only come for a good time. Some women were covered, he said, with their entire fortune in gold cloth or silver, constellated with jewels and looking as if they were going to a wedding instead of a bath. In a thousand people, there was never any discord, jealousy, or quarreling, not even a murmur. How different it is with us in Italy, mused Poggio, we who think evil of everything, and instead of being content – like these people – in order to make a fortune upset heaven and earth.

He added: "One finds here Virgins of Vesta too, or rather of Flora, and abbots, monks, friars and priests behaving with far less decorum than the rest, and as they bathe in the midst of the women, with their hair also adorned with silk ribbons, they seem to have stripped off every religious characteristic."

The Council ground on. In its efforts to stamp out heresy, Constance not only burned Huss and Jerome, but punished the English reformer, John Wycliffe, who had died thirty years before. (Wycliffe is the one that posterity would call the First Protestant.) Since little, in the physical sense, remained of him by now, he was condemned to have his bones dug up and burned, provided that this could be done without disturbing good Christian bones alongside him. The Council also managed to get rid of two Popes, but the third one, he of Avignon, refused to go away and disappear. He and the Popes of the Avignon line continued to reign on. Meanwhile the Council elected Martin V as Pontiff.

When the Council closed on April 22, 1418, Poggio remained in the city until May 16. Because of troubles in Italy's Papal States, Martin could not go back to Rome, and Poggio accompanied him on various peregrinations which finally led to Milan and Mantua. After an impulsive visit to England, where he was friendless, bookless, and without funds, Poggio went back to Italy, becoming Pope Martin's secretary toward the end of 1420.

Prior to Martin's time, Poggio and his friends had been wont to foregather in a secluded room at the Papal Court. They called this room the Lie Factory (*Bugiale*) and here they would tell one another the Latin pleasantries which Poggio afterward collected in his Joke Book. "We collected news of the day," Poggio wrote, "and conversed on various subjects, mostly with a view to relaxation, but sometimes also with serious intent. Nobody was spared, and whatever met with our disapprobation was freely censured. Oftentimes the Pope himself was the first subject-matter of our criticism. Many people attended our parties, lest they should themselves be the objects of our first chapter. Foremost among the relaters were Razello . . . Antonio Lusco . . . and the Roman Cincio . . . I have also added some good things of my own. Now that those boon companions have departed this life, the Bugiale has come to an end. Whether men or the times are to be held responsible, it is a fact that genial talk and merry confabulation have gone out of fashion."

Humor is seldom viable. Like charm, perfume and style, its substance is soon lost, and few will laugh today at Poggio's Joke Book as it now stands, although it might provide occasion for *aggiornamento*. Among the non-pornographic anecdotes in the *Facetiae* is Poggio's tale of the gallant Cardinal. Urging the soldiers into battle, the Cardinal exhorts them not to fear death. Should they fall, he assures them, they will sup with God. At this, the men call upon him to join them in the fray. "Thank you," is the Cardinal's reply, "but I have just eaten my fill."

Sometimes as they stood outside the Papal Palace, discussing literary affairs, Poggio and his cronies would be joined by the youthful Thomas Parentucelli, secretary to one of the Cardinals. Thomas would trot up on his mule, accompanied by two servants carrying the books that he had inevitably purchased along the way. The son of a village doctor from Sazano, young, poor and plebeian, this book-lover subsequently, in 1447, became Pope Nicholas V. He then filled his court with humanists, and modelled everything on antiquity and paganism. He founded the Vatican Library, and incidentally distributed largesse to Poggio.

Later on, Poggio was caught by a band of roving soldiers, whereupon he, as widely known for thrift as for scarcity of funds, had the pain of buying himself loose. He was next in Florence, carrying on a fierce paper war with the young Francesco Filelfo, who had prudently fled the city when his enemy, Cosimo de' Medici returned to power. (Of Cosimo, Filelfo wrote: "Cosimo uses dagger and poison against me; I use my mind and my pen against him. I do not want Cosimo's friendship, and I despise his enmity.") A clean sample of Poggio's invective, addressed to Filelfo, is as follows: "If a few men still frequent your house and evince respect for you, it can only be those who afterward, in exchange for your insufferable ravings, compensate themselves with your wife . . ." After a good many of these interchanges over a period of years, the two became fast friends.

In 1436 Poggio bought a country house in Tuscany in the Arno region and the Magistrates of Florence exempted him and his numerous progeny from paying taxes. He was now fifty-five, installed in a beautiful retreat furnished with antique statuary and other works of art, and he felt the time had come to do something about his mistress, Luccia, and their fourteen natural children. True, when the Cardinal of Sant' Angelo reproached him for his way of life – Luccia, all the offspring – Poggio simply replied: "I have children . . . I have had them by a concubine, as has been the way of ecclesiastics since the world began."

Finally, however, he decided to regularize everything. In December, 1435, he married Vaggia de Buondelmonte, who was not only eighteen but brought a dowry of 600 florins. We hear no more of Luccia, the married woman with whom he had lived thirty years and by whom he had produced the fourteen children. As with Petrarch's offspring before him, Poggio's had been legitimized by the Pope. There were only four of them left when he separated from Luccia, but a new family of six soon grew up around him. Unfortunately for the moralists, Poggio's marriage was happy, although one biographer claims that his death at seventy-nine was premature, and brought on by Vaggia's excessive affection.

Should an Old Man Get Married? addressed to Cosimo de' Medici, is one of Poggio's famous pieces and a theme obviously close to his heart. The gist of it is that an old man should preferably marry a young virgin. Like soft wax, says Poggio, the young virgin will take on the imprint of his character and wishes. She will naturally "disdain the seduction of voluptuous pleasures which she knows nothing about," and will be all prudence, moderation, wise counsel and fertility. Poggio's arguments in favor of old bridegrooms are hard to answer: an old man's record is known, while a young man is an uncertain quantity. The young are exposed to worse health hazards than the old. Anyone who has managed to reach fifty knows how to live a long time and is tough and viable; the old man has as it were a "certificate of longevity." No one can make pronouncements as to how long he will live, a young man may die, an old man may well be around long enough to see his children grow up. But even if he dies beforehand, he will enjoy the best part of his children, their childhood, before they get old enough to rebel and turn against their parents. An old father is a better teacher for his children; in such a household, comments the author of the *Facetiae*, children "don't even know, having never had an example of it in the home, what is a shameful act, an indecent word." How faithful are old men, rapturously declares Poggio. Besides, it cheers them up to take a young bride. As to the argument that an old man is not particularly assiduous as a husband, one learns from the example set by animals that the actual begetting of offspring is all that is required, and in any event the ancient must teach his bride continence. Poggio's thesis is solidly predicated on the belief that the young woman will be like soft wax. It is better, he thoughtfully adds, for the old man not to arouse nostalgia by marrying a widow.

On April 24, 1453, Poggio was made Chancellor of the Florentine Republic, and left the Papal Court after fifty years of service, Nicholas V permitting him to retain the honorary title of Apostolic Secretary. Among his latest activities was the waging of a literary war with the philologist and critic, Laurentius Valla (the same who exposed the "Donation of Constantine" as a forgery), which became so vicious that the polemicist Filelfo, of all people, stepped in as a mediator, addressing the contestants a lengthy epistle on the advantages of moderation.

Poggio died October 30, 1459 while working on a Latin history of Florence, which his son Giacomo Bracciolini subsequently completed and translated into Italian.

The author of the *Facetiae* was buried with much solemnity on November 2 in Florence's Church of the Holy Cross. His grateful fellow-citizens put up a statue to him on the façade of the Church of Santa Maria del Fiore, and by an accident which he would have appreciated, in the course of structural changes the statue was transferred elsewhere in the church and Poggio became part of a group of the Twelve Apostles.

Saint and Friar

Vincent Ferrer and Thomas Conecte were early-day preachers in what was already a time-honored tradition. For their respective attempts to improve medieval conduct, one is revered as a saint, the other was burned at the stake in Rome by order of the papal authorities. This paradox is all the greater because the sainted evangelist spent several decades working against the popes of Rome, he being a supporter of the popes of Avignon. This was during the Great Schism of the West – that forty-year split in the Church when the occidental Christian world was divided first between two rival lines of popes, and later among three.

When still in his teens, Vincent developed a reputation for conversions and miracle-working. He was a Dominican, born in Valencia, Spain, in 1352, and his record says he piled up miracles by the tens of thousands: 58,400 public miracles, to be exact, or a minimum of eight per day for twenty years. To these should be added all the unlisted others which came to him as naturally as breathing. He had miracle apprentices to handle the extra ones, and it was said to be a miracle when he was not performing a miracle.

This man who spent most of his life exhorting people to be good, and especially to be penitent, himself set the example of abstinence and simplicity. Though he was actually a complicated individual, a politician as well as a preacher, no one would have guessed this as he traveled the dusty roads. He went about in white wool with black cloak and cowl. When the cowl was back you saw a high forehead above the snapping black eyes, light hair, a tonsure, pale cheeks. Thickset as he got to middle age, he could be seen on many a narrow path bouncing along on a small donkey, seated well toward the back in the Moorish fashion. From the rear you saw only the donkey's hind legs and its tasseled tail, above it the bulky, wool-swathed evangelist. By his appearance he might have been taken for any poor friar, but the Chancellor of the University of Paris saw him otherwise. "You are the Angel of the Apocalypse," he told Vincent in a letter.

As the future saint travelled about – from Spain to Brittany, in Italy, in southern France – he gathered followers, and eventually these formed a company of flagellants – self-whippers – who went with him from place to place, often several hundred strong. They were made up of both men and women, clothed in white and black like their leader. They slept in the open, on the ground, and ate what was offered them along the way, for they were not allowed to beg.

When Vincent was about to preach he would lead a procession of flagellants through the crowds lining the way to the church. They came singing a hymn that he had composed, a hymn to God's mercy. Their faces were veiled, their backs bare, ready for the scourge. At the church steps they fell silent, the last words, "Lord God, mercy . . . mercy . . . mercy . . ." dying away in the still air. They knelt and took a firm grip on their scourges. Then the rhythmic whipping began, rising in force until it sounded like a heavy fall of rain.

Sometimes the crowds would do as they saw done. When Vincent preached at Toulouse in 1415, there were booths along his way, selling hair shirts and disciplines, and the streets were soon covered with a red slime.

The saint's preaching included that always popular, equally futile, damnation of women's cosmetics. He told of hearing in confession that this one painted her face, or that one dyed her hair – because of a young husband. He asked the individual women in the crowd, "Are you bald, that you must hang blond curls over your temples? If you are dark, doesn't your husband already know this? Aren't you really trying to entrap another man? . . . You don't come out of the house all dressed in finery to please your husband. Oh no, it's not for him, poor fellow . . ." Surprisingly, he also seemed to disapprove of too much clothing. He criticized the amount of cloth that went into a fashionable woman's dress; enough for four dresses, he complained.

In spite of Vincent's bitter condemnation of beauty aids, he must have recognized the need for a woman to be beautiful. Encountering one whose husband regularly flogged her because she was so ugly, the saint with a touch turned her into the belle of Valencia, so that it became proverbial there to say of an ugly woman, "What she needs is the hand of Saint Vincent."

Among his miracles was that once, with a few drops of holy water, he saved the vines of Piedmont from a tempest. Holy water of course was even then old as the hills; ritual purification before entering a sacred place could be read of in Numbers 19, while the Greeks and Romans had placed lustral water in a vessel at the temple door, so that those entering might symbolically cleanse themselves by dipping in their fingers and sprinkling their clothes.

All who flocked to hear him – Italians, Germans, English, Portuguese and the like – could miraculously understand his Spanish tongue, and those on the outer fringes of the crowd of maybe ten thousand could hear him best. All were, on occasion, disconcerted to see him sprout wings in mid-sermon and temporarily float away. In Pamplona he was once directed to interrupt his speech and was guided, the audience following, to a mansion from which issued two voices in "licentious conversation." Operating through the door, Saint Vincent turned their owners into statues; marble ones. Also in Pamplona, at a prostitute's deathbed, the saint obtained a full pardon for the unfortunate – a letter from Heaven written in gold; there was no question as to its being authentic – it was signed by the Trinity. In Morella he resurrected a baby, not only dead but already in part cooked to a turn by its cannibal mother, and as a modern writer on this event assures us by way of proof, the house is still there.

Another miracle out of so many was the inducing of a husband to stay at home. "Have a cup of water handy," Saint Vincent directed the wife, "and when your husband comes in, take a mouthful and hold it in your mouth without swallowing."

Even more noteworthy was the time when Vincent had promised his superior to stop performing miracles and a builder fell off a scaffold. "Wait!" he cried to the hurtling workman. "Wait till I ask permission!" The builder, duly arrested in mid-hurtle, waited. Vincent ran for permission and rescued him by remote control.

Throughout the phenomenal accounts of miraculous and multiple conversions of Muslims, heretics and Jews (including the Chief Rabbi of Valladolid), one thing we can be sure of: Saint Vincent was a personality, a healer, doubtless a psychic – he read minds, and though far away he knew at once of his parents' death – and had the magnetism to attract the people of his times.

Upon the saint's death in 1419 there was unseemly scuffling between the Dominicans and the Franciscans over the body. Friars and lay clergy fought on the stairs and out into the street. Nor did the struggle over Vincent end with his burial in the cathedral at Vannes in northwestern France. For two centuries Valencia tried to get him home. A hundred years after his death, a small group of Valencians secretly made their way to Vannes, intending to retrieve their saint. But a church official learned of this in time to remove the body and hide it in his house. Another century passed before Valencia resigned itself to Nicholas V's papal bull ordering that Vincent should stay forever in Vannes.

It would be pleasant to report that some splendid miracle had occurred at the time of Saint Vincent's passing. Unfortunately, the record is rather ordinary. A cloud of white butterflies did float into the room where his body lay and remained by him for some time, fluttering. But other dead personages, possibly less worthy, had attracted similar swarms. Nor was the fragrance which emanated from his mortal remains and spread throughout the town more than might have been expected. And the same is true of the miracle of the candles – good enough for some saints, perhaps, but hardly a satisfactory curtain for one who had stopped a falling workman in mid-air: two candles, once lighted for a mass by Vincent himself, had been kept as holy mementoes but had disappeared. At the moment of the saint's death they were again to be seen in their accustomed places, burning bright.

Friar Thomas Conecte took up where Saint Vincent had left off, and did what he could to purify the third decade of the fifteenth century. His was the commoner touch – more like the modern Billy Graham and his predecessors, the revivalists of the nineteenth century – in that he had no company of flagellants, and created no flood of miracles. A Carmelite friar from Brittany, he acquired considerable fame throughout Flanders and in the Amiens region. This fame was to be his downfall. This and making the mistake of going to Rome.

When Thomas was due in a town, the chief burghers would have a scaffold erected for him in the handsomest square, install an altar on the scaffold and decorate the whole with rich tapestries. Friar Conecte would arrive and say mass there, attended by some of his monks and disciples, who usually followed him around on foot. He himself travelled on a small mule.

The friar would then get down to business and condemn everyone's vices, always a popular move. He made, however, one wasteful error: he attacked the women's hats. These were the hennins, which remained in style from 1375 to 1480, and were not, actually, queer compared with the general run of women's headgear down the ages: a fact which casts a cynical reflection on the male, since hats are designed to attract the beholder.

The hennin has been variously described as a beehive, or conical, or two-horned. Hassall quotes Riley to the effect that the conical headdress of the late fifteenth century was Burgundian, and was worn only for a short period but has "become the ignorant person's idea of medieval fashion . . ." The truth seems to be that the average hennin was much like the present headgear of certain European nuns, projecting upwards and outwards like great horns; Salzman says in those days a wearer could only with difficulty pass through doorways. This headgear, made more singular by plucking out or shaving the hair to carry the forehead up toward the crown of the head, was denounced by preachers and laughed at by satirists in vain. (When, conversely, masses of hair were the style, false hair and even wool were added. At all times, of course, paint and powders were available to help out.)

Monstrelet describes the procedures of Friar Conecte as follows: "Having said mass on this platform, he then preached long sermons, blaming the vices and sins of each individual, more especially those of the clergy, who publicly kept mistresses, to the breach of their vows of chastity. In like manner, he blamed greatly the noble ladies, and all others who dressed their heads in so ridiculous a manner, and who expended such sums on the luxuries of apparel. He was so vehement against them that no woman thus dressed dared to appear in his presence, for he was accustomed, when he saw any of them with such dresses, to incite the little boys to torment and plague them, giving them certain days of pardon for so doing, and which he said he had the power of granting. He ordered the boys to shout after them, *Au hennin, au hennin!* so that the ladies were forced to seek shelter in places of safety. These cries caused many tumults between those who raised them and the servants of the ladies."

The result was that in Friar Conecte's audiences, there was soon not a hennin to be seen, the ladies coming to hear him "in caps somewhat like those worn by peasants and people of low degree."

The friar, however, had learned about women from nobody. True, the fine ladies, briefly "ashamed by the abusive expressions of the preacher" wore simple caps. "But this reform lasted not long, for as snails, when anyone passes by them, draw in their horns, and when all danger seems over, put them forth again – so these ladies, shortly after the preacher had quitted their country, forgetful of his doctrine and abuse, began to resume their former colossal headdresses, and wore them even higher than before."

Not only the mass but the quality were very much in favor of Friar Conecte. As crowds followed him, a knight or some other personage of rank led his mule "on foot to the house wherein he was to lodge, which was commonly that of the richest burgher in the town; and his disciples, of whom he had many, were distributed among the best houses, for it was esteemed a great favor when one of them lodged in the house of any individual."

Having arrived there, the preacher would retire to a private chamber and see no one except members of the family, saving all his strength for the multitudes. He would then proceed to his scaffold as usual. "At the conclusion of his sermons, he earnestly admonished the audience on the damnation of their souls, and on pain of excommunication, to bring to him whatever backgammon boards, chess boards, ninepins or other instruments for games of amusement they might possess. In like manner did he order the women to bring their hennins – and having caused a great fire to be lighted in front of his scaffold, he threw all those things into it."

For some four years or so he kept on, making many widely discussed sermons, in city after city. His voice must have been powerful, as he had audiences of up to twenty thousand people. Nothing escaped him. He divided the men from the women by a cord, "for he said he had observed some sly doings between them while he was preaching."

Famous as the preacher who had defeated the hennin, he then went to Rome, during the popedom of Eugenius IV. This was his mistake. Eugenius sent for him to come and preach a sermon. Aware that his orthodoxy might be in question, Friar Conecte begged off twice – pleading illness. The third time, Eugenius sent a high official, the papal treasurer, to fetch him. Observing the treasurer's advent below, Friar Conecte jumped out of the window. He was pursued and soon caught, however, and was carried before the pope. The cardinals of Rouen and Navarre were charged by Eugenius with "investigating" the friar's doctrines, which meant with finding something off-color. And sure enough he was pronounced "guilty of heresy, and of death, and in consequence to be publicly burnt in the city of Rome."

Friar Conecte was thus, unfortunately, thrown into a bonfire himself, after the chess sets, the backgammon boards, the ninepins – and the hennins.

Laugh When I Would Weep

France's first professional woman writer was an Italian. Of Pisan birth, she became the prototype of all the French literary women and *femmes savantes*, coming down to us from the late Middle Ages as the first woman in France with wide learning and a real passion for study. Nor is her title clouded by mentioning a writer from two centuries earlier, Marie de France, who lived in England. And, of course, the "first medieval dramatist," a nun called Hroswitha of Gandersheim, was not French.

It has been loftily said of Christine de Pisan that the excuse for her verses was the necessity of raising her children. This sort of comment is typical of comfortable male critics. Whole sections of history will have to be rewritten some day, in a form purged of masculine bias. In fact, so many kinds of prejudice have affected historians that we see former times only through the waviest pane of glass. The black, the woman, the oriental, the adherent of a religion other than the given writer's, know how false the presentation of history can be, even from honest pens. The historian, that semi-detached observer, should carefully examine his mind, to discover his prejudices; these could then be listed in the back of the book, like the Errata.

An illustrated manuscript shows Christine in a tight gown, steeple hat and wimple, standing tall and graceful at a desk, writing under the guidance of three pretty ladies in crowns, they being the Three Virtues – Reason, Justice and Righteousness. A companion picture shows her raising up the wall of her book, the *Cité des Dames*. Dressed as before, she stands, trowel in hand, while a crowned woman, who symbolizes this work in which Christine defends womankind against the attacks of the *Romaunt of the Rose*, brings her the great building blocks.

The daughter of Thomas of Pisa, Christine was born in Venice in 1364, some say a year earlier, but spent most of her life in France. In 1402 she wrote that she had been a widow thirteen years; elsewhere she affirms that her husband died when she was twenty-five; and as with other women, people have gradually guessed her age by combining such unrelated dates.

Thomas was called *il Pisano* and in France this became Pisan. He had served as Counselor to the Republic of Venice, where he married. Sought after by Charles V and Louis of Hungary at once, he had chosen Paris, arriving there in 1368 to act as the King's physician (he was later promoted to counselor) and astrologer. Christine says that in the Muses' Fountain he had discovered two jewels, more precious far than carbuncles and rubies: one told him the future, and it was astrology; the other empowered him to heal all ills, and it was medicine.

There were astronomers in those days as well as astrologers, and one could be what was called a "practitioner of heavenly bodies" without foretelling events. But Aristotle's *primum mobile* was the outermost sphere, the heaven of the fixed stars, and derived its circular motion, "the most perfect of motions," immediately from God, and carried the fixed stars along in its daily turning. The stars were thus go-betweens linking God and His creation; acquiring their motion from Him, they pushed all the rest along. Heavenly bodies were the springs of human action, and events were tied to what they were doing at a given time. Many a prince had his official astrologer, as did the Italian cities and most Popes; for it was vital to know at what precise moment some important matter should be undertaken, and how else could they find out? People laughed at the Church Fathers' dim view of the stars. Even religions depended on the planets; they were born through Jupiter's conjunction with the other six (there could, therefore, never be but six religions, since there were only the seven planets). It was Jupiter's conjunction with Mercury that created Christianity; with Saturn, Judaism; with Venus, Islám.

Christine was five years old when she was brought to Paris. They reared her well, in bookish surroundings that included her father's Italian library. At fifteen she married Étienne de Castel, a young French gentleman and scholar "whose qualities surpassed his possessions." Christine, in other words, was poor, and that is why her name has come down to us.

The King gave Étienne work to do; he became a royal notary and secretary. But Charles died in 1380 and, wrote Christine, "that opened the door to all our misfortunes." Her father's revenues stopped: a hundred pounds a month and as much again in gifts and perquisites. He died leaving as a legacy to Christine and her husband, his wife and two sons. Nine years after Charles, the husband she loved was carried off at thirty-four, willing Christine a daughter, two sons and some long and costly lawsuits.

"I had to work," she wrote, "something I, brought up spoiled and indulged, had never learned, and I had to guide the ship without a captain . . ."

She tells us that she always wore on her head a chaplet, given her as a girl by her prudent mother, that was set with three diamonds to symbolize discretion.

There were only a few things that a woman of her type and station could set her hand to. She began to write – to produce both poetry and prose, her first work, *A Hundred Ballads*, being published in 1394.

Christine knew small Latin and no Greek, but the royalty and nobility of France had been seeing to it that Greek and Latin works were put into French. She read copiously. At the time, it was customary for an author to copy generous sections out of another's work and pass it off as his own, a practice called *piscari* – going fishing. One cannot, then, always be certain whose thoughts were whose. Christine's *Book of Chivalry and Feats of War* includes long passages from H. Bonet's *The Tree of Battles*, which itself includes whole pages from Jean de Legnano's *Tractatus de bello*; but Christine says that as she lay dreaming, a sage appeared and told her to "pluck from *The Tree of Battles*," and that when she demurred, he insisted, reminding her how Jean de Meung had taken over, from Guillaume de Lorris, the *Romaunt of the Rose*.

She was *not*, Ernest Nys maintains, the center of Louis d'Orléans' opulent and brilliant group, but he did grant her one audience, and she had various other noble patrons; for example she wrote a life of Charles V for his brother, the Duke of Burgundy. She held with working quietly by herself, and wrote: "Seneca tells us that he closed his door in order to be of use to all, since in this retreat he composed valuable remedies and salutary preparations for the soul."

By 1405 she had completed fifteen books, and was widely admired, except for the usual backbiters who averred that "knowledge cannot come from a woman," and that her books were ghosted by scholars and priests. One of the nobles who helped her was the British envoy to Paris, the Earl of Salisbury; he took her eldest son, Jean de Castel, into his household, and the mother's heart must have been briefly content; but nothing was certain in those times, and after the Duke of Lancaster had dethroned Richard II and become Henry IV, the Earl of Salisbury had his head cut off. Later, Christine sent Jean to the Duke of Orléans; and in 1418 the gifted man, who wrote *Poem of the Pine*, was named secretary to the Dauphin, Charles de France. He died in 1426. The other son died very young and the daughter went into a nunnery.

It was in her *Epistle to the God of Love* that Christine attacked the *Romaunt of the Rose*. She advised her son Jean to keep away from the hated *Romaunt* if he would lead a chaste life, and to read the *Divine Comedy* instead. Her *Cité des Dames* (whose title, it is said, may have been suggested by Augustine's *City of God*) is a collection of the deeds of noted women. It describes among other great ladies the fair Novella, daughter of a lawyer of Bologna, who, when her father was otherwise engaged, would be sent by him to teach his pupils, she conducting the class from behind a little curtain, "lest the beauty of her keep her hearers from thinking."

Christine's works include opinions on such topics as social and political organization, the class system, war and peace. Wycliffe had recently denounced war as unlawful, and as theft on a grand scale, but Christine maintained that just wars, by chiefs of state, as opposed to private wars, were legitimate.

From 1392 to 1422, Charles VI, who had succeeded his

father, Charles V, was subject to crises of madness called the *folie furieuse*. The ship of state, like Christine's life, was captainless, and many a feudal lord played sovereign, even dispatching ambassadors abroad and making pacts. Christine composed some further writings, and then, as she aged, retired into a convent. Here, out of love for the Maid of Orléans, she wrote her *Dittié à la louange de Jeanne d'Arc*. It is believed that she died in 1431.

Her life is somehow the story of many a woman's: of anguish at losing the man she loved, of panic at being left alone; she knew that sorrow of the gently-born new-poor, whose hands are unskilled. She knew the prejudice which even now directs its scorn at women. She was a foreshadowing, not only of France's glittering women scholars, but of such spiritual descendants as Ṭáhirih and Mary Wollstonecraft and Florence Nightingale and Lucy Stone. Somehow she sent her name down the ages.

"A woman has nothing but her affections," Florence Nightingale says in *Cassandra*, "and this makes her at once more loving and less loved." There is the same wistfulness in Christine, a lonely feeling that many women still experience, and that shows in such lines of hers as these:

> I only sing to hide:
> Mine eyes would sooner weep.
> None knows what sorrows deep
> In my poor heart abide.
> And here is all my woe:
> There's none to pity me.
> The harder road I go,
> The fewer friends I see.
> Then setting tears aside,
> For me my anguish keep,
> And laugh when I would weep.
> Both rhyme and beat denied,
> I only sing to hide.

VII

Two Loves

"It seemed to me that your person, your least motion, had a more than human importance in the world. My heart was like dust rising after your footsteps. You seemed like moonlight on a summer evening, when everything is fragrances and quiet shadows and whitenesses and infinity; and the delights of the flesh and of the spirit were all included for me in your name, which I would repeat over and over and try to kiss as it passed my lips.

"Sometimes your words come back to me, like a faraway echo, like the sound of a bell brought by the wind; and I think you are here, when I read about love in the books . . . All that people disparage in them as exaggerated, you caused me to feel."

The nineteenth-century Frenchman, Flaubert, who wrote these words, was skilled in human love. But the thirteenth-century Persian, Rúmí, could have told him human love was only like the wooden sword a soldier puts in his son's hands, or the rag doll given to a little girl; it was only a kind of sample or lesson.

Grown men and women look rather foolish, clutching their wooden swords and their rag dolls.

The meaning is not that they shouldn't love each other. These days, in a world dying of hate, you're grateful even for the initials carved in a heart on a park bench, because at least they spell a truce. But the Persian meant that this love between men and women isn't the point. The point is something quite different, and romantic love, like the love of money and of fame, is put there so we'll miss it.

The world dangles love, or money, or fame in front of us so that our eyes will follow them mechanically and miss what is going on. We live out our days grabbing at toys and loudly lamenting that the painted wooden sword won't cut and the rag doll won't come to life.

Why are we so easy to fool? All of us, wise and otherwise: because a sailor whistling at a girl is not always much different from a scholar working for another degree. Not that there is anything necessarily wrong with a blonde or a Ph.D., but still, they aren't the point.

People who get everything describe how empty everything is. A successful sculptor tells how he dreamed he was eating glass grapes. A millionaire says he can't stay awake – there is nothing to stay awake for. A wage-earner says he is too busy keeping alive to worry about reasons.

You look at people's faces and see the strain which is the mark of current man. Then you look at a tree moving, or at silver light wiped flat on the bay; you see the drifting and settling, the leafing and withering, the world going about its business, over and above current man. (It may be rage at these orderly procedures that makes man want to destroy nature as well as himself.)

Perhaps you are thinking: if the show isn't about men and women and money and prestige, what is it about then?

Well, it is hiding something much more desirable than what we have. It is keeping us away from the one thing that would make the rest worth getting. Of course, if we prefer to be fooled, that is our affair; no one can force us to look twice.

They don't chain bees to flowers; birds aren't timeclocked while they feed their young; you can't flog a poet into writing a deathless sonnet. We go by drives and urges; it has to be natural. If we have an urge to see what is back of life we shall look twice, but no one can force us to.

The secret is right out in the open, but you can't see it. But then, you can't see love or courage either; all you can actually see is an example: a mother holding her child; a picture of the Marines raising the flag on Suribachi. You have an example of the thing. If a person who didn't know English asked you what "courage" is, for instance, you could show him the picture of the Marines, being fired on and still raising the flag.

All you can have of this hidden thing in the world is an example too.

The example is a man, a person. He is a man who talks and acts in a strange way. The people in charge of things, especially the clergy, say he is crazy. They do not think he is crazy, however; they do not put him in an asylum. They arrest him. Then they either jail him or shoot him or send him away to die; once they took him and drove nails through his hands and feet. They are mortally afraid of him because he comes between them and the people and breaks up their arrangements; he is a threat to their toys.

He does not ask the authorities for their approval. He says his say. He says that he comes from the Lord and Owner of the world. When people ask to see this Owner now, the man tells them that he himself is reflecting Him, the way a face shines in a mirror; he tells the people to look at him and be like him because he has come into the world to reflect its Lord.

The people look at him and find that they love him. They love him better than their wives and children, better than drink or money or a place in the community. They see that whatever this Lord of the world may be, He is better to love than anything else.

And so they remember the man for a long, long time. They tell their children what he was like and the word is passed along down the years, because the memory is too sweet to lose. But after a while, after hundreds of years, his name is only a confusion in their minds; some say he never existed at all, and others say he was only one of themselves, and still others turn him into a statue of wax or stone. By now his voice is only an echo, or like the sound of a bell drifting by on the wind.

Perhaps you are thinking: I know this all happened once, but it was a long time ago. I know that once a Man came into the world who really loved people, so that they felt it and loved Him, and tried to live the way He asked. But it could only happen once, and it was way back, a long time ago.

If you think this, you would be wrong. It happened many

times, not once. A Man like this was born in 1817. He drew so many people to Him that the authorities said He was a magician; they said He put a philtre in His tea, and gave it to the people to make them love Him. Later they said He wanted to tear down the Government. His disciples knew that the magic was not in the tea, and that He had bidden them to observe the law of the land. But the others chained Him underground, and then they sent Him away; He was a prisoner all the rest of His life; He was sent here and there over the earth, and He never saw His country again.

Wherever He came, the people would not leave Him alone. They went to Him the way iron filings go to a magnet; by a natural law, they went straight to Him. They forgot their own selves; they forgot how dangerous it was to love Him. They did not care when the authorities struck at them and killed them, because death had no heartache any more.

Then He grew old and bowed down with suffering and He died, but this love which He had created was left for a legacy. It was in 1892 that He died, in the Holy Land, and today the story of His life is known all around the world. His name was Bahá'u'lláh, which means The Glory of God; His followers are called Bahá'ís, those who follow and belong to The Glory of God. Bahá'ís are people whom The Glory of God has taught to live in a new way. He has shown them how to stand as one brotherhood amongst all the contending peoples of the earth; how to obey their rules of righteous living though all mankind try to corrupt them; how to form into spiritual communities where men and women and children of all colors and classes, religions and nativities, are at peace together. He has fastened their minds on God, and set His love in their hearts, whether they are rich or poor, black or white, from East or West.

What if we don't listen, what if we don't turn to this God Who loves and watches over us, and to this Man Whom He has sent to call us back to Him? Well, even so there is the same old show as always, you are probably thinking; the same old merry-go-round of love and money and fame; the same old galloping wooden horses, bobbing and going round again; same old brass ring.

A few years ago, say in our grandfathers' time, you might have been right. But today, the machinery has broken down; the music has stopped; the carousel is on fire. Our old world vanishes today; it will never spin round again. If we choose, we die with it, curling away in the smoke.

But if we prefer to live, here and hereafter, we have only to turn in the direction of the mercy of God. He will not shut us away; "He, verily, loveth the one that turneth towards Him."[1] We have only to listen to His voice, as He speaks through all His Prophets, and to practice the Law He has laid down for us today. This Law which will make the planet safe for humanity; which will protect man from his own law of hate and blood and death.

Here are words the Prophets have spoken, about that other love, waiting for man out there in the universe:

"I am the Lord thy God . . . Thou shalt have no other gods before me."[2]

"My soul waiteth for the Lord more than they that watch for the morning; I say, more than they that watch for the morning."[3]

"Praises, and songs, and adorations do we offer to Ahura-Mazda, and to Righteousness the Best . . . And to thy good kingdom, O Ahura-Mazda! may we attain forever . . . So mayest Thou be to us our life, and our body's vigour, O Thou most beneficent of beings, and that for both the worlds!"[4]

"Amitâbha, the unbounded light, is the source of wisdom, of virtue, of Buddhahood . . . what is more wondrous, more mysterious, more miraculous than Amitâbha?"[5]

"Thou shalt love the Lord thy God with all thy heart, and with all thy soul, and with all thy mind."[6]

"For the kingdom . . . is God's, and God hath power over all things . . . Hast thou not seen how all in the Heavens and in the Earth uttereth the praise of God? – the very birds as they spread their wings?"[7]

These lines are taken from Moses and David and Zoroaster, from Buddha and Christ and Muḥammad. To these are now added the words of Bahá'u'lláh:

"What power can the shadowy creature claim to possess when face to face with Him Who is the Uncreated?"[8]

"Those hearts . . . that are aware of His Presence, are close to Him."⁹

"How can I claim to have known Thee, when the entire creation is bewildered by Thy mystery, and how can I confess not to have known Thee, when, lo, the whole universe proclaimeth Thy Presence . . . ?"¹⁰

"Whoso hath known Him shall soar in the immensity of His love, and shall be detached from the world and all that is therein."¹¹

"My remembrance of Thee, O my God, quencheth my thirst, and quieteth my heart. My soul delighteth in its communion with Thee, as the sucking child delighteth itself in the breasts of Thy mercy; and my heart panteth after Thee."¹²

The choice is ours to make, between these two loves. We should not make it lightly. If we choose the one, we shall have both; and if we choose the other, it will slip away and betray us at the close.

> *I look on thee – on thee –*
> *Beholding, besides love, the end of love,*
> *Hearing oblivion beyond memory;*
> *As one who sits and gazes from above,*
> *Over the rivers to the bitter sea.*¹³

Notes and References

Victoriana

1. John Richard Green (1837–83), famed English historian who wrote *History of the English People.*
2. See Philip Henry Savage, *Poems* (Copeland & Day, Boston 1898). Also *Letters of Louise Imogen Guiney* (Harper & Brothers, New York and London 1926), Vol. II, p. 2.

Looking for Pedro de Luna

1. See 'Abdu'l-Bahá, *The Secret of Divine Civilization* (Bahá'í Publishing Trust, Wilmette 1970), pp. 89–91.

The Diamond Bough

1. Accounts of the Siamese Twins vary, but see Irving and Amy Wallace, *The Two* (Simon & Schuster, New York 1978).
2. Marie-Henri Beyle (de Stendhal), *On Love* (Horace Liveright, New York 1927); also translated by H.B.V. under C. K. Scott-Moncrieff (Liveright Publishing Corp. 1947).
3. 'Abdu'l-Bahá, *The Promulgation of Universal Peace* (Bahá'í Publishing Trust, Wilmette 1982), p. 43.
4. Shoghi Effendi, *Citadel of Faith* (Bahá'í Publishing Trust, Wilmette 1970), p. 125.
5. *Promulgation,* p. 270.
6. ibid. p. 75.
7. ibid. p. 9.
8. ibid. p. 291.
9. Shoghi Effendi, *God Passes By* (Bahá'í Publishing Trust, Wilmette, rev. edn 1953), p. 241.
10. 'Abdu'l-Bahá, *The Wisdom of 'Abdu'l-Bahá* (Bahá'í Publishing Trust, Wilmette), p. 167; *Paris Talks* (Bahá'í Publishing Trust, London 1972), p. 180.
11. The Báb, *Selections from the Writings of The Báb* (Bahá'í World Centre, Haifa 1976), p. 59.
12. Nabíl-i-A'zam, *The Dawn-Breakers* (Bahá'í Publishing Trust, Wilmette 1974), title page.
13. ibid. p. 373.

14. Bahá'u'lláh, *Gleanings from the Writings of Bahá'u'lláh* (Bahá'í Publishing Trust, Wilmette 1976), p. 90.
15. *Dawn-Breakers*, p. 675.
16. See ibid. pp. 31ff for this and for account which follows.
17. *God Passes By*, p. 34.
18. ibid., p. 32.
19. *Dawn-Breakers*, pp. 397–8.
20. *God Passes By*, p. 137.
21. *Promulgation of Universal Peace*, p. 34.
22. *The Wisdom of 'Abdu'l-Bahá*, p. 169; *Paris Talks*, p. 181.

The Star Servant

1. Shoghi Effendi, *Messages to America 1932–1946* (Bahá'í Publishing Committee, Wilmette 1947), p. 30.
2. Rúḥíyyih Rabbani, *The Priceless Pearl* (Bahá'í Publishing Trust, London 1969), p. 106.
3. *Messages to America*, p. 40.
4. *God Passes By*, pp. 386–7.

The Smoke and Din of Battle

1. Shoghi Effendi, *Bahá'í Administration* (Bahá'í Publishing Trust, Wilmette 1968), p. 64.
2. Bahá'u'lláh, *Epistle to the Son of the Wolf* (Bahá'í Publishing Trust, Wilmette 1976), p. 25.

For John, With Love

1. The other finishing school with which Louise was connected was Rosemary Hall, Connecticut.
2. This letter is dated March 3, 1927. It says in part: "The last meeting of the National Assembly received the interesting suggestion that steps be taken by the friends along the Pacific Coast to organize a summer Bahá'í community along the lines of Green Acre . . . We hope that conditions will make it possible for some such informal center to come into being in the near future and we appreciate what splendid results it would have for the Cause throughout the Pacific states."
3. It will be recalled that Julien Viaud owes his pseudonym to the Tahitian people, who in 1872 named him Pierre Loti, *loti* meaning "rose" in Tahitian.
4. Louise writes, April 13, 1947, that she is still in touch with Ariane. Earlier, she wrote me of Suzell Marchal (daughter of the man she describes as "the wonderful Mr Ernest Marchal"), "a 6 months old baby when my husband and I came to Tahiti in 1920 . . . In her letter she asked me if she may have our friendship and would we correspond with her? Her letter was fragrant with the *parfum* of pressed blossoms of the national flower of Tahiti . . ." Louise mentions as other Tahitian Bahá'ís George Spitz and Rene Gasse, and as others deeply interested

Martial Yorss and Ernest Marchal. Still another who knew of the Faith was Alexandre Drollet, a fine old man, born in Tahiti and government interpreter there.

5. "Deeply grieve great loss his magnificent spirit. Services immortal. Assure you loving sympathy fervent prayers. Shoghi."

Juliet Remembers Gibran

1. Barbara Young, in *This Man from Lebanon: A Study of Kahlil Gibran* (Knopf, New York 1945), p. 68, has written: "In his later years he liked to talk about the years in Paris and the early years in New York, of his first studio, which he called 'my little cage,' and then the spacious one, higher up in the building, a great room where he felt a new freedom, where he said, 'I can spread my wings.'

   "It was in this studio that the drawing was made of the revered Abdul Baha in 1912. The saintly man had indicated that seven in the morning was the hour at which he would consent to sit for his portrait. Telling about it, Gibran said, 'I remained awake all night, for I knew I should never have an eye or a hand to work with if I took my sleep.' "

2. The Bahá'í teaching, like the Christian, is that the Manifestation of God is the way to God. Jesus said, "I am the door . . ." (John 10:7).

3. Bahá'u'lláh and the Báb are the two Manifestations of God for today. 'Abdu'l-Bahá is the Exemplar and Interpreter of the Bahá'í Faith.

Two Loves

1. *Gleanings*, p. 291.
2. Exodus 20:2–3.
3. Psalm 130:6.
4. S. A. Kapadia, *The Teachings of Zoroaster*, pp. 71–2.
5. P. Carus, *The Gospel of Buddha*, pp. 151–2.
6. Matthew 22:37.
7. Qur'án 3:186; 24:41.
8. Bahá'u'lláh, *Prayers and Meditations* (Bahá'í Publishing Trust, Wilmette) p. 149.
9. *Gleanings*, p. 186.
10. ibid. p. 63.
11. ibid. p. 205.
12. *Prayers and Meditations*, p. 195.
13. Elizabeth Barrett Browning, *Sonnets from the Portuguese*, No. 15.